D0090555

Never Eat Alone

Never Eat Alone

And Other Secrets to Success, One Relationship at a Time

KEITH FERRAZZI

with Tahl Raz

CURRENCY · DOUBLEDAY

NEW YORK   LONDON   TORONTO   SYDNEY   AUCKLAND

A CURRENCY BOOK
PUBLISHED BY DOUBLEDAY
a division of Random House, Inc.

CURRENCY is a trademark of Random House, Inc., and
DOUBLEDAY is a registered trademark of Random House, Inc.

Cataloging-in-Publication Data is on file with the Library of Congress

ISBN: 0-385-51205-8

Book design by Fearn Cutler de Vicq

PRINTED IN THE UNITED STATES OF AMERICA

First Edition: March 2005
All trademarks are the property of their respective companies.

SPECIAL SALES
Currency Books are available at special discounts for bulk
purchases for sales promotions or premiums. Special editions,
including personalized covers, excerpts of existing books, and
corporate imprints, can be created in large quantities for special
needs. For more information, write to Special Markets, Currency
Books, specialmarkets@randomhouse.com.

22 21 20 19 18 17

For Mom and Dad

Contents

SECTION THREE

Turning Connections into Compatriots

SECTION FOUR

Trading Up and Giving Back

The Mind-Set

CHAPTER 1

Becoming a Member of the Club

Relationships are all there is. Everything in the universe only exists because it is in relationship to everything else. Nothing exists in isolation. We have to stop pretending we are individuals that can go it alone.

—Margaret Wheatley

How on earth did I get in here?" I kept asking myself in those early days as an overwhelmed first-year student at Harvard Business School.

There wasn't a single accounting or finance class in my background. Looking around me, I saw ruthlessly focused young men and women who had undergraduate degrees in business. They'd gone on to crunch numbers or analyze spreadsheets in the finest firms on Wall Street. Most were from wealthy families and had pedigrees and legacies and Roman numerals in their names. Sure, I was intimidated.

How was a guy like me from a working-class family, with a liberal arts degree and a couple years at a traditional manufacturing company, going to compete with purebreds from McKinsey and Goldman Sachs who, from my perspective, seemed as if they'd been computing business data in their cribs?

It was a defining moment in my career, and in my life.

I was a country boy from southwestern Pennsylvania, raised in a small, hardworking steel and coal town outside of Latrobe called Youngstown. Our region was so rural you couldn't see another house from the porch of our modest home. My father worked in the local steel mill; on weekends he'd do construction. My mother cleaned the homes of the doctors and lawyers in a nearby town. My brother escaped small-town life by way of the army; my sister got married in high school and moved out when I was a toddler.

At HBS, all the insecurities of my youth came rushing back. You see, although we didn't have much money, my dad and mom were set on giving me the kind of opportunities my brother and sister (from my mom's previous marriage) never got. My parents pushed me and sacrificed everything to get me the kind of education that only the well-to-do kids in our town could afford. The memories rushed back to those days when my mother would pick me up in our beat-up blue Nova at the bus stop of the private elementary school I attended, while the other children ducked into limos and BMWs. I was teased mercilessly about our car and my polyester clothes and fake Docksiders—reminded daily of my station in life.

The experience was a godsend in many ways, toughening my resolve and fueling my drive to succeed. It made clear to me there was a hard line between the haves and the have-nots. It made me angry to be poor. I felt excluded from what I saw as the old boys' network. On the other hand, all those feelings pushed me to work harder than everyone around me.

Hard work, I reassured myself, was one of the ways I'd beaten the odds and gotten into Harvard Business School. But there was something else that separated me from the rest of my class and gave me an advantage. I seemed to have learned something long before I arrived in Cambridge that it seemed many of my peers had not.

As a kid, I caddied at the local country club for the homeowners and their children living in the wealthy town next to mine. It made me think often and hard about those who succeed and those who don't. I made an observation in those days that would alter the way I viewed the world.

During those long stretches on the links, as I carried their bags, I watched how the people who had reached professional heights unknown to my father and mother helped each other. They found one another jobs, they invested time and money in one another's ideas, and they made sure their kids got help getting into the best schools, got the right internships, and ultimately got the best jobs.

Before my eyes, I saw proof that success breeds success and, indeed, the rich *do* get richer. Their web of friends and associates was the most potent club the people I caddied for had in their bags. Poverty, I realized, wasn't only a lack of financial resources; it was isolation from the kind of people that could help you make more of yourself.

I came to believe that in some very specific ways life, like golf, is a game, and that the people who know the rules, and know them well, play it best and succeed. And the rule in life that has unprecedented power is that the individual who knows the right people, for the right reasons, and utilizes the power of these relationships, can become a member of the "club," whether he started out as a caddie or not.

This realization came with some empowering implications. To achieve your goals in life, I realized, it matters less how smart you are, how much innate talent you're born with, or even, most eye-opening to me, where you came from and how much you started out with. Sure all these are important, but they mean little if you don't understand one thing: You can't get there alone. In fact, you can't get very far at all.

Fortunately, I was hungry to make something of myself (and, frankly, even more terrified that I'd amount to nothing). Otherwise, perhaps I would have just stood by and watched like my friends in the caddy yard.

I first began to learn about the incredible power of relationships from Mrs. Pohland. Caryl Pohland was married to the owner of the big lumberyard in our town, and her son, Brett, who was my age, was my friend. They went to our church. At the time, I probably wanted to be Brett (great athlete, rich, all the girls falling over him).

At the club, I was Mrs. Pohland's caddie. I was the only one who cared enough, ironically, to hide her cigarettes. I busted my behind to help her win every tournament. I'd walk the course the morning before to see where the tough pin placements were. I'd test the speed of the greens. Mrs. Pohland started racking up wins left and right. Every ladies day, I did such a great job that she would brag about me to her friends. Soon, others requested me.

I'd caddie thirty-six holes a day if I could get the work, and I made sure I treated the club caddie-master as if he were a king. My first year, I won the annual caddie award, which gave me the chance to caddie for Arnold Palmer when he came to play on his hometown course. Arnie started out as a caddie himself at the Latrobe Country Club and went on to own the club as an adult. I looked up to him as a role model. He was living proof that success in golf, and in life, had nothing to do with class. It was about access (yes, and talent, at least in his case). Some gained access through birth or money. Some were fantastic at what they did, like Arnold Palmer. My edge, I knew, was my initiative and drive. Arnie was inspirational proof that your past need not be prologue to your future.

For years I was a de facto member of the Pohland family, splitting holidays with them and hanging out at their house nearly every day. Brett and I were inseparable, and I loved his family like my own. Mrs. Pohland made sure I got to know everyone in the club that could help me, and if she saw me slacking, I'd hear it from her. I helped her on the golf course, and she, in appreciation of my efforts and the care I bestowed upon her, helped me in life. She provided me with a simple but profound lesson about the power of generosity. When you help others, they often help you. Reciprocity is the gussied-up word people use later in life to describe this ageless principle. I just knew the word as "care." We cared for each other, so we went out of our way to do nice things.

Because of those days, and specifically that lesson, I came to realize that first semester at business school that Harvard's hyper-competitive, individualistic students had it all wrong. Success in any field, but especially in business, is about working *with* people, not against them. No tabulation of dollars and cents can account for one immutable fact: Business is a human enterprise, driven and determined by people.

It wasn't too far into my second semester before I started jokingly reassuring myself, "How on earth did all these *other* people get in here?"

What many of my fellow students lacked, I discovered, were the skills and strategies that are associated with fostering and building relationships. In America, and especially in business, we're brought up to cherish John Wayne individualism. People who consciously court others to become involved in their lives are seen as schmoozers, brown-nosers, smarmy sycophants.

Over the years, I learned that the outrageous number of misperceptions clouding those who are active relationship-builders is equaled only by the misperceptions of how relationship-building is done properly. What I saw on the golf course—friends helping friends and families helping families they cared about—had nothing to do with manipulation or quid pro quo. Rarely was there any running tally of who did what for whom, or strategies concocted in which you give just so you could get.

Over time, I came to see reaching out to people as a way to make a difference in people's lives as well as a way to explore and learn and enrich my own; it became the conscious construction of my life's path. Once I saw my networking efforts in this light, I gave myself permission to practice it with abandon in every part of my professional and personal life. I didn't think of it as cold and impersonal, the way I thought of "networking." I was, instead, *connecting*—sharing my knowledge and resources, time and energy, friends and associates, and empathy and compassion in a continual effort to provide value to others, while coincidentally increasing my own. Like business itself, being a connector is not about managing transactions, but about managing relationships.

People who instinctively establish a strong network of relationships have always created great businesses. If you strip business down to its basics, it's still about people selling things to other people. That idea can get lost in the tremendous hubbub the business world perpetually stirs up around everything from brands and technology to design and price considerations in an endless search for the ultimate competitive advantage. But ask any accomplished CEO or entrepreneur or professional how they achieved their success, and I guarantee you'll hear very little business jargon. What you will mostly hear about are the people who helped pave their way, if they are being honest and not too caught up in their own success.

After two decades of successfully applying the power of relationships in my own life and career, I've come to believe that connecting is one of the most important business—and life—skill sets you'll ever learn. Why? Because, flat out, people do business with people they know and like. Careers—in every imaginable field—work the same way. Even our overall well-being and sense of happiness, as a library's worth of research has shown, is dictated in large part by the support and guidance and love we get from the community we build for ourselves.

It took me a while to figure out exactly how to go about connecting with others. But I knew for certain that whether I wanted to become president of the United States or the president of a local PTA, there were a lot of other people whose help I would need along the way.

Self-Help: A Misnomer

How do you turn an acquaintance into a friend? How can you get other people to become emotionally invested in your advancement? Why are there some lucky schmos who always leave business conferences with months' worth of lunch dates and a dozen potential new associates, while others leave with only indigestion? Where are the places you go to meet the kind of people who could most impact your life?

From my earliest days growing up in Latrobe, I found myself absorbing wisdom and advice from every source imaginable— friends, books, neighbors, teachers, family. My thirst to reach out was almost unquenchable. But in business, I found nothing came close to the impact of mentors. At every stage in my career, I sought out the most successful people around me and asked for their help and guidance.

I first learned the value of mentors from a local lawyer named George Love. He and the town's stockbroker, Walt Saling, took me under their wings. I was riveted by their stories of professional life and their nuggets of street-smart wisdom. My ambitions were sown in the fertile soil of George and Walt's rambling business escapades, and ever since, I've been on the lookout for others who could teach or inspire me. Later in life, as I rubbed shoulders with business leaders, store owners, politicians, and movers and shakers of all stripes, I started to gain a sense of how our country's most successful people reach out to others, and how they invite those people's help in accomplishing their goals.

I learned that *real* networking was about finding ways to make *other* people more successful. It was about working hard to *give* more than you get. And I came to believe that there was a litany of tough-minded principles that made this softhearted philosophy possible.

These principles would ultimately help me achieve things I didn't think I was capable of. They would lead me to opportunities otherwise hidden to a person of my upbringing, and they'd come to my aid when I failed, as we all do on occasion. That aid was never in more dire need than during my first job out of business school at Deloitte & Touche Consulting.

By conventional standards, I was an awful entry-level consultant. Put me in front of a spreadsheet and my eyes glaze over, which is what happened when I found myself on my first project, huddled in a cramped, windowless room in the middle of suburbia, files stretching from floor to ceiling, poring over a sea of data with a few other first-year consultants. I tried; I really did. But I just couldn't. I was convinced boredom that bad was lethal.

I was clearly well on my way to getting fired or quitting.

Luckily, I had already applied some of the very rules of networking that I was still in the process of learning. In my spare time, when I wasn't painfully attempting to analyze some data-ridden worksheet, I reached out to ex-classmates, professors, old bosses, and anyone who might stand to benefit from a relationship with Deloitte. I spent my weekends giving speeches at small conferences around the country on a variety of subjects I had learned at Harvard mostly under the tutelage of Len Schlessinger (to whom I owe my speaking style today). All this in an attempt to drum up both business and buzz for my new company. I had mentors throughout the organization, including the CEO, Pat Loconto.

Still, my first annual review was devastating. I received low marks for not doing what I was asked to do with the gusto and focus that was expected of me. But my supervisors, with whom I had already developed relationships and who were aware of all my extracurricular activities, had another idea. Together, we cooked up a job description that previously did not exist at the company.

My mentors gave me a $150,000 expense account to do what I had already been doing: developing business, representing the firm with speaking engagements, and reaching out to the press and business world in ways that would strengthen Deloitte's presence in the marketplace. My supervisors' belief in me paid off. Within a year, the company's brand recognition in the line of business on which I focused (reengineering) moved from bottom of the consulting pack to one of the top of the industry, achieving a growth rate the company had never known (though, of course, it wasn't all my doing). I went on to become the company's chief marketing officer and the youngest person ever tapped for partner. And I was having a blast—the work was fun, exciting, interesting. Everything you could want in a job.

While my career was in full throttle, in some ways it all seemed like a lucky accident. In fact, for many years, I couldn't see exactly where my professional trajectory would take me—after Deloitte, a crazy quilt of top-level jobs culminating in my founding my own company. It's only today, looking in the rearview mirror, that it makes enormous sense.

From Deloitte, I became the youngest chief marketing officer in the Fortune 500 at Starwood Hotels & Resorts. Then I went on to become CEO of a Knowledge Universe (Michael Milken)– funded video game company, and now, founder of my own company, Ferrazzi Greenlight, a sales and marketing consulting and training firm to scores of the most prestigious brands, and an advisor to CEOs across the world. I zigged and zagged my way to the top. Every time I contemplated a move or needed advice, I turned to the circle of friends I had created around me.

At first I tried to draw attention away from my people skills for fear that they were somehow inferior to other more "respectable" business abilities. But as I got older, everyone from well-known CEOs and politicians to college kids and my own employees came to me asking for advice on how to do those things I had always loved doing. *Crain's* magazine listed me as one of the forty top business leaders under forty, and the World Economic Forum labeled me as a "Global Leader for Tomorrow." Senator Hillary

Clinton asked me to use my connecting skills to raise money for her favorite nonprofit organization, Save America's Treasures. Friends and CEOs of Fortune 500 companies asked if I could help them throw more intimate dinner parties for their lead prospects and clients in key regions of the country. MBA students sent me e-mails hungry to learn the people skills their business schools weren't teaching them. Those turned into formal training courses now taught at the most prestigious MBA programs in America.

The underlying "softer" skills I used to arrive at my success, I learned, were something others could benefit from learning.

Of course, building a web of relationships isn't the only thing you need to be successful. But building a career, and a life, with the help and support of friends and family and associates has some incredible virtues.

1. It's never boring. Time-consuming, sometimes; demanding, perhaps. But dull, never. You're always learning about yourself, other people, business, and the world, and it feels great.
2. A relationship-driven career is good for the companies you work for because everyone benefits from your own growth—it's the value you bring that makes people want to connect with you. You feel satisfaction when both your peers and your organization share in your advancement.
3. Connecting—with the support, flexibility, and opportunities for self-development that come along with it—happens to make a great deal of sense in our new work world. The loyalty and security once offered by organizations can be provided by our own networks. Lifetime corporate employment is dead; we're all free agents now, managing our own careers across multiple jobs and companies. And because today's primary currency is information, a wide-reaching network is one of the surest ways to become and remain thought leaders of our respective fields.

Today, I have over 5,000 people on my Palm who will answer the phone when I call. They are there to offer expertise, jobs, help, encouragement, support, and yes, even care and love. The very successful people I know are, as a group, not especially talented, educated, or charming. But they all have a circle of trustworthy, talented, and inspirational people whom they can call upon.

All of this takes work. It involves a lot of sweat equity, just as it did for me back in the caddie yard. It means you have to think hard not only about yourself but about other people. Once you're committed to reaching out to others and asking for their help at being the best at whatever you do, you'll realize, as I have, what a powerful way of accomplishing your goals this can be. Just as important, it will lead to a much fuller, richer life, surrounded by an ever-growing, vibrant network of people you care for and who care for you.

This book outlines the secrets behind the success of so many accomplished people; they are secrets that are rarely recognized by business schools, career counselors, or therapists. By incorporating the ideas I discuss in this book, you too can become the center of a circle of relationships, one that will help you succeed throughout life. Of course, I'm a bit of a fanatic in my efforts to connect with others. I do the things I'm going to teach you with a certain degree of, well, exuberance. But by simply reaching out to others and recognizing that no one does it alone, I believe you'll see astounding results, quickly.

Everyone has the capacity to be a connector. After all, if a country kid from Pennsylvania can make it into the "club," so can you.

See you there.

CHAPTER 2

Don't Keep Score

There is no such thing as a "self-made" man. We are made up of thousands of others. Everyone who has ever done a kind deed for us, or spoken one word of encouragement to us, has entered into the make-up of our character and of our thoughts, as well as our success.

—George Burton Adams

When I give talks to college and grad students, they always ask me, What are the secrets to success? What are the unspoken rules for making it big? Preferably, they'd like my response wrapped up in a tight package and tied with a neat little bow. Why not? I wanted the same thing at their age.

"So you want the inside scoop," I respond. "Fair enough. I'll sum up the key to success in one word: generosity."

Then I pause, watching the faces of the kids in the crowd as they look back at me with quizzical expressions. Half the group thinks I'm about to tell them a joke; the other half thinks they would have been better off getting a beer rather than attending my talk.

I go on to explain that when I was young, my father, a Pennsylvania steelworker, wanted more for me than he ever had. And he expressed this desire to a man whom up until that moment he had never met, the CEO of his company, Alex McKenna. Mr. McKenna liked my dad's moxie and helped me get a scholarship to one of the best private schools in the country, where he was a trustee.

Later, Elsie Hillman, chairwoman of the Pennsylvania Republican Party, whom I first met after she read in the *New York Times* about my unsuccessful bid for New Haven City Council in my sophomore year at Yale, lent me money and advice and encouraged me to attend business school.

By the time I was your age, I tell the students, I had been afforded one of the best educational opportunities in the world, almost purely through the generosity of others.

"But," I continue, "here's the hard part: You've got to be more than willing to accept generosity. Often, you've got to go out and ask for it."

Now I get that look of instant recognition. Almost everyone in the room has had to reach out for help to get a job interview, an internship, or some free advice. And most have been reluctant to ask. Until you become as willing to ask for help as you are to give it, however, you are only working half the equation.

That's what I mean by connecting. It's a constant process of giving and receiving—of asking for and offering help. By putting people in contact with one another, by giving your time and expertise and sharing them freely, the pie gets bigger for everyone.

This karma-tinged vision of how things work may sound naïve to those who have grown cynical of the business world. But while the power of generosity is not yet fully appreciated, or applied, in the halls of corporate America, its value in the world of networks is proven.

For example, I enjoy giving career advice and counseling. It's almost a hobby. I've done this with hundreds of young people, and I get enormous satisfaction hearing from them later on as their careers progress. There are times when I can make a big difference in a young person's life. I can open a door or place a call or set up an internship—one of those simple acts by which destinies are altered. But too often the offer is refused.

The recipient will say, "Sorry, but I can't accept the favor because I'm not sure I'll ever be able to repay you"; or "I'd rather not be obligated to anyone, so I'll have to pass." Sometimes, they'll insist right there and then that they return the favor somehow. To me, nothing is as infuriating as encountering such blindness about how things work. Nor is it, as one might assume, a generational issue. I've gotten similar reactions from people of all ages and in all walks of life.

A network functions precisely because there's recognition of mutual need. There's an implicit understanding that investing time and energy in building personal relationships with the right people will pay dividends. The majority of "one percenters," as I call the ultra-rich and successful whom many of my mentees aspire toward, are one percenters because they understand this dynamic—because, in fact, they themselves used the power of their network of contacts and friends to arrive at their present station.

But to do so, first you have to stop keeping score. You can't amass a network of connections without introducing such connections to others with equal fervor. The more people you help, the more help you'll have and the more help you'll have helping others. It's like the Internet. The more people who have access, and use it, the more valuable the Internet becomes. I now have a small army of former mentees, succeeding in any number of industries, helping me to mentor the young people that come to me today.

This is not softhearted hokum; it's an insight that hard-headed business people would do well to take seriously. We live in an interdependent world. Flattened organizations seek out strategic alliances at every turn. A growing pool of free agents are finding they need to work with others to accomplish their goals. More than ever before, zero-sum scenarios where only one party wins often mean, in the long run, that both parties will lose. Win/win has become a necessary reality in a networked world. In a hyperconnected marketplace, cooperation is gaining ground on competition.

The game has changed.

In 1956, William Whyte's bestselling book *The Organization Man* outlined the archetypal American worker: We donned our gray suit for a large corporation, offering our loyalty in exchange for job security. It was glorified indentured servitude, with few options and few opportunities. Today, however, employers offer little loyalty, and employees give none. Our careers aren't paths so much as landscapes that are navigated. We're free agents, entrepreneurs, and intrapreneurs—each with our own unique brand.

Many people have adapted to these new times with the belief that it's still a dog-eat-dog world, where the meanest, baddest dog in the neighborhood wins. But nothing could be further from the truth.

Where employees once found generosity and loyalty in the companies we worked for, today we must find them in a web of our own relationships. It isn't the blind loyalty and generosity we once gave to a corporation. It's a more personal kind of loyalty and generosity, one given to your colleagues, your team, your friends, your customers.

Today, we need each other more than ever.

Sadly, plenty of people still function as if it were 1950. We have a tendency to romanticize independence. Most business literature still views autonomy as a virtue, as though communication, teamwork, and cooperation were lesser values. To such thinkers, interdependence is just a variation of outright dependence. In my experience, such a view is a career-killer.

Autonomy is a life vest made out of sand. Independent people who do not have the skills to think and act interdependently may be good individual producers, but they won't be seen as good leaders or team players. Their careers will begin to stutter and stall before too long.

Let me give you an example. When I was at Deloitte, I was working on a project for the largest HMO in the country, Kaiser Permanente, forcing me to travel between their two headquarters in San Francisco and Los Angeles, and back to my home in Chicago on the weekend.

It was clear to me early on that I hoped to use the consulting world as a gateway into some other field. Since I was in Los Angeles, I wondered how I might begin to create inroads into the entertainment industry. I wasn't looking to accomplish anything in particular; I just knew that I was interested in the industry, and when the day came to move on, I wanted to break into Hollywood without having to deliver some agent's mail.

Ray Gallo, my best friend from my undergraduate days, was practicing law in Los Angeles, so I called him to get some advice.

"Hey, Ray. Who do you know in the entertainment world that I can talk to for some advice about breaking into the industry? You know any people who'd be open for a short lunch?"

"There's a guy named David who I know through mutual friends who also went to HBS. Give him a call."

David was a smart entrepreneur doing some creative deals in Hollywood. In particular, he had a close connection with a senior executive at one of the studios whom he had also gone to school with. I was hoping I might get a chance to get to know both of them.

David and I met for a cup of coffee at an outdoor café in Santa Monica. He was dressed in very dapper casual L.A. attire. I wore a suit and tie, befitting the buttoned-down Midwestern consultant that I was at the time.

After a good deal of back-and-forth, I asked David a question.

"I'm thinking about transitioning into the entertainment industry at some point. Is there anyone you know who you think could lend some helpful advice?" I was a good friend of a close friend of his. This seemed like a mild request given the strength of our meeting.

"I do know somebody," he told me. "She is a senior executive at Paramount."

"Great, I'd love to meet her," I said excitedly. "Is there any chance of arranging a quick introduction? Maybe you could pass on an e-mail?"

"I can't," he told me flatly. I was shocked, and my face showed it. "Keith, here's the situation. It's likely that at some point I'm going to need something from this person or want to ask a personal favor. And I'm just not interested in using the equity that I have with this individual on you, or anyone else, for that matter. I need to save that for myself. I'm sorry. I hope you understand."

But I didn't understand. I still don't. His statement flew in the face of everything I knew. He thought of relationships as finite, like a pie that can only be cut into so many pieces. Take a piece away, and there was that much less for him. I knew, however, that relationships are more like muscles—the more you work them, the stronger they become.

If I'm going to take the time to meet with somebody, I'm going to try to make that person successful. But David kept score. He saw every social encounter in terms of diminishing returns. For him, there was only so much goodwill available in a relationship and only so much collateral and equity to burn.

What he didn't understand was that it's the exercising of equity that builds equity. That's the big "ah-ha" that David never seemed to have learned.

Jack Pidgeon, the former headmaster of the Kiski School in southwestern Pennsylvania, where I went to high school, taught me that lesson. He'd built an entire institution on his asking people not "How can you help *me*?" but "How can I help *you*?"

One of the many times Jack came to my aid was when I was a sophomore in college. I'd been enlisted to work during the summer for a woman who was running for Congress against a young Kennedy. Running against a Kennedy in Boston, and for Jack

Kennedy's former congressional seat to boot, was for many people a lost cause. But I was young and naïve and ready for battle.

Unfortunately, we barely had time to don our armor before we were forced to wave the white flag of surrender. A month into the campaign, we ran out of money. Eight other college kids and I were literally thrown out of our hotel room, which doubled as our campaign headquarters, in the middle of the night by a general manager who had not been paid in too long a time.

We decided to pack our duffel bags into a rented van, and not knowing what else to do, we headed to Washington, D.C. We innocently hoped we could latch onto another campaign. Boy, we were green.

In the middle of the night, at some anonymous rest stop on the way to Washington, I called Mr. Pidgeon from a pay phone. When I told him about our situation, he chuckled. Then he proceeded to do what he has done for several generations of Kiski alums. He opened his Rolodex and started making calls.

One of those people he called was Jim Moore, a Kiski alum who was the former Assistant Secretary of Commerce in the Reagan administration. By the time our caravan of lost souls made it to D.C., we all had places to stay and we were on our way to getting summer jobs. I'm pretty sure that Mr. Pidgeon had made a few similar calls for Jim in his day.

Mr. Pidgeon understood the value of introducing people to people, Kiski boy to Kiski boy. He knew not only the impact it would have on our individual lives, but that the loyalty such acts engender would ultimately reap rewards for the nearly bankrupt, small, five-building facility in southwestern Pennsylvania he was trying to establish.

And so it has. Jim and I are now on the Board of Directors at our alma mater. And if you were around when Jack first took over the school, today you'd barely recognize the place, with its ski slopes, golf course, fine arts center, and the sort of sophisticated technology that makes it look like some midwestern MIT.

My point is this: Relationships are solidified by trust. Institutions are built on it. You gain trust by asking not what people can do for you, to paraphrase an earlier Kennedy, but what you can do for others.

In other words, the currency of real networking is not greed but generosity.

When I look back on all the people who have taught me invaluable lessons about creating lasting relationships—my father, Elsie, my mentees and the college kids I speak with, Ray, Mr. Pidgeon, the people I've worked with—I come away with several fundamental insights and observations:

1. Yesterday we had the new economy. Today we have the old economy (again!), and no one can predict what's going to be thrown at us next. Business cycles ebb and flow; your friends and trusted associates remain. A day might well come when you step into your boss's office some afternoon to hear, "I'm sorry to have to tell you this, but . . ." Tough day, guaranteed. The experience will be a whole lot easier to handle, however, if you can make a few calls and walk into someone's office soon after to hear, "I've been waiting for this day to come for a long time. Congratulations . . ."

   Job security? Experience will not save you in hard times, nor will hard work or talent. If you need a job, money, advice, help, hope, or a means to make a sale, there's only one surefire, fail-safe place to find them—within your extended circle of friends and associates.

2. There's no need to ponder whether it's their lunch or yours. There's no point in keeping track of favors done and owed. Who cares?

   Would it surprise you if I told you "Hollywood" David isn't doing that well any longer? David hoarded the relational equity he had until he eventually looked around and discovered there was nothing more to hoard. Ten years after I met him at that Santa Monica café, I haven't heard from him. In fact, no one else I know has heard from him either. Like so many industries, entertainment is a small world.

Bottom line: It's better to give before you receive. And never keep score. If your interactions are ruled by generosity, your rewards will follow suit.

3. The business world is a fluid, competitive landscape; yesterday's assistant is today's influence peddler. Many of the young men and women who used to answer my phones now thankfully take my calls. Remember, it's easier to get ahead in the world when those below you are happy to help you get ahead, rather than hoping for your downfall.

Each of us is now a brand. Gone are the days where your value as an employee was linked to your loyalty and seniority. Companies use branding to develop strong, enduring relationships with customers. In today's fluid economy, *you* must do the same with *your network*.

I would argue that your relationships with others are your finest, most credible expression of who you are and what you have to offer. Nothing else compares.

4. Contribute. It's like Miracle-Gro for networks. Give your time, money, and expertise to your growing community of friends.

5. In thinking about what Jack Pidgeon did for me and countless others, and the legacy he will leave behind because of it, I've become more convinced than ever that sharing what I've learned from him about reaching out to others is the greatest way to repay my former headmaster. Thanks again, Mr. Pidgeon.

CHAPTER 3

What's Your Mission?

"Would you tell me, please, which way I ought to go from here?"

"That depends a good deal on where you want to get to," said the Cat.

"I don't much care where—" said Alice.

"Then it doesn't matter which way you go," said the Cat.

—Alice's Adventures in Wonderland BY LEWIS CARROLL

D o you want to become a CEO or a senator? Rise to the top of your profession or to the top of your child's school board? Make more money or more friends?

The more specific you are about what you want to do, the easier it becomes to develop a strategy to accomplish it. Part of that strategy, of course, is establishing relationships with the people in your universe who can help you get where you're going.

Every successful person I've met shared, in varying degrees, a zeal for goal setting. Successful athletes, CEOs, charismatic leaders, rainmaking salespeople, and accomplished managers all know what they want in life, and they go after it.

As my dad used to say, no one becomes an astronaut by accident.

My own focus on goal setting started early. As a Yale undergrad, I thought I wanted to become a politician, a future governor of Pennsylvania. (I really was that specific, and that naïve.) But I learned that the more concrete my goal, the more I could accomplish toward it. In my sophomore year, I became chairman of Yale's political union, where so many alumni had cut their teeth before going on to careers in politics. When I became interested in joining a fraternity, I didn't simply join the first organization available to me. I researched which fraternity had the most active politicians as alumni. Sigma Chi had a rich tradition and an alumni roster of impressive leaders. But the fraternity wasn't chartered at Yale at that time. So we founded a chapter.

Eventually I ran for New Haven City Council. I lost, but in the process met everyone from William F. Buckley and Governor of Pennsylvania Dick Thornburg to the president of Yale, Bart Giamatti. I made regular visits to see Bart up until he died; he was a virtual oracle of advice and contacts for me. Even then, I recognized how something as simple as a clearly defined goal distinguished me from all those who simply floated through school waiting for things to happen. Later, I would apply this insight with even more vigor.

At Deloitte & Touche, for example, it was one of the ways I differentiated myself from the other postgrad consultants. I knew I needed a focus, a direction that I could pour my energies into. An article by Michael Hammer that I read in business school gave me that focus. Coauthor of *Reengineering the Corporation,* Hammer's ideas were taking the business world by storm and were on the verge of creating a new segment for consulting services.

Here was a chance to become an expert on a relatively new body of knowledge and research that was quickly becoming in hot demand. I read all the case studies and attended every conference or lecture I could. Wherever Michael Hammer was, there was I. Over time, he thankfully saw me less as a stalker and more as a pupil and friend. My access to Michael Hammer, and my growing knowledge in the field, helped me broker a much stronger relationship between my company and one of the business world's most influential and respected thinkers. Publicity and profits followed for Deloitte as they became a company at the forefront of the reengineering movement. And with that success, my career, which had once been on shaky ground, began to soar.

Countless books have been written about goal setting over the last few decades. Yes, it really *is that* important. Over the years, I've refined my own goal-setting process into three steps. But the key is to make setting goals a habit. If you do that, goal setting becomes a part of your life. If you don't, it withers and dies.

Step One: Find Your Passion

The best definition of a "goal" I've ever heard came from an extraordinarily successful saleswoman I met at a conference who told me, "A goal is a dream with a deadline." That marvelous definition drives home a very important point. Before you start writing down your goals, you'd better know what your dream is. Otherwise, you might find yourself headed for a destination you never wanted to get to in the first place.

Studies indicate that well over 50 percent of Americans are unhappy at work. Many of these people are doing well, but they are doing well at something they don't enjoy. How we got ourselves into such a situation isn't difficult to understand. People get overwhelmed by the decisions they have to make about their jobs, their families, their businesses, their futures. There are too many choices, it seems. We end up shifting our focus to talents we don't have and careers that don't quite fit. Many of us respond by simply falling into whatever comes down the pike without ever asking ourselves some very important questions.

Have you ever sat down and thought seriously about what you truly love? What you're good at? What you want to accomplish in life? What are the obstacles that are stopping you? Most people don't. They accept what they "should" be doing, rather than take the time to figure out what they *want* to be doing.

We all have our own loves, insecurities, strengths, weaknesses, and unique capabilities. And we have to take those into account in figuring out where our talents and desires intersect. That intersection is what I call your "blue flame"—where passion and ability come together. When that blue flame is ignited within a person, it is a powerful force in getting you where you want to go.

I think of the blue flame as a convergence of mission and passion founded on a realistic self-assessment of your abilities. It helps determine your life's purpose, from taking care of the elderly to becoming a mother, from being a top engineer to becoming a writer or a musician. I believe everyone has a distinct mission inside of him or her, one that has the capacity to inspire.

Joseph Campbell, who coined the phrase "follow your bliss" in the early 1900s, was a graduate student at Columbia University. His blue flame, he decided, was the study of Greek mythology. When he was told there was no such major, he devised his own plan.

After graduation, he moved into a cabin in Woodstock, New York, where he did nothing but read from nine in the morning until six or seven each night for five years. There isn't exactly a career track for lovers of Greek myth. Campbell emerged from the woods a very, very knowledgeable man, but he still had no clue what to do with his life. He persisted in following his love of mythology anyway.

The people who met him during this time were astonished by his wisdom and passion. Eventually, he was invited to speak at Sarah Lawrence College. One lecture led to another, until finally, when Campbell looked up one day twenty-eight years later, he was a famous author and professor of mythology, doing what he loved, at the same school that had given him his first break. "If you follow your bliss, you put yourself on a kind of track that has been there all the while, waiting for you, and the life that you ought to be living is the one you are living."

So how do you figure out your bliss?

Campbell believed that deep within each person, there's an intuitive knowledge of what she or he wants most in life. We only have to look for it.

Well, I agree with Dr. Campbell. All good decisions, I'm convinced, come from good information. Deciding on your passion, your bliss, your blue flame is no different. There are two aspects to getting good information. One part comes from within you; the other part comes from those around you.

1. Look inside

There are many ways to conduct a self-assessment of your goals and dreams. Some people pray. Others meditate or read. Some exercise. A few seek long periods of solitude.

The important thing when conducting an internal review is to do without the constraints, without the doubts, fears, and expectations of what you "should" be doing. You have to be able to set aside the obstacles of time, money, and obligation.

When I'm in the right frame of mind, I start to create a list of dreams and goals. Some are preposterous; others are overly pragmatic. I don't attempt to censure or edit the nature of the list—I put anything and everything down. Next to that first list, I write down in a second column all the things that bring me joy and pleasure: the achievements, people, and things that move me. The clues can be found in the hobbies you pursue and the magazines, movies, and books you enjoy. Which activities excite you the most, where you don't even notice the hours that pass?

When I'm done, I start to connect these two lists, looking for intersections, that sense of direction or purpose. It's a simple exercise, but the results can be profound.

2. Look outside

Next, ask the people who know you best what they think your greatest strengths and weaknesses are. Ask them what they admire about you and what areas you may need help in.

Before long, you'll find that the information you're getting from your own review and the input you receive from others will lead you to some very concrete conclusions about what your mission or direction should be.

Some of the business world's toughest CEOs and entrepreneurs are big believers in this notion of the blue flame—although they probably don't call it that.

James Champy, celebrated consultant and coauthor of *Reengineering the Corporation*, claims that success is first and foremost a matter of our dreams. In his book *The Arc of Ambition*, Champy found that the abilities of successful leaders like Ted Turner, Michael Dell, and Jack Welch are less important than the fact that each shares a clearly defined mission that drives him in all that he does.

When Champy asked Michael Dell where he found the ambition to build Dell computers, the CEO started to talk about business cycles and technology. Then he stopped.

"You know where I think the dream really came from?" he said. He described driving to school through the suburbs of Houston and ogling the office buildings with their great flagpoles. Dell wanted a flagpole. He wanted that kind of presence. To him, it was a symbol of success, and it drove him to envision starting up his own company before he could legally order a drink. Today, he has three flagpoles. I've spoken to Michael a number of times about his strategy at Dell, and it's amazing how each and every time this dream comes through clearly.

Human ambitions are like Japanese carp; they grow proportional to the size of their environment. Our achievements grow according to the size of our dreams and the degree to which we are in touch with our mission.

Coming up with goals, updating them, and monitoring our progress in achieving them is less important, I believe, than the process of emotionally deciding what it is you want to do.

Does that mean a hopeless dreamer could have run GE as well as Neutron Jack? Of course not. The transformation of a dream into reality requires hard work and discipline.

"Welch might resent the fact that I say, 'Jack, you're a dreamer,'" says Champy. "But the truth is he's a disciplined dreamer. He has the ability and sensibility that allows him to walk into various industries and see where the opportunities are."

Disciplined dreamers all have one thing in common: a mission. The mission is often risky, unconventional, and most likely tough as hell to achieve. But it *is* possible. The kind of discipline that turns a dream into a mission, and a mission into a reality, really just comes down to a process of setting goals.

Step Two: Putting Goals to Paper

Turning a mission into a reality does not "just happen." It is built like any work of art or commerce, from the ground up. First, it must be imagined. Then, one needs to gather the skills, tools, and materials needed. It takes time. It requires thought, determination, persistence, and faith.

The tool I use is something I call the Relationship Action Plan.

The Plan is separated into three distinct parts: The first part is devoted to the development of the goals that will help you fulfill your mission. The second part is devoted to connecting those goals to the people, places, and things that will help you get the job done. And the third part helps you determine the best way to reach out to the people who will help you to accomplish your goals.

It's a bare-bones, straightforward worksheet, but it has been extraordinarily helpful to me, my sales staff, and many of my friends.

In the first section, I list what I'd like to accomplish three years from today. I then work backward in both one-year and three-month increments to develop mid- and short-term goals that will help me reach my mission. Under each time frame, I create an "A" and a "B" goal that will meaningfully contribute to where I want to be three years from now.

A close friend, Jamie, offers a good example of how this works. Jamie was struggling to find direction in her life. She had graduated with a Ph.D. in history from Harvard, thinking she'd become a professor. But she found academia too stuffy. She gave business a shot, but found the world of commerce unrewarding. So Jamie spent several months living in Manhattan thinking about where she was going in life, until it occurred to her that what she really wanted to do was teach children.

I asked Jamie to give my Relationship Action Plan a try. She was skeptical at first. "That may be good for MBA types, but I'm not sure it works for people like me," she insisted. Nonetheless, she agreed to try it.

So she set about filling out the worksheet. Her "A" goal three years forward was to be a teacher. Her three-year "B" goal was to be a teacher in a well-respected district located in a place she wanted to live. Then she filled in her short-term A and B goals.

In ninety days, she wanted to be well on her way toward becoming certified as a high school teacher, enrolling in some type of program that would help professionals transition into the field of education. In a year, she wanted to be teaching full-time; she made a list of some of the best high schools in Manhattan that she might enjoy working at.

In the second part of the Plan, broken up in similar time increments, she had to name several people for each A and B goal who she thought could get her one step closer to making her goal a reality.

Jamie did her research and found the contact for a program

that places midcareer professionals into teaching positions. She also found out the names of the people at each of the best high schools she had listed who were responsible for hiring. Finally, she found the number for an organization that provides teaching certification courses.

Within a couple of weeks, Jamie was on her way. She started to see the symbiotic relationship between goal setting and reaching out to the people who can help us achieve those goals. The more she accomplished, the bigger her teaching network grew. The bigger her teaching network grew, the closer she came to accomplishing her three-year goals.

Ultimately, the third stage helps you assess which of the strategies I'll show you in the following chapters will be most successful. With some people, it will require you cold-call them (which we'll talk more about later). Others you'll be able to reach through friends of friends; still others might best be acquainted through a dinner party or conference. I'll teach you how to utilize all these methods and more.

Jamie is now a tenured high school history teacher in one of the best high schools in the country, in Beverly Hills, California. And she loves the job.

This process can be used by almost anyone, whatever your career. After completing the worksheet, you'll have a mission. You'll have the names of flesh-and-blood people who can help you take the next step in achieving that mission. And you'll have one, or perhaps several, ways to reach out to them.

The purpose of this exercise is to show that there is a *process*, a system if you will, involved in building a network. It's not magical; it's not reserved for a select few born with an inherent gift for being social. Connecting with others really just involves having a predetermined plan and carrying it out, whether you want to be a ninth-grade history teacher or start your own business.

Moreover, you can apply the worksheet to every aspect of your life: to expand your network of friends, further your education, find a lifelong partner, and search for spiritual guidance.

Once you have your plan, post it in a place (or places) where you will see it on a regular basis. Share your goals with others. This is very powerful and perhaps one of the most rewarding aspects of having clear goals—there are hidden opportunities waiting to be accessed in everyone if you just tell them what you want.

Make a plan for yourself now, before going on to the next chapter. I like to keep some variation of mine in my Palm to remind myself regularly what I need to be accomplishing, and whom I need to reach out to. A few years ago, I laminated a small version of the sheet and kept it in my wallet.

But your goals *must be in writing*. Have the conviction to put your intentions to paper. An unwritten wish is just a dream. In writing, it's a commitment, a goal.

Here are a few other criteria to consider when filling out your Relationship Action Plan, or RAP:

- Your goals must be specific. Vague, sweeping goals are too broad to be acted upon. They must be concrete and detailed. Know what steps you'll take to achieve your goal, the date by which it will be accomplished, and the measurement you'll use to gauge whether you've achieved the goal or not. I tell my salespeople that setting a goal like "I'm going to have my best quarter ever" is not enough. Will they make $100,000 or $500,000?

- Your goals must be believable. If you don't *believe* you can reach them, you won't. If your goal is to increase the revenue of your business to five million dollars in a year, and you only achieved revenue of one million last year, you're setting yourself up for failure. Instead, set your goal at one and one-half million dollars for the year—and beat the heck out of it.

- Your goals must be challenging and demanding. Step out of your comfort zone; set goals that require risk and uncertainty. And when you achieve your goal, set another one. One of the best salesmen I've ever met is a man my father knew named Lyle, who sold books door-to-door. He would set annual sales goals for himself, write them down, and place them wherever he could: in his wallet, on his refrigerator, in his desk. Inevitably, he'd reach his goal months ahead of schedule. Then he'd simply write down another one. The man was never satisfied. What matters is the goal setting, Lyle would say, not the goal getting. He may have been the only door-to-door book salesman in Pennsylvania—or anywhere else, for that matter—who died a rich man.

Next, take *ACTION*! It's called a Relationship *Action* Plan for a reason. To prepare yourself to run a marathon, you must get out there and jog every day. With a plan in place, it's up to you to start reaching out. Every day!

Step Three: Create a Personal "Board of Advisors"

Goals, like everything else I write about in this book, aren't achieved alone. With a plan in place, you're going to need reinforcement to stay focused. As in any business, even the best-conceived plans benefit from external vetting.

It helps to have an enlightened counselor, or two or three, to act as both cheerleader and eagle-eyed supervisor, who will hold you accountable. I call this group my Personal Board of Advisors. It may be made up of family members; perhaps someone who's been a mentor to you; even an old friend or two.

My board came to my own aid at a critical juncture in my career after I left Starwood Hotels and Resorts, the company that owns such brands as the W Hotel and the Westin. I was adrift. For the first time in my life, I couldn't lay claim to a title or a job. I had to reassess my mission.

I had come to Starwood from Deloitte to accept what was an irresistible offer: to be the youngest chief marketing officer in a Fortune 500 company (a goal I had set for myself three years earlier) and reinvent the way an industry thought about marketing.

But my new job didn't go exactly as planned.

Juergen Bartels, the president at Starwood who recruited me, promised to mentor me and pave my way toward becoming a future leader of the company. My goals for the company were large and required changing an entire company's way of thinking.

Up until that point, marketing in the hospitality industry was a regional affair, often left to individual hotels. But the cost of that arrangement was a lack of company-wide brand consistency. Our plan was to consolidate our marketing functions under one roof with a global outlook. Rather than allow each of our regions around the world to set their own individual marketing strategies, I wanted to centralize our marketing operations more in order to clarify our message and create greater impact in the marketplace with a cohesive brand. After all, our primary customers—business travelers—were increasingly global and expected consistency.

Shortly after I was hired, however, Juergen Bartels left the company. Corporations, like any bureaucracy, tend to resist change, especially when the change doesn't have the support of top management. It became clear, a year into my job, that under the new president I wouldn't be able to garner the kind of support within the company I needed for such a radical reorganization.

The new president made it clear that we would not be moving forward with our plan to reorganize the marketing department. The writing was on the wall for the plan and for me personally. Without the go-ahead needed to make the kind of bold decisions that I felt would ultimately lead to company success and a more senior personal position, I knew I wouldn't be able to reach my goals there.

I was shocked. I left work early that particular day and jogged mile after mile through the beautiful paths of New York's Central Park. Exercise has always been a refuge where I do some of my best thinking. But some ten miles later, I was still in shock.

The next morning, as I walked into the office, I knew that my future was somewhere else. All the accoutrements of a top executive's life—the large, cushy office, the mahogany furniture, the corporate jet, the fancy title on the door—meant nothing if I couldn't implement the ideas that made work fun, creative, and exciting. I officially resigned soon after, and if I hadn't, I know I wouldn't have been long for the company anyway.

It was time for me to establish a new goal. Should I seek out another position as chief marketing officer, proving myself by building bigger and better brands, striving for greater revenue (and profits), and helping to turn a company into a brand icon? Or should I set my sights even higher? My ultimate goal was to become a CEO. But it seldom happens for those in marketing. I had spent the greater part of my career convincing top management that marketing can and should directly influence all operating activities, yet I was not responsible for all of them.

To truly define the brand, the ultimate marketing job was to be the CEO. If I chose the latter direction, what else did I need to learn to become CEO? What were my chances of getting such a job? What sacrifices or risks were involved?

Honestly, these questions weren't clear to me at the time. In the wake of my disappointment, after years of go-go-go, I felt lost. I needed to figure out what I wanted to be all over again.

And I was scared. For the first time in ages, I had no company to attach to my name. I loathed the thought of meeting new people without a clear explanation of what I did.

Over the next few months, I had hundreds of conversations with the people I trust. I took a Vipassana meditation retreat where I sat for ten hours each day for ten days straight—in silence. For a guy like me, who can't shut up, it was torture. I wondered if I might fritter away all my time thinking. I wondered if I should go back to Pennsylvania and find a smaller pond to inhabit.

During that time I wrote a detailed twelve-page mission statement asking such questions as What are my strengths? What are my weaknesses? What are the various industry opportunities available to me? I listed the venture capitalists I wanted to meet, the CEOs I knew, the leaders I could turn to for advice, and the companies that I admired. I left all my options open: teacher, minister, politician, chief executive officer. For each potential new direction, I filled out a Relationship Action Plan.

When everything was laid out, I reached out to my personal board of advisors. I didn't have the qualifications to be appointed a CEO with a major corporation. Yet when I looked inside myself, that was exactly what I wanted to do.

Sitting down with Tad Smith, a publishing executive and one of my best friends and advisors, I was told I had to get over the prestige of working for a Fortune 500 company. If I wanted to be CEO, I had to find a company I could grow with.

It was exactly the advice I needed to hear. I had been too focused on big companies. While the dot-com crash had made entering the digital world a whole lot less palatable, there were still some very good companies in need of business fundamentals. Now I knew this was where I needed to look, and I began refining my action plan.

From that day on, many of the calls I made, and the meetings and conferences I attended, were aimed at finding the right small company to call home. Three months later, I had five job offers.

One of the people I reached out to was Sandy Climan, a well-known Hollywood player who once served as Michael Ovitz's

right-hand man at Creative Artists Agency and who then ran an
L.A.-based venture capital firm called Entertainment Media Ventures. I had gotten to know Sandy during my time with Deloitte,
when I was exploring paths into the entertainment world. Sandy
introduced me to the people at a company called YaYa, one of the
investments in his firm's portfolio.

YaYa was a marketing company pioneering the creation of
online games as advertising vehicles. They had a good concept and
the strength of committed employees and founders. They needed
a bigger vision to get the market's attention, some buzz for their
then-unknown product, and someone who could use all that to
sell, sell, sell.

In November 2000, when the YaYa board offered me the CEO
position, I knew it was the right fit. The company was located in
Los Angeles, and it offered the sort of unconventional route into
the entertainment world I had been looking for and a chance to
bring my experience as a marketer to the CEO job.

If Virginia Can Do It, You Can Too

A few months ago, a friend of mine told me about a woman named
Virginia Feigles, who lived not too far away from where I grew up.
He had been inspired by her tale of triumph. Hearing her story, I felt
the same way.

At forty-four, Feigles decided she no longer wanted to be a hair-
dresser; she wanted to be an engineer. From the get-go, there were
naysayers, people who insisted it couldn't be done. Their negativity
simply provided more fuel for her fire.

"I lost a lot of friends during this whole thing," Feigles says. "People become jealous when you decide to do what no one thought
you would, or could. You just have to push through."

Her adventure reads like a Cliffs Notes guide to career management where a bold mission and a commitment to reach out to oth-

ers combine to create opportunities previously unavailable to a high school graduate. It also conveys a harsh dose of reality: Change is hard. You might lose friends, encounter seemingly insurmountable obstacles, and face the most troubling hurdle of all—your own self-doubt.

Feigles had always planned to go to college. Raised by a single mother in small-town Milton, Pennsylvania, the opportunities were slim. She was married by seventeen and pregnant a year later. She worked full time as a hairstylist in her husband's salon and raised her only son. Twenty years went by. With her second divorce, Feigles rethought her life. Growth, she reflected, came only from change. And change came only from new goals.

She was working part-time as a secretary at the chamber of commerce when she realized life had more to offer. "I just thought, 'This is stupid. Why am I on the wrong end of this? Not everyone who has a Ph.D. in physics is Albert Einstein.'"

While it's true not every engineer is a genius, they all know algebra—something Feigles couldn't claim. So she buckled down and learned the subject within a few months.

After a summer stint at community college, she decided to apply to a top-tier civil engineering school at Bucknell University. The associate dean, Trudy Cunningham, didn't sugarcoat the situation.

"When she arrived, I told her that life was about to get hard. She's an adult with a life, an apartment, a car, and she was competing with kids who were living in dorms and having their meals cooked."

Luckily, Feigles had always been an avid connector all her life. She was a member of a number of community organizations, serving on the boards of the YMCA, Milton Chamber of Commerce, and Parks and Recreation Committee. She also had stints serving as president of the Garden Club and the Milton Business Association. She had supportive friends and advisors all around.

For the other students, the end of class meant keg parties and football games. For her, it meant a night working at the salon followed by grinding study sessions. Feigles doesn't remember a day she didn't think of quitting.

She remembers getting back her first physics test. She failed.

"Another student thought it was the end of the world. I told her not to worry, I wasn't about to commit suicide," she recalls with the wry insight reserved for someone who's been through it. She ended up with a C in the class.

Many sleepless nights and several Cs later, Feigles found herself among 137 other engineers in the graduating class of 1999. No one was more astonished than the graduate herself: "I just kept on thinking, 'What have I done?' And then repeating to myself, 'I've done it, I've actually done it!'"

With her goals completed, her network has grown—and not only in terms of friends and new business contacts. Today, she's newly married—to her former boss at the chamber of commerce—and busy with a budding career at the state's Department of Transportation. Recently she became chairperson of the Planning Commission, where she used to take notes as a secretary.

Reaching your goals can be difficult. But if you have goals to begin with, a realizable plan to achieve them, and a cast of trusted friends to help you, you can do just about anything—even becoming an engineer after the age of forty.

CONNECTORS' HALL OF FAME PROFILE

Bill Clinton

"Know your mission in life."

In 1968, when William Jefferson Clinton was a Rhodes Scholar at Oxford University, he met a graduate student named Jeffrey Stamps at a party. Clinton promptly pulled out a black address book. "What are you doing here at Oxford, Jeff?" he asked.

"I'm at Pembroke on a Fulbright," Jeff replied. Clinton penned "Pembroke" into his book, then asked about Stamps's undergraduate school and his major. "Bill, why are you writing this down?" asked Stamps.

"I'm going into politics and plan to run for governor of Arkansas, and I'm keeping track of everyone I meet," said Clinton.

That story, recounted by Stamps, epitomizes Bill Clinton's forthright approach to reaching out and including others in his mission. He knew, even then, that he wanted to run for office, and his sense of purpose emboldened his efforts with both passion and sincerity. In fact, as an undergraduate at Georgetown, the forty-second president made it a nightly habit to record, on index cards, the names and vital information of every person whom he'd met that day.

Throughout his career, Clinton's political aspirations and his ability to reach out to others have gone hand-in-hand. In 1984, when he was governor of Arkansas, he attended, for the first time, a national networking and thought leadership event called Renaissance Weekend in Hilton Head, South Carolina. Clinton secured an invitation through his friend, Richard Riley, who was then governor of South Carolina. Attending Renaissance Weekend was like a trip to a toy store for a guy like Clinton, who wasted no time meeting others and making friends. Here's how a *Washington Post* article from December 1992 describes Clinton in action at the event:

Many guests, reflecting on Clinton's presence, remember images more than words: how he would roam from discussion to discussion and take a spot at the side of the room, leaning casually against the wall; how he would seem to know everyone, not just from their name tags, but remember what they did and what they were interested in. "He hugs you," said Max Heller, the former mayor of Greenville. "He hugs you not only physically, but with a whole attitude."

What Heller is referring to is Clinton's unique ability to create an almost instantaneous intimacy with whomever he's talking to. Clinton doesn't just recall your personal information; he uses the information as a means to affirm a bond with you.

From Clinton, two lessons are clear: First, the more specific you are about where you want to go in life, the easier it becomes to develop a networking strategy to get there.

Second, be sensitive to making a real connection in your interactions with others. There is almost an expectation among us that whoever becomes rich or powerful can be forgiven for high-handed behavior. Clinton illustrates how charming and popular you can become, and remain, when you treat everyone you meet with sincerity.

CHAPTER 4

Build It Before You Need It

Build a little community of those you love and who love you.

—Mitch Albom

Forget the images we all have in our heads of the desperate, out-of-work individuals scooping up every business card in sight while fervently mingling at business conventions and job-hunting events. The great myth of "networking" is that you start reaching out to others only when you need something like a job. In reality, people who have the largest circle of contacts, mentors, and friends know that you must reach out to others long before you need anything at all.

George, for example, is a smart guy in his twenties who was introduced to me through a mutual friend. George worked in public relations in New York and aspired to start his own PR business. He asked me to lunch one day looking for advice and encouragement.

Ten minutes after we sat down, I knew he was on the wrong track.

"Have you started to reach out to potential clients?" I asked.

"No," he told me. "I'm taking it step by step. My plan is to work my way up in my current company to a point where I can afford to leave. Then I'll incorporate, get an office, and start searching for my first customers. I don't want to start meeting with potential clients until I can present myself as a credible PR person with my own firm."

"You've got it totally backwards," I told him. "You're setting yourself up for failure."

My advice was to start finding future clients today. Had he thought about what kind of industry he wanted to specialize in? Had he thought about where the top people in that industry hang out? Once he could answer those questions, the next step was to go hang with this new circle of people.

"The most important thing is to get to know these people as friends, not potential customers," I said. "Though you're right about one thing: No matter how friendly you are, if the people you approach are any good at what they do, they won't hire you right off the bat to do their PR. Which is why you should offer your services for free—at least at first. For instance, maybe you can volunteer your time to a nonprofit organization they're involved in, or aid in publicizing a school fundraiser their kids are involved in."

"But won't my employer be angry at my expending so much energy on other things?" George asked.

"Doing good work for your employer comes first," I told him. "Finding time to manage your outside work is your responsibility. Concentrate on an industry that your present employer doesn't service. Remember, if you haven't done the necessary legwork on the day you decide to open your own business, you'll be back at your old job in no time flat."

"So I should work for these people for *free*?"

"Absolutely," I said. "Today you are unproven, and breaking in is tough. Eventually you'll have a growing circle of people who have seen your work and who believe in you. That's the kind of connections you're looking to create if you're going to start a business, or if you're looking to change jobs or careers.

"At some point, while you're still working for your current employer, start looking to turn one of your contacts into a real, paying client. Once you've got an established client that will provide references and create some word-of-mouth, you're halfway home. Then, and only then, is it time to go back to your company and ask to go half time, or better yet, turn them into your second big client. If you quit at that point, you've hedged your bets. You have a group of people who will help transition you into a new career."

The last half hour of our lunch was spent thinking about all the people he already knew who could help him get started. I offered a name or two from my own network, and George's confidence started to soar. I'm confident that now, when he reaches out, his interactions won't be tainted by desperation. He'll be looking for ways to help others, and everyone can benefit from a little bit of that.

The ideas behind starting a business aren't that different from the ideas that will make you a hot commodity within your company—not to mention give you job security. I know that's hard to believe given the current job environment. According to a recent study of business school programs, the percentage of MBAs in 2004 who were without a job three months after graduation tripled from the year before to an alarming 20 percent. Scores of people are out of work or living in dread that the ax will fall on their heads. A blizzard of pink slips has convinced job seekers that they must do more than scan the help-wanted ads or send résumés.

Too often, we get caught up efficiently doing ineffective things, focusing solely on the work that will get us through the day. The idea isn't to find oneself another environment tomorrow—be it a new job or a new economy—but to be constantly creating the environment and community you want for yourself, no matter what may occur.

Creating such a community, however, is not a short-term solution or one-off activity only to be used when necessary. The dynamics of building a relationship is necessarily incremental. You can only truly gain someone's trust and commitment little by little over time.

Right now, there are countless ways you can begin to create the kind of community that can help further your career. You can: (1) create a company-approved project that will force you to learn new skills and introduce you to new people within your company; (2) take on leadership positions in the hobbies and outside organizations that interest you; (3) join your local alumni club and spend time with people who are doing the jobs you'd like to be doing; (4) enroll in a class at a community college on a subject that relates to either the job you're doing now or a job you see yourself doing in the future.

All of these suggestions will help you meet new people. And the law of probability ensures that the more new people you know, the more opportunities will come your way and the more help you'll get at critical junctures in your career.

My first year in business school, I started consulting with my friend Tad Smith, who is now President of the Media Division at the large magazine publishing company Reed Business Information. The idea wasn't to create a sustainable consulting company that we would run after school. Instead, we wanted to offer our knowledge and work ethic to small companies for cut-rate prices. In exchange, we'd learn about new industries, gain real-world skills, and have a list of references and contacts when we graduated, as well as make some ready cash.

What about the world you inhabit right now? Are you making the most of the connections you already have?

Imagine, for a moment, that all your family and friends and associates are a part of a garden. Take a stroll through that relationship garden. What do you see?

If you're like most people, you see a tiny parcel of cleanly cut grass that represents the usual suspects of an ordinary Rolodex. It consists of your immediate friends, coworkers, and business partners: the most obvious people.

Your real network, however, is an overgrown jungle with an infinite variety of hidden nooks and crannies that are being neglected.

Your potential for connecting is at this moment far bigger than you realize. All around you are golden opportunities to develop relationships with people you know, who know people you don't know, who know even more people.

There are a number of things that you can do to harness the power of your preexisting network. Have you investigated the friends and contacts of your parents? How about your siblings? Your friends from college and grad school? What about your church, bowling league, or gym? How about your doctor or lawyer or realtor or broker?

In business, we often say that your best customers are the customers you have now. In other words, your most successful sales leads come from the selling you've already done. The highest returns don't come from new sales; they come on top of the customer base you've already established. It's easiest to reach out to those people who are at least tangentially part of your network.

The big hurdles of networking revolve around the cold calls, meeting of new people, and all the activities that involve engaging the unknown. But the first step has nothing to do with strangers; you should start connecting with the people you *do* know.

Focus on your immediate network: friends of friends, old acquaintances from school, and family. I suspect you've never asked your cousins, brothers, or brothers-in-law if they know anyone that they could introduce you to to help fulfill your goals.

Everyone from your family to your mailman is a portal to an entirely new set of folks.

So don't wait until you're out of a job, or on your own, to begin reaching out to others. You've got to create a community of colleagues and friends *before* you need it. Others around you are far more likely to help you if they already know and like you. Start gardening now. You won't believe the treasures to be found within your own backyard.

CHAPTER 5

The Genius of Audacity

Seize this very minute; what you can do, or dream you can, begin it; Boldness has genius, power and magic in it.

—Johann Wolfgang von Goethe

My father, Pete Ferrazzi, was a first-generation American, a Merchant Marine sailor in World War II, and an uneducated steelworker whose world was hard hours and low wages. He wanted more for me, his son. He and I were inseparable when I was growing up (his friends called me "re-Pete" because he took me everywhere with him). He knew I would have a better life if he could help me find a way out of our working-class heritage.

But my dad didn't know the exits. He'd never been to college. He knew nothing of country clubs or private schools. He could picture only one man who would have the sort of pull that could help me: his boss. Actually, the boss of his boss's boss—Alex McKenna, CEO of Kennametal, in whose factory my dad worked.

The two men had never met. But Dad had a clear sense of how the world worked. He'd observed, even from the plant floor, that audacity was often the only thing that separated two equally talented men and their job titles. So he asked to speak with McKenna. McKenna, upon hearing the request, was so intrigued that he took the meeting. In the course of the meeting, he agreed to meet me—but nothing more.

It turned out that McKenna liked me—partly because of the way I had come to his attention. He served on the board of a local private elementary school, the Valley School of Ligonier, where all the wealthy families sent their children; by reputation it was one of the best elementary schools in the country. Strings were pulled, and Mr. McKenna got us an appointment with Peter Messer, the headmaster.

The day I enrolled in the Valley School, on scholarship, I entered a new world that set me on an entirely new course, just as my father had hoped. I got one of the best educations in America, starting with Valley School, then Kiski School, Yale University, and on to Harvard Business School. And it would never have happened if my father hadn't believed that it never hurts to ask.

As I look back on my career, it was the single most important act in my life. Moreover, the lesson I learned from my father's action, like no other, informed all that I have done since.

My father simply couldn't be embarrassed when it came to fulfilling his family's needs. I remember once we were driving down the road to our home when Dad spotted a broken Big Wheel tricycle in someone's trash. He stopped the car, picked it up, and knocked on the door of the home where the discarded toy lay waiting to be picked up.

"I spotted this Big Wheel in your trash," he told the owner. "Do you mind if I take it? I think I can fix it. It would make me feel wonderful to give my son something like this."

What guts! Can you imagine such a proud, working-class guy approaching that woman and, essentially, admitting he's so poor that he'd like to have her garbage?

Oh, but that's not the half of it. Imagine how that woman felt, having been given an opportunity to give such a gift to another person. It surely made her day.

"Of course," she gushed, explaining that her children were grown and that years had passed since the toy had been used.

"You're welcome to the bicycle I have, too. It's nice enough that I just couldn't throw it away . . ."

So we drove on. I had a "new" Big Wheel to ride and a bike to grow into. She had a smile and a fluttering heart that only benevolence breeds. And Dad had taught me that there is genius, even kindness, in being bold.

Every time I start to set limits to what I can and can't do, or fear starts to creep into my thinking, I remember that Big Wheel tricycle. I remind myself how people with a low tolerance for risk, whose behavior is guided by fear, have a low propensity for success.

The memories of those days have stuck with me. My father taught me that the worst anyone can say is no. If they choose not to give their time or their help, it's their loss.

Nothing in my life has created opportunity like a willingness to ask, whatever the situation. When I was just an anonymous attendee at the World Economic Forum in Switzerland, I walked onto a hotel bus and saw Nike founder Phil Knight. Knight was like a rock star to me, given his extraordinary success at creating and building Nike, and the many marketing innovations he introduced over the years. Was I nervous? You bet. But I jumped at the opportunity to speak with him, and made a beeline for the seat next to his. Later, he would become YaYa's first blue-chip customer. I do this sort of thing all the time, whatever the situation.

Sometimes I fail. I've got an equally long list of people I've attempted to befriend who weren't interested in my overtures. Audacity in networking has the same pitfalls and fears associated with dating—which I'm not nearly as good at as I am the business variety of meeting people.

Sticking to the people we already know is a tempting behavior. But unlike some forms of dating, a networker isn't looking to achieve only a single successful union. Creating an enriching circle of trusted relationships requires one to be *out there*, in the mix, all the time. To this day, every time I make a call or introduce myself to people I don't know, the fear that they might reject me is there. Then I remember the Big Wheel my father got me, and push ahead anyway.

Most of us don't find networking the least bit instinctive or natural. Of course, there are individuals whose inherent self-confidence and social skills enable them to connect with ease.

Then there are the rest of us.

In the early days at YaYa, I was worried for the company's survival. For the first time in my career, I had to reach out to a lot of people I didn't know, representing an unknown company, pushing a product that was untested in the marketplace. It was uncomfortable. I didn't want to cold-call executives from BMW and MasterCard and pitch them my wares. But you know what? Pushing to get into BMW was not that difficult when the alternative was laying off a bunch of my staff or failing in the eyes of my board and investors.

Mustering the audacity to talk with people who don't know me often simply comes down to balancing the fear I have of embarrassment against the fear of failure and its repercussions. For my father, either he asked or his family didn't have. For me, I either ask or I'm not successful. That fear always overrides my anxiety about rejection or being embarrassed.

Ultimately, everyone has to ask himself or herself how they're going to fail. We all do, you know, so let's get that out of the way. The choice isn't between success and failure; it's between choosing risk and striving for greatness, or risking nothing and being certain of mediocrity.

For many people, the fear of meeting others is closely tied to the fear of public speaking (a fear that consistently beats out death as the one thing we dread most). Some of the world's most famous speakers admit to feeling similar anxiety. As Mark Twain said, "There are two types of speakers: those that are nervous and those that are liars."

The best way to deal with this anxiety is to first acknowledge that our fear is perfectly normal. You are not alone. The second thing is to recognize that getting over that fear is critical to your success. The third is to commit to getting better.

Here are a few things you can do today to make good on that commitment and get more comfortable at being audacious in social situations:

- *Find a role model.*

We're predisposed to seek out people like us—shy people tend to congregate with other shy people, and outgoing people congregate with outgoing people—because they unconsciously affirm our own behaviors. But everyone knows that one person within their group of friends and associates who seems to engage others with little or no fear. If you're not yet ready to take the big leap of addressing new people on your own, let these people help you and show you the way. Take them with you, when appropriate, to social outings and observe their behaviors. Pay attention to their actions. Over time, you'll adopt some of their techniques. Slowly, you'll build up the courage to reach out by yourself.

- *Learn to speak.*

Many businesses have responded to the nearly infinite number of people who recognize they need to become better speakers. These educational organizations realize you're not looking to give speeches to an audience of a thousand people (at least initially). Most people who come to them for help are looking to gain self-confidence and some trusty tools for overcoming shyness. They don't offer one or two simple quick-fix cure-alls. What they do offer is a chance to practice, in a nonintimidating environment, with an instructor who can guide and push you. There are hundreds of coaches and schools devoted to this type of training. One of the most well known is the Toastmasters Club. They're sure to have a local chapter in your area. It is a well-run organization that has helped millions of people hone their speaking skills and overcome their fears.

- *Get involved.*

You'll feel most comfortable when you're doing something you enjoy with others who share your enthusiasm. Any hobby is an opportunity to get involved: stamp collecting, singing, sports, literature. Clubs develop around all of these interests. Join up. Become an active member. When you feel up to it, become one of the leaders of the group. This last step is crucial. Being a leader in life takes practice—so practice! The possibilities for making new contacts and reaching out to others will grow and grow.

- *Get therapy.*

I know, I know, you're probably thinking, "He wants me to go to therapy to become better at talking to people?" Let me explain. One, I think merely acting on the desire to be better than you are now, no matter the venue, is a very important commitment. Two, some of the most successful people I know have been to a therapist at one point in their lives or another. I'm not suggesting therapy will make you a better people person, but it might help you address your own fears and social anxieties in a more productive way. Many studies funded by the National Institute of Mental Health report a high success rate using counseling to alleviate the conditions that normally inhibit a shy person.

- *Just do it.*

Set a goal for yourself of initiating a meeting with one new person a week. It doesn't matter where or with whom. Introduce yourself to someone on the bus. Slide up next to someone at the bar and say hello. Hang out at the company water cooler and force yourself to talk to a fellow employee you've never spoken with. You'll find that it gets easier and easier with practice. Best of all, you'll get comfortable with the idea of rejection. With that perspective, even failure becomes a step forward. Embrace it as learning. As the playwright Samuel Beckett wrote, "Fail, fail again. Fail better."

Fear debilitates. Once you realize there's no benefit to holding back, every situation and every person—no matter how seemingly beyond your reach—becomes an opportunity to succeed.

The Madam of Moxie

When it comes to improving your speaking skills, no one is better than DeAnne Rosenberg, a thirty-two-year career counselor and owner of her own management consulting firm, DeAnne Rosenberg Inc. Rosenberg is the madam of moxie, and for good reason.

In 1969, she read a *Wall Street Journal* article that noted the absence of a female voice in the American Management Association.

"They were interviewing the then president of the A.M.A., who was quoted as saying, 'We haven't found a woman who can speak authoritatively in public about management,'" Rosenberg recalls.

She cut the article out and sent a letter to the A.M.A. telling them to look no further. Two weeks went by and her letter went unanswered.

"Well, that wouldn't do," she snaps. "I wrote another letter straight to the president, effectively telling them to put up or shut up."

Two days later, the president of the association called to say that they had scheduled her for a lecture. DeAnne went on to become the first woman to speak on behalf of the A.M.A.

The lesson from that fateful series of events remains with her: The recipe for achievement is a medley of self-assuredness, dogged persistence, and audacity. Encounters of the audacious kind, as DeAnne learned, are what successful careers are built upon. In her many years teaching others to overcome their fears, she's created a time-tested script that anyone can use when meeting someone for the first time.

I found the script helpful. I think it can help a lot of you as well, and I gratefully offer it to you here:

1. State the situation. "You go right in and hit them with how you see it in the cold light of day, without being too inflammatory or dramatic," says Rosenberg. She made it clear to the A.M.A. that a) having no women speakers was wrong, and b) hiring her would be a step in the right direction. It makes sense that before you can speak persuasively—that is, before you speak from a position of passion and personal knowledge—you need to know where you stand.

2. Communicate your feelings. We downplay the influence of emotions in our day-to-day contacts, especially in the business world. We're told that vulnerability is a bad thing and we should be wary of revealing our feelings. But as we gain comfort using "I feel" with others, our encounters take on depth and sincerity. Your emotions are a gift of respect and caring to your listeners.

3. Deliver the bottom line. This is the moment of truth when you state, with utter clarity, what it is you want. If you're going to put your neck on the line, you'd better know why. The truth is the fastest route to a solution, but be realistic. While I knew Phil Knight of Nike wasn't going to buy anything based on one five-minute conversation on a bus in Davos, Switzerland, I did make sure to get his e-mail and tell him that I'd like to follow up with him again sometime. Then I did so.

4. Use an open-ended question. A request that is expressed as a question—one that cannot be answered by a yes or no—is less threatening. How do you feel about this? How can we solve this problem? The issue has been raised, your feelings expressed, your desires articulated. With an open-ended suggestion or question, you invite the other person to work toward a solution with you. I didn't insist on a specific lunch date at a specific time with Phil. I left it open and didn't allow our first exchange to be weighted down by unnecessary obligations.

CHAPTER 6

The Networking Jerk

Ambition can creep as well as soar.

—EDMUND BURKE

He is the man or she is the woman with a martini in one hand, business cards in the other, and a prerehearsed elevator pitch always at the ready. He or she is a schmooze artist, eyes darting at every event in a constant search for a bigger fish to fry. He or she is the insincere, ruthlessly ambitious glad-hander you don't want to become.

The networking jerk is the image that many people have when they hear the word "networking." But in my book, this breed of hyper-Rolodex-builder and card-counter fails to grasp the nuances of authentic connecting. Their shtick doesn't work because they don't know the first thing about creating meaningful relationships.

As I learned the hard way.

If you knew me as a younger man, you may not have liked me. I'm not sure I liked myself that much. I made all the classic mistakes of youth and insecurity. I was pretty much out for myself. I wore my unquenchable ambition on my sleeve, befriending those above me and ignoring my peers. Too often people put on one face with their subordinates, another with their boss, and another one yet with their friends.

When I became responsible for marketing at Deloitte, I suddenly had a lot of people reporting to me. I had some very big ideas about what I wanted to do—things that never had been done from a marketing standpoint in the world of consulting. And now finally I had a team with which to execute them. But instead of viewing my employees as partners to be wooed in achieving my long-term objectives and theirs, I saw them as called upon to carry out my tasks.

Add to this my young age (I was twenty years younger than any other member of the executive committee), and you can understand why the resistance among my staff was holding all of us back. Tasks that I thought should have taken hours ended up taking days. I knew I needed to do something, so I reached out to an executive coach, Nancy Badore, who had been coaching high-level CEOs before there was a name for such a thing.

The day of our first meeting, sitting in my office, we barely had a chance to exchange pleasantries before I blurted out, "What do I need to do to become a great leader?"

She looked around my office for a few moments and said nothing. When she finally spoke, it struck me to the core. "Keith, look at all the pictures on your wall. You talk about aspiring to become a great leader, and there's not one picture in your whole office of anybody but you: you with other famous people, you in famous places, you winning awards. There's not one picture in here of your team or of anything that might indicate what your team has accomplished that would lead anybody like me to know that you care for them as much as you care for yourself. Do you understand that it's your team's accomplishments, and what they do because of you, not for you, that will generate your mark as a leader?"

I was floored by her question. She was absolutely right. Had I shown the genuine concern I had for the lives my employees led outside of work? Why hadn't I made an effort to make them part of the leadership? I'd been doing it with my bosses from day one.

I realized then my long-term success depended on everyone around me. That I worked for them as much as they worked for me!

Politicians understand this in a way too few executives grasp: We vote for the people we like and respect. Great companies are built by CEOs who inspire love and admiration. In today's world, mean guys finish last.

My friend and author Tim Sanders taught me there are two reasons for the end of the era of mean business. First, we live in a new "abundance of choice in business" in everything from products to career paths. Choice spells doom for difficult colleagues and leaders. "At a time when more of us have more options than ever, there's no need to put up with a product or service that doesn't deliver, a company that we don't like, or a boss whom we don't respect," he writes. The second reason is what he calls the "new telegraph." "It's almost impossible for a shoddy product, a noxious company, or a crummy person to keep its, his, or her sad reality a secret anymore. There are too many highly opinionated and well-informed people with access to e-mail, instant messaging, and the Web."

The bottom line is if you don't like someone, it's easier than ever to escape him. When you don't have others' interests at heart, people will find out sooner rather than later. Our culture demands more of us these days. It demands that we treat each other with respect. That every relationship be seen in mutually beneficial terms.

When you look back upon a life and career of reaching out to others, you want to see a web of friendships to fall back on, not the ashes of bad encounters. Here are a few rules I can suggest from personal experience to ensure that you never become a Networking Jerk:

1. Don't schmooze.

Have something to say, and say it with passion. Make sure you have something to offer when you speak, and offer it with sincerity. Most people haven't figured out that it's better to spend more time with fewer people at a one-hour get-together, and have one or two meaningful dialogues, than engage in the wandering-eye routine and lose the respect of most of the people you meet. I get e-mails all the time that read, "Dear Keith, I hear you're a good networker. I am, too. Let's sit down for fifteen minutes and a cup of coffee." Why? I ask myself. Why in the world do people expect me to respond to a request like that? Have they appealed to me emotionally? Have they said they could help me? Have they sought some snippet of commonality between us? I'm sorry, but networking is not a secret society with some encoded handshake practiced for its own virtue. We must bring virtue to it.

2. Don't rely on the currency of gossip.

Of course, using gossip is easier. Most people lap up such information. But it won't do you any good in the long run. Eventually the information well will run dry as more and more people realize you're not to be trusted.

3. Don't come to the party empty-handed.

Who are the stars of today's Internet world? Bloggers. Those free-wheeling cybernauts who set up sites and online journals to provide information, links, or just empathy to a community of like-minded individuals. They do it for free, and they're often rewarded with a devout following of people who, in return, offer as much as they receive. It's a loop. In connecting, as in blogging, you're only as good as what you give away.

4. Don't treat those under you poorly.

Soon enough, some of them will become "overlings." In business, the food chain is transient. You must treat people with respect up and down the ladder. Michael Ovitz, the famed Hollywood superagent, was said to be a master networker. A scathing and relatively recent *Vanity Fair* profile, with dozens of anonymous and not-so-anonymous sources taking shots at the man, was a very public expression of a dazzling career that had gone somehow horribly wrong. People asked what happened? Ovitz has some amazing interpersonal skills, but he wielded them disingenuously. People he no longer needed he treated with indifference, or worse. It wasn't surprising that these same people not only reveled in, but may have also contributed to, his fall.

5. Be transparent.

"I am what I am," the cartoon character Popeye used to say. In the information age, openness—whether it concerns your intentions, the information you provide, or even your admiration—has become a valuable and much-sought-after attribute. People respond with trust when they know you're dealing straight with them. At a conference, when I run into someone I've been dying to meet, I don't hide my enthusiasm. "It's a pleasure to finally meet you. I've admired your work from afar for quite some time and been thinking how beneficial it might be if we could meet one another." Coy games may work in a bar, but not when you're looking to establish a deeper, more meaningful connection.

6. Don't be too efficient.

Nothing comes off as less sincere than receiving a mass e-mail addressed to a long list of recipients. Reaching out to others is not a numbers game. Your goal is to make genuine connections with people you can count on.

I'm embarrassed by the way I learned this lesson. I had always heard that sending out holiday/New Year's greeting cards was a good idea. So I began a practice when I graduated from Yale to send a holiday card to everyone in my contact database. By the time I was at Deloitte, that list was thousands of people long and I was hiring temp help to address and even sign the cards at year's end. Well, we all can see this coming. The intention was good enough until a college roommate noted (actually gibed) how appreciative he was to get not one but actually three cards one year . . . all with different signatures. It's not about mass, it's about a real connection.

If you're not making friends while connecting, best to resign yourself to dealing with people who don't care much about what happens to you. Being disliked will kill your connecting efforts before they begin. Alternatively, being liked can be the most potent, constructive force for getting business done.

CONNECTORS' HALL OF FAME PROFILE

Katharine Graham (1917–2001)

"Cultivate trust in everyone."

Tragedy transformed Katharine Graham from wife to publisher overnight. She took over the *Washington Post* in 1963 after the death of her husband, Philip Graham. Her shy and quiet demeanor seemed unfit to deal with the demands of one of the most important newspapers in the country. Graham proved everyone wrong. She helped to build one of the great newspapers and most successful businesses in America. During her era, the *Post* published the Pentagon Papers, took President Nixon head-on over Watergate, and ruled Washington's political and media scene in a style that was inimitably her own.

In fact, it was this style that is her most lasting legacy. Running the *Post* with compassion, kindness, and sincerity, Graham became a powerful figure. Graham's influence gave her an ability to empower others—from the highest echelons of society to its lowest—with a sense of dignity and respect.

Richard Cohen, a columnist for the *Washington Post*, wrote the following a few days after Graham's funeral:

On a beastly July Sunday some years ago, I returned to Washington from the beach and took a taxi to the parking garage across the street from the *Washington Post* where I kept my car. A tent had been erected on the *Post*'s own parking lot. It was for a company party, given for people whose names you never hear—those un-bylined, non-TV-appearing types who take the ads or deliver the paper or maybe just clean the building. In the heat, I saw Katharine Graham plodding toward the party.

She was old by then, and walking was difficult for her. She pushed her way up the ramp, moving in a laborious fashion. She had a farm in Virginia, a house in Georgetown, an apartment in New York and, most significantly that hideously hot day, a place on the water in Martha's Vineyard. Yet here she was—incredibly, I thought—doing the sort of thing vice presidents-for-smiling do in other companies.

Analyze the life of Katharine Graham, and one inescapable theme emerges: Despite a lifetime free from financial worry, and a social status bordering on royalty, she made friends with *everyone*—not just those who could assist her newspaper or augment her position within the Beltway.

Most reports on her funeral mentioned celebrity names like Henry Kissinger, Bill Clinton, Bill Gates, Warren Buffett, and Tom Brokaw. But you don't have to do much heavy lifting before you find an extensive list of *non*-celebrity attendees. Here's a sampling:

- Irvin Kalugdan, a Fairfax County special-education teacher who founded a student break-dancing team with a $350 *Washington Post* grant
- Rosalind Styles, from the Frederick Douglass Early Childhood and Family Support Center, for which Graham had helped raise money
- Henrietta Barbier of Bethesda, a woman retired from the Foreign Service, belonged to a weekly bridge club of about sixty women at the Chevy Chase Women's Club. She said Graham never missed a session: "She was bright about the game, and she took lessons, and she was serious."

All of which reveals an inner truth about the skill of reaching out to others: Those who are best at it don't network—they make friends. They gain admirers and win trust precisely *because* their amicable overtures extend to everyone. A widening circle of influence is an unintended result, not a calculated aim.

Graham's relationship with former Secretary of State Henry Kissinger, more than anyone, highlighted her flare for friendship qua friendship, as opposed to friendship for ulterior purposes.

On the surface, the two seemed the unlikeliest of pals: After all, the crucial moments of Graham's career were stunning blows to Kissinger's. First, in 1971, there was Graham's decision to publish the Pentagon Papers, confidential documents detailing the U.S. involvement in the Vietnam War. A year later the *Post*, at Graham's behest, began its Watergate investigations. Both led to the embarrassment of the Nixon administration in which Kissinger served.

Yet there was Kissinger, the first speaker to eulogize Graham at her funeral. He and Graham frequently attended movies together.

How did Graham form such an alliance, such a friendship? How did she create connections with everyone from anonymous teachers to the world's most famous and powerful? By knowing her boundaries and cultivating trust in others; by being discreet; by the sincerity of her intentions; by letting the other person know she had his or her best interests at heart.

In an interview with CNN, Kissinger remarked: "It was a strange relationship in the sense that her paper was on the opposite side from my views very often, but she never attempted to use our friendship for any benefit for her newspaper. She never asked me for special interviews or anything of that kind."

The Skill Set

CHAPTER 7

Do Your Homework

Spectacular achievement is always preceded by spectacular preparation.

—Robert H. Schuller

W hom you meet, how you meet them, and what they think of you afterward should not be left to chance. As Winston Churchill would tell us, preparation is—if not the key to genius— then at least the key to sounding like a genius.

Before I meet with any new people I've been thinking of introducing myself to, I research who they are and what their business is. I find out what's important to them: their hobbies, challenges, goals—inside their business and out. Before the meeting, I generally prepare, or have my assistant prepare, a one-page synopsis on the person I'm about to meet. The only criterion for what should be included is that I want to know what this person is like as a human being, what he or she feels strongly about, and what his or her proudest achievements are.

Sure, you should also be up-to-date on what's happening within the company of a person you want to establish a relationship with. Did the person have a good or bad quarter? Do they have a new product? Trust me, *all* people naturally care, generally above and beyond anything else, about what it is *they* do. If you are informed enough to step comfortably into their world and talk knowledgeably, their appreciation will be tangible. As William James wrote: "The deepest principle in human nature is the craving to be appreciated."

These days, doing such research is easy. Here are a few places to start:

- The Internet. Be sure to check out the company's Web site. Use search engines, like Google, to check a person's affiliations. Going to a meeting without Googling someone is unacceptable.

- The public library, where you'll find books, periodicals, magazines, trade journals, etc. Check for articles written by or about the people you intend to meet. If there aren't any, read up on the person's industry or type of job. Most of this can be found online, too.

- Literature from the company's public relations department. Call and explain that you have a scheduled meeting and would like some background information.

- Annual reports. They'll give you a good idea of where a company is headed and what challenges and opportunities lie ahead.

Setting out to know someone inevitably means understanding what their problems or needs are. At work, it may be their product line. But as you talk with the person, you'll also find out that perhaps their kids are hoping to land an internship, that they themselves have health issues, or they just want to cut strokes off their golf game. The point is, you have to reach beyond the abstract and get to someone as an individual. Find a way to become part of those things that are of most interest to them, and you will have found a way to become part of their life.

Recently, I took part in a roundtable discussion sponsored by the Milken Institute's Global Conference in Los Angeles, an annual three-day gathering that brings together the world's top thinkers and CEOs to work over global problems. There were fifteen participants, each one an executive of a company far bigger than my own.

In many settings, I probably wouldn't have been rubbing elbows with them, but because I had helped organize the conference (always an advantage), I was invited to participate.

The events were planned with a CEO's tight schedule in mind. There was a brief mixer before the event to allow the participants to mingle and get to know one another. Then a panel discussion on the future of marketing, given the challenges facing big brands. Afterward, a short dinner.

In other words, there was about a three-hour window of opportunity where I could hope to establish a foundation for one or two relationships.

A successful conference's agenda is always created to maximize the participants' time. My own goal at such conferences is to maximize the brief windows of opportunity I might get to become intimate with other interesting people I haven't met before.

Food, I find, has a unique ability to facilitate conversation. People are usually open, even eager, to be amused while eating. Meals at conventions, however, are problematic. They're rushed, frenetic affairs that call for gracious, but unobtrusive, small talk. You're never sure where you'll end up sitting. And among strangers, it's usually difficult to focus beyond the people sitting either to your left or right.

And during the panel, people are focused on their own presentations.

That left the mixer. During mixers, I like to hang out near the bar. Virtually everyone gets a drink at some point. Throughout the day, I had also scouted out which rooms the people I wanted to meet were holding court in for the day, and arranged my schedule so I could be there as they were walking in or out. It sounds a bit manipulative, but really, it's just putting yourself in the right position at the right time.

The challenge in such circumstances, as it is in every conversation, is to try to transcend the trivialities of polite chitchat. I had gotten to know the lead organizer of the event during the preceding months, and based on casual conversation I generally knew who was coming—not privileged information but useful in my preparation. My office compiled simple bios of the VIPs who were coming in case I ended up meeting them or sitting next to them. My assistant prepared a few one-pagers on the one or two individuals I especially wanted to meet.

This is all part of what I call just doing your homework. That alone, however, is not enough. The idea is to find a point of common ground that is deeper and richer than what can be discovered in a serendipitous encounter. Armed with knowledge about a person's passions, needs, or interests, you can do more than connect; you'll have an opportunity to bond and *impress*.

A master politician like Winston Churchill planned his public encounters in the same way. Churchill today is known as an oratory genius, master of the art of repartee—the kind of fantastic dinner guest who captures everyone's undivided attention. What is less known—but which Churchill acknowledged in his own writing—is the blood, sweat, and tears of preparation that went into the making of a single sentence or the delivery of a clever joke. Churchill realized the power of knowing his audience and knowing how to push their buttons.

So how did I do?

I discovered that one of the CEOs, John Pepper, was also a fellow graduate of Yale. I had admired him since I was an undergrad and had seen him speak on campus. The former CEO of Procter

& Gamble, Pepper was committed to human rights and making sure the story of the Underground Railroad was preserved in a museum devoted to the subject he was founding in Cincinnati. Pepper was known for his leadership and the innovations in marketing he had brought to Procter & Gamble. Even now, after stepping down, he continued to be a powerful influence on P&G's board and on the boards of several other companies.

Knowing he had attended Yale, I knew that he'd have a bio listed on the Yale University Web site. So I tapped into my alumni network for more information. There, I found a treasure trove of old college affiliations and interests. It turned out we had both been in Berkeley College at Yale. That meant he must have known Robin Winks, a warmly admired and much-respected professor for whom I had worked while in college. When I brought up our many common experiences, we hit it off.

By the end of our conversation, John was giving me insightful advice about and contacts for my young company (YaYa at the time). He invited me to keep in touch in the coming years. I hoped our paths would cross many more times over the years, and they certainly have. When Professor Winks—Robin—passed away just a week later, we shared our memories of him. A few months later, I met a successful businessman from Cincinnati who was bragging about the museum enshrining the Underground Railroad and I made a point of putting him in touch with John Pepper for fundraising. I've probably introduced two or three potential donors to John in the last year.

I had no affiliations or organizations in common with the other CEO I wanted to meet. Luckily, a random Google search revealed that she had run the New York City Marathon the previous year. I know firsthand how much commitment and sacrifice it takes to train day in and day out to run and complete a marathon. I had tried—and failed. I had begun to train for a marathon one year, but my knees started to act up, to my disappointment. By the way, I'm always looking for good advice on how I might someday be able to run a marathon.

When I ran into this CEO, I said, "You know, I don't know how you do it. I like to think I'm in great shape, but the training for a marathon killed me. I had to stop."

Of course, she was surprised. "How the heck did you know I ran a marathon?" she happily quipped.

I never shy away from mentioning the research I've done. "I always make a special effort to inquire about the people I'd like to meet." Inevitably, people are flattered. Wouldn't you be? Instantly, the other person knows that rather than suffering through a strained half hour with a stranger, they're able to connect with someone with whom they share an interest, someone who has gone out of his way to get to know them better.

As it happened, the day before I had gone through "Barry's Boot Camp," a tough-as-nails but totally exhilarating exercise regimen in West Hollywood, not far from the conference. I said, "If you want an amazing and different workout sometime, you should consider boot camp." In return, I received some welcome advice for extending my running regimen. Later, she tried boot camp with me and loved it.

To this day, each time she and I meet, we talk about Barry's Boot Camp and I give her my progress report on my goal of running a marathon. And what I have found with those I've converted to my boot camp workout is that when they visit L.A., they might not have time to take a meeting or lunch with others, but they often do make one nonbusiness detour—and we have one hardcore workout together.

Once again, your goal in such a setting is to transform what could be a forgettable encounter into a blossoming friendship. There are shortcuts in my system, but this isn't one of them. I wouldn't have been able to reach out to these individuals, and truly connect, without doing my homework.

CHAPTER 8

Take Names

Once you've taken the time to figure out what your mission is and where you want to get to, the next step is to identify the people who can help you get there.

The successful organization and management of the information that makes connecting flourish is vital. Tracking the people you know, the people you want to know, and doing all the homework that will help you develop intimate relationships with others can cause one heck of an information overload. How do you manage it? Luckily, today we have a whole new set of software and hardware tools that can help us deal with the task in an orderly fashion.

But you don't need the latest and greatest gadgets. Ink and paper are a perfectly suitable way to keep track of the new people in your expanding social life. I'm a list-taking madman, and you should become one, too.

My experience at YaYa is a good example of how lists help people achieve their goals. On my last day at Starwood, I made more than forty phone calls. One of them was to Sandy Climan. What's interesting about the call, and the dozens of others like it I made that day, is that long before any of these people knew me, many of them had been on one of many lists I'd been keeping for years.

It was Sandy who eventually recruited me to YaYa. It didn't hurt that one of the other investors with a stake in the company, Knowledge Universe, was backed by the famed financier Michael Milken, who ultimately became a mentor of mine whom I'd met through a mutual nonprofit interest.

In November 2000, the YaYa board named me CEO and handed me two goals: establish a viable business model, and either find a major investor or sell the company to a well-heeled strategic acquirer. At the time, YaYa had the technology to invent online games that corporations could use to attract and educate their customers, but the company had no customers—or revenue.

First, I sat down and established ninety-day, one-year, and three-year goals in my Relationship Action Plan. Each goal required me to connect with and develop different parts of my network.

In ninety days, I had to establish credibility with the board, gain the trust of my employees, and set a clear direction for the business.

In a year, I wanted to have enough blue-chip accounts to be close to profitability and moving toward making the company attractive for potential acquisition. Most important, I had to prove to the outside world that YaYa was producing something worthwhile. The concept of *advergaming*, which wasn't even a word then, was not considered a viable segment of the advertising market. Interactive ads were hopelessly ineffective, and banner ads on Web sites were now considered an industry joke. We had to differentiate ourselves.

I wanted a business model in place three years down the road that could function without me, gain liquidity for my investors, and solidify the company's standing as a thought leader in the online marketing arena.

To make these goals possible, I mapped out the most important players in both the online and games industries, from CEOs and journalists to programmers and academics. My goal was to get to know almost all of them within a year.

To create excitement around our product, I wrote down a list of people I called "influentials": the early adopters, journalists, and industry analysts that help spread the initial buzz about a product or service. Next, I made a list of potential customers, potential acquirers, and people who might be interested in funding us down the road. (In creating *your* own categories, each should correspond to your own goals.)

When you make such lists, it's important you name the actual decision makers, and not just an organization. The point here is to have a readily accessible and specific list of names.

At the outset, concentrate on the people who are already part of your existing network. I bet you have no idea how vast and widespread it really is. As I noted in the previous chapter, take the time to list people such as:

Relatives

Friends of relatives

All your spouse's relatives and contacts

Current colleagues

Members of professional and social organizations

Current and former customers and clients

Parents of your children's friends

Neighbors, past and present

People you went to school with

People you have worked with in the past

People in your religious congregation

Former teachers and employers

People you socialize with

People who provide services to you

Next, I enter the gathered names into a database. (I tend to use Microsoft's Outlook, but there are plenty of programs out there that are just as good.) I then create call sheets by region, listing the people I know and those I'd like to know. When I'm in a given town, I'll try to phone as many people as I can. I have the numbers in my Palm and BlackBerry; both devices have unique and important functionality to me, so I've kept both.

I also print out and carry these lists around with me wherever I go. They focus my efforts in cabs between meetings. I have something palpable to encourage me to reach out. Some of the lists you create will be related to your action plans; others are more general, helping you to stay connected. The way you organize your lists can be fluid. I have lists by geographical location, by industry, by activity (other runners, for instance, or people who like to go out on the town), whether they're an acquaintance or friend, and so on.

Adding to the names on your lists is simply a matter of looking in the right place. In the beginning stages at YaYa, I read all the trade magazines having to do with advertising and games. If I read about someone who fell into one of my categories, I'd put him on a list and find out his contact information.

When you're looking for people to reach out to, you'll find them everywhere. One great resource for making lists is—it almost sounds absurd—other people's lists. Newspapers and magazines do rankings of this sort all the time.

Long before I became one of *Crain's* "40 Under 40," for example, I had been ripping out that list for years. I clip out lists of top CEOs, most admired marketers, the nation's most progressive entrepreneurs—all of these kinds of lists are published in local and national publications; every industry has something similar.

You want not only to know who the players in your field are

but eventually to be recognized as one of those players. The people who are on *Crain's* "40 Under 40" aren't necessarily the forty best businesspeople. They are, however, probably the forty most connected. And they probably all have lunched with one another at one time or another. When you get to know these people, and the people they know (including the journalists at *Crain's* responsible for the "40 Under 40"), you're that much more likely to be on the list yourself the next time it appears.

There's another category you might want to add, something I call my "aspirational contacts." There are those extremely high-level people who have nothing to do with my business at hand but are just, well, interesting or successful or both. The people on that list may be anyone from heads of state and media moguls, to artists and actors, to people others speak highly of. I list these people, too.

If you could see my Palm, I could show you the contact information for Richard Branson, chairman of the Virgin empire. Now, I don't know Richard Branson . . . yet. But I want to. If you scroll down a bit farther, you'll find Howard Stringer, CEO of Sony Corp. of America. He was on my aspirational list once. I now know Howard.

People get a chuckle out of this, but the results speak for themselves.

Remember, if you're organized, focused, and a stickler for taking names, there's no one that's out of reach.

As for me, my three years at YaYa came to a close. In 2002, *Forbes* magazine reported on our extraordinary rise to success as a start-up that had come from nowhere with a totally new concept. The concept of advergaming gained a cultural currency in the marketplace, and the term is now used by CEOs and journalists alike. The other day I overheard a CEO, who didn't know we had created the word, bragging about the innovative tool called "advergaming" that had led to a measurable increase in the sales and recognition of his product. As planned, YaYa was ultimately sold to a public company, giving investors access to the liquid currency they were looking for and giving YaYa the operating capital it needed. And it's clear that without that bunch of lists to thank, YaYa would never have made it beyond the first year of operations.

CHAPTER 9

Warming the Cold Call

Cold calls turn even the most competent of souls into neurotic messes. I can relate to those who go catatonic at the very idea of calling a stranger.

So how do you manage a cold call?

First, it's all about attitude. Your attitude. You're never going to be completely ready to meet new people; there is no perfect moment. Your fears will never be completely quieted, because inviting rejection is never going to be appealing. There are always a hundred reasons to procrastinate. The trick is to just plunge right in. Remember, if you don't believe you are going to get what you want from the call, you probably won't. So, in the words of *Caddy Shack,* "Be the ball." You have to envision yourself winning to win.

You have to view getting to know new people as a challenge and an opportunity. The very idea should spark your competitive fires, silencing the wallflower in all of us that shies away from socially adventuresome behavior.

And second, cold calls are for suckers. I don't call cold—ever.

I've created strategies that ensure every call I make is a warm one.

Let me give you an example. Jeff Arnold, founder of WebMD, is a friend. He had recently bought out the rights and patents for a technology that puts digital content on a miniature DVD disk for a unique delivery. One use for this technology is placing these small disks on the lids of fountain beverages. Picture getting a soda from McDonald's; on the top of your drink is a small diskette containing games, music, and/or videos. With 20 billion or so fountain beverages sold each year, this is a compelling new form to get digital content into people's hands.

In talking with Jeff and his partner, Thomas Tull, I was told about the deal they had just closed with a movie theater company to distribute their DVDs on beverages sold at theaters. Jeff and Thomas thought that, given the demographics of moviegoers, a company like Sony Electronics could stand to benefit from this new distribution technology. But they didn't know whom to contact at Sony and came to me for thoughts.

I had met Sir Howard Stringer, CEO of Sony, a number of times, so I put a call into his office. But instead of just waiting for Howard to get back to me, I wanted to find a few other paths as well. At the time, I couldn't think of anyone else within my network of contacts who could hook me up with the right decision maker within Sony. When no one responded to my phone calls or e-mails, I researched which agencies serviced Sony, and I found that Brand Buzz, a marketing agency within advertising giant Young & Rubicam, counted Sony as one of its top clients.

Furthermore, the person who was CEO of Brand Buzz at the time, John Partilla, is a close friend of mine.

So I called him. "Hey, John, I've got two things for you. One, I want you to meet a buddy of mine named Jeff Arnold. He's brilliant and creative and you should know him. He's the guy who founded WebMD and he's started a new company, Convex Group, which may need your services down the line. And two, Convex is putting out this incredible technology that distributes digital content in a new way. I think Sony would appreciate being aware of it."

In a sense, by reaching out in this way, I was offering John two opportunities: a chance to know someone of importance and interest, perhaps for new business, through Jeff, and a chance to look good with the business he already had—Sony—by bringing them new opportunities.

John was happy to make the connection. He knew the perfect guy, the new head of Media & Internet Strategies at Sony, Serge Del Grosso. I asked John to send a brief introductory e-mail ahead of my call and CC me in the process. By having him copy me on the e-mail, in all subsequent correspondence to Serge, I could include John, and put some urgency behind our meeting. Tacitly, as a result, both John and I were now waiting for a meeting with Serge.

As with so many business dealings, that alone didn't do the deed. Serge was busy, and I heard nothing back from him or his administrative assistant after several e-mails. This isn't unusual. Frequently, people won't get back to you. You have to put your ego aside and persist in calling or writing. And when you do finally connect, don't sabotage your efforts by expressing how annoyed you are that they didn't get back to you as quickly as you would have liked. Nor should you apologize for your persistence. Just dive in as if you caught him on the first call. Make it comfortable for everyone.

Setting up such meetings takes time. It is up to you to take the initiative. Sometimes, you have to be aggressive. After a few weeks of no reply, I called Sony information and eventually got Serge's direct line. When I call someone directly whom I haven't spoken with before, I try to call at an unusual time. Someone who is busy is more likely to pick up their own phone at 8:00 A.M. or 6:30 P.M. Plus, they're probably less stressed out since they're not facing typical nine-to-five pressures.

I called in the early morning, but got Serge's voice mail. So I left a message: "I just want to reiterate my excitement regarding our meeting. I've never heard John talk so flatteringly of a business associate. I understand how busy you must be. I haven't heard from your administrative assistant, but I'm sure I will. See you soon." At no point do you want your interactions to become strained. Creating and maintaining a sense of optimism and gentle pressure around the appointment is all part of the dance.

When I still didn't hear from his office, I called Serge's direct line after hours, around 6 P.M. This time, Serge picked up the phone himself and I gave him the pitch.

"Hi, Serge. It's Keith Ferrazzi. John's talked highly of you for some time, and I've finally got a nice excuse to give you a call. I'm calling for my friend Jeff Arnold, the founder of WebMD, who has a new, very powerful way to distribute digital content. With some of the new products you'll be launching this quarter, it could make for the perfect partnership. I'll be in New York next week. Let's get together. Or, if getting together this trip isn't convenient, I'll make room in my schedule for whenever it's more convenient for you."

In fifteen seconds, I used my four rules for what I call *warm* calling: 1) Convey credibility by mentioning a familiar person or institution—in this case, John, Jeff, and WebMD. 2) State your value proposition: Jeff's new product would help Serge sell his new products. 3) Impart urgency and convenience by being prepared to do whatever it takes whenever it takes to meet the other person on his or her own terms. 4) Be prepared to offer a compromise that secures a definite follow-up at a minimum.

The result? I was in Serge's office the next week. And, while his budgets didn't allow a short-term application, he totally understood the power of the medium for his audience. Don't be surprised if sometime soon your movie-theater beverage has a cool little DVD on the lid brimming over with some of Sony's newest technology.

Here are some of the rules I follow fleshed out in more detail:

1. Draft off a reference.

The reason a cold call feels like torture was set out in vivid detail fifty or so years ago in an advertisement, recalled by Harvey Mackay, in his book *Swim with the Sharks*. It pictures a corporate killjoy facing the reader, who is cast in the role of the salesman. The killjoy says:

> I don't know who you are.
>
> I don't know your company.
>
> I don't know what your company stands for.
>
> I don't know your company's customers.
>
> I don't know you company's products.
>
> I don't know your company's reputation.
>
> Now—what was it you wanted to sell me?

You can see the total lack of credibility one has when making a cold call. Credibility is the first thing you want to establish in any interaction, and ultimately, no one will buy from you unless you establish trust. Having a mutual friend or even acquaintance will immediately make you stand out from the other anonymous individuals vying for a piece of someone's time.

What do I mean by that? If you are calling on behalf of the president, I guarantee you Mr. Killjoy on the other end of the line will listen to what you have to say. Drafting off the brands of others, whether personal references or organizations, is a helpful tactic to get past someone's initial reluctance.

Most of us, however, don't work for Microsoft or know the

president of the organization we're trying to reach out to. Our task, then, is to tap our network of friends, family, clients, neighbors, classmates, associates, and church members to find a path back to the person we're trying to reach. When you mention someone both of you have in common, all of a sudden the person you're calling has an obligation not only to you but also to the friend or associate you just mentioned.

Today, finding a line into someone's office is a lot easier than when I started out.

Again, the wonderfully effective search engine Google.com is nearly invaluable in this process. Do a name search and you'll likely find where a person went to school, what his or her interests are, and what boards he or she sits on—you'll get a perspective on the person's life that should give you ideas on where a mutual contact might be found. What sports do they play? What nonprofits do they care about? Do you know other people involved in similar causes?

A whole host of new companies, like Spoke and LinkedIn, specialize in helping you find connections to people you want to get in touch with. A company called Capital IQ aggregates market data and information on executives, for example, to make it very easy to find out whom they know that you know. Other companies, like Friendster, Ryze, and ZeroDegrees, help to broker connections inside and outside of companies around the world. Some of these networks are better for finding a date, so you'll have to see for yourself which one makes more sense for you.

People used to say there were only six degrees of separation between anyone in the world. Today, we're only one or two mouse clicks away.

2. State your value.

Acquiring a reference or institution to draft off of is only a starting point. It will help you get your foot in the door. Once you have someone's commitment to hear you out for thirty seconds, you'll need to be prepared to deliver a high-value proposition. You've got very little time to articulate why that person should not try to get off the phone as quickly as possible. Remember, it's all about them. What can you do for them?

When researching for a connection to the people you want to meet, first do some reconnaissance about the company and industry they're selling in. Selling is, reduced to its essence, solving another person's problems. And you can only do that when you know what those problems are. When I finally got a chance to talk with Serge, for instance, I already knew he was preparing to launch some new products in the upcoming quarter, and in the busy holiday season he was going to need something that would really stand out. I also knew his target audience aligned well with those going to the theaters.

I can cut through the clutter of other cold calls by personalizing my call with specific information that shows I'm interested enough in their success to have done some homework.

3. Talk a little, say a lot. Make it quick, convenient, and definitive.

You want to impart both a sense of urgency and a sense of convenience. Instead of closing with "We should get together some time soon," I like to finalize with something like "I'm going to be in town next week. How about lunch on Tuesday? I know this is going to be important for both of us, so I'll make time no matter what."

You will, of course, need to provide enough information about your value proposition to make the person want to spend some time talking. But also, don't talk too much. If you launch into a long sales pitch without finding out the other person's thoughts, you can turn them off immediately. It is a dialogue, not a scripted monologue. Even my fifteen-second intro above left time for the casual "ah huh, yes" or "hmm" from the other person. Don't ever talk *at* someone. Give them time to come along with you.

Remember, in most instances, the sole objective of the cold call is, ultimately, to get an appointment where you can discuss the proposition in more detail, not to close the sale. In my experience, deals, like friendships, are made only one-to-one, face-to-face. Take as little time as possible in your cold call to ensure that the next time you speak to them it's in their office, or better yet, over some linguine and wine.

4. Offer a compromise.

In any informal negotiation, you go big at the outset, leaving room for compromise and the ability to ratchet down for an easier close. I closed my pitch to Serge by suggesting that even if he didn't want to hear anything about digital content, I'd love to get together with him just to meet, given our mutual friend's admiration and respect.

Robert B. Cialdini's book *The Psychology of Persuasion* shows how compromise is a powerful force in human relations. An example used to illustrate this idea concerns Boy Scouts, who are often turned down initially when trying to sell raffle tickets. It has been statistically shown, however, that when the Scout then offers candy bars instead, a less costly item, customers will buy the candy even if they don't really want it. In giving in to the concession, people feel as if they're holding up their social obligation to others. So remember, try for a lot—it will help you settle for what it is you really need.

CHAPTER 10

Managing the Gatekeeper— Artfully

L et's face it, having a list of names of people you want to reach in business, and a plan for what to say to them when you've got them on the phone, doesn't mean much if you never get them on the phone. Half the difficulty in reaching out to others is actually reaching somebody at all. It's even more difficult when that somebody is a Big Kahuna with a thicket of protective voice mailboxes, blind e-mail addresses, and defensive assistants running interference.

So how do you open the door?

First, make the gatekeeper an ally rather than an adversary. And never, *ever* get on his or her bad side. Many executive assistants are their bosses' minority partners. Don't think of them as "secretaries" or as "assistants." In fact, they are associates and lifelines.

Every time I have ever tried to go head-to-head with an administrative assistant, I've lost. It's like that childhood game: rock, paper, scissors. Well, in this game, as Mary Abdo taught me, the "associate" trumps all.

Mary was the assistant to Pat Loconto, the CEO of Deloitte

(and I guess still is, even though Pat is retired), and in the beginning, we got along great. I remember once finishing up a dinner with Pat and Mary. Mary had to leave early, so I walked her outside while she got a taxi. The next day, I called to say thanks for arranging such a wonderful evening.

Apparently, people rarely called Mary to thank her for organizing events, and she was very grateful. She even bragged the next morning to Pat about how much she liked me.

Mary was a blast: fun and full of energy and wonderful stories. In my early days at Deloitte, when I'd call Pat, I'd spend an extra few minutes kibitzing. "Mary, you're a hoot to talk to." Looking back, my relationship with Mary was clearly one of the most important reasons I was given such easy access to Pat. And my relationship with Pat was one of the most important relationships of my business life.

However, with Mary and me there was a time when all that began to change. I had just become chief marketing officer.

At that time, I got my very own full-time administrative assistant, who I'll call Jennifer. I thought Jennifer was everything I'd want in an assistant: smart, organized, efficient. We got along great. The only problem was she didn't get along with Mary—at all.

Mary managed all the administrative assistants in our executive suite. Almost immediately, Jennifer and Mary were butting heads. Jennifer was digging in her heels and not letting up. I just thought they'd work it out eventually.

"It's all a power play. She's wasting my time," Jennifer complained.

I wanted to be supportive. Jennifer's complaints and concerns seemed reasonable to me, but I was hearing only one side of the story. I encouraged Jennifer to work harder at the relationship. And one day, after I had been pulled into the middle of another bout between them, I asked Mary if she could just work harder to get along with Jennifer.

Mary didn't take my suggestion well. Before long, getting on Pat's calendar became more and more difficult. Bypassing corporate bureaucracy, which was a breeze in the past, now became impossible. My expense accounts were getting micro-scrutinized, taking up my time, and the pressure on Jennifer was greater than ever, which made her react even worse.

I'd had enough. I went up to Pat's office and said bluntly, "Look, Mary, this has to stop."

If I thought Mary had been upset before—yikes!—it was nothing compared to her ire now.

Office life became a nightmare for a period of time.

Finally, Pat drew me aside. "Keith," he said, "you've gone about this all wrong. Now this whole ordeal is making *my* life difficult. Think about it: I get to hear all this from Mary's side as well about your administrative assistant, and I don't really want to have to deal with this. Second of all, you're being stupid. Mary likes you and always has. Do yourself a favor. Do *me* a favor. Whatever it takes, smooth things over with Mary. When it comes to these issues, she runs this place."

Personally, I had always cared for and respected Mary, but now I learned something else—an assistant like Mary has enormous power. Secretaries and assistants are more than just helpful associates to their bosses. If they are any good, they become trusted friends, advocates, and integral parts of their professional, and even personal, lives.

One day Jennifer, who was as loyal to me as Mary was to Pat, came to me and offered to resign. "Listen, I'm miserable and your career is going to be jeopardized if all this doesn't get straightened out," she told me. It was an amazingly gracious gesture, as well as a way to restore sanity in her life. I promised to help find Jennifer another job (which she did quickly), and we remain good friends to this day.

When I went to hire my next assistant, I did two things. First, I asked if Mary would prescreen all candidates and rank her top choices. I went with her first choice. I also told my new administrative assistant to do whatever Mary instructed. It didn't take long for me to make up with Mary, either. Pat was right: Mary *did* like me and I just had to better understand her role. Pat started getting my messages again and all of our lives were so much easier.

As important as gatekeepers are within an organization, they're that much more important when you're working from the outside.

At about the same time, Kent Blosil, an advertising sales representative for *Newsweek* magazine, was one of twenty ad salespeople banging on my door looking to make a sale. But I had a media buyer at the agency whom we paid to take those meetings for me, and as a rule, I never met with ad sales reps.

Kent was different. He knew the kind of influence a gatekeeper wields.

Kent would call Jennifer once a week. He was deferential and overwhelmingly kind. Every so often, he would surprise her with a box of chocolates or flowers or something. Still, despite my assistant's suggestions, I saw no reason to take the meeting.

Jennifer persisted, however, and Kent must've been scheduled into my calendar on ten different occasions without my knowledge. Each time, I'd cancel. But she'd just keep plugging her good friend into my schedule because she felt he was different and had a more innovative approach than the others.

"Have him go meet with my buyer," I finally said one day.

"No, you're going to meet with him. You can take five minutes out of your day. He's very nice and creative and worth five minutes." So I relented.

Kent certainly was nice, but he also came to the meeting prepared with a deep understanding of my business and an interesting value proposition. At our meeting, almost the first thing out of his mouth was "If it's okay with you, I would like to introduce you to the top three senior editors of *Newsweek*. Would you be interested in that?" As someone who relied on getting the media to cover Deloitte's intellectual property, this was an important offer.

"Of course," I told him.

"By the way, we're having a conference in Palm Springs where some other CMOs are getting together with our editors and reporters. It's going to be a really good conference about media strategies in the New Economy. Can I put you on the guest list?" He was offering a real business value, as many of the other CMOs would also be Deloitte customers. It would be a personal networking opportunity among my peers.

"Yeah, I'd like to go to that."

"Also, I know your media guy has been evaluating a proposal we put in a few months ago. I'm not going to waste your time with the details. I just want you to know that it would be great if we could do business together sometime." That was it. That was Kent's five-minute sales pitch. It was 98 percent value-add for me, 2 percent sales pitch by him.

I called our media guy after Kent left my office. "Go to *Newsweek*," I told him. "Quote them a fair price relative to the other magazines we were considering, and give them our business in this segment. Make it work." And you know that when Kent went to another magazine, so did my business.

My point? Always respect the gatekeeper's power. Treat them with the dignity they deserve. If you do, doors will open for you to even the most powerful decision makers. What does it mean to treat them with dignity? Acknowledge their help. Thank them by phone, flowers, a note.

And yes, there are times, of course, where the situation calls for more than niceties and pleasant gifts. At times, you'll need to use street smarts to get a meeting.

Last summer, I met a former Disney executive on a flight to New York. In the course of our conversation, I mentioned that I was a fairly new transplant to Los Angeles and I was always looking to meet good, smart people. She suggested that I might like to get to know an up-and-coming executive by the name of Michael Johnson, the president of Walt Disney International.

There wasn't anything obvious that Johnson could do for my company or me at that point, but I felt he was someone I should meet. I was running a computer games company, and who could say whether Disney might someday be interested in the video games space. The only problem was getting through Johnson's gatekeeper; at a huge company like Disney, that's often a big problem.

I called Michael Johnson when I got home from my travels and, unsurprisingly, got a neutral to cold reception.

"I'm sorry, Mr. Johnson is traveling, and he'll be gone all month," his administrative assistant told me.

"That's okay," I replied. "Why don't you tell him a friend of Jane Pemberton's called. Please tell him to call me back when he gets a chance."

With a first call you don't want to come off as aggressive. Remember, you never, ever want to anger the gatekeeper.

My second call was more of the same: establishing my presence and making it known I wouldn't go away.

"Hi, this is Keith Ferrazzi. I'm just calling back because I haven't heard from Michael." Here, again, without being too pushy, you begin to create the presumption that his return call is imminent and expected. Johnson's gatekeeper politely took down my message and thanked me for calling. I asked for his e-mail address, but she wouldn't give it to me, stating privacy concerns.

On the third attempt, she was less polite. "Listen," she told me with a little edge in her voice, "Mr. Johnson is very busy and I don't know who you are." Now, I could either match her tone and this would spiral downward, or . . .

"Oh, I'm really sorry, I'm a personal friend of a friend of his. I just moved into the city, and Jane suggested that I should meet Michael, and honestly, I don't even know why besides the fact that Jane is a good friend of Michael's. Maybe you're right. Maybe it's all wrong. Maybe Michael doesn't know Jane well and he wouldn't want to meet me. I apologize if this is the case."

By being so candid and even vulnerable, I put the assistant on alert. She now fears that perhaps she's been too gruff, perhaps inappropriate, to a friend of a friend of her boss. After all, I'm just a guy following a friend's advice. Most likely she'll back off, worried that she's closed the gate too tight. Then I made a suggestion: "Why don't I just send Michael an e-mail?" And at this point, she's thinking, "I want to be out of the middle of this thing." So, finally, I got his e-mail address.

The e-mail I sent was simple: "Dear Michael, I'm a friend of Jane's, and she suggested I talk with you . . . Jane thinks we should know each other." If I had had something specific to discuss, I would have put it right up front, but the best value proposition I had was the mutual friend who felt this would be a win-win.

It's sometimes effective to utilize several forms of communication when trying to reach an important new contact. An e-mail, letter, fax, or postcard often has a better chance of landing directly in the hands of the person you're trying to reach.

Johnson's reply was cordial and short. "When convenient, I'd be happy to meet."

So I went back to his assistant with the information that Michael said he'd be happy to meet and that I was now calling to find out when. And finally, we did in fact meet.

Situations that call for this amount of maneuvering are, unfortunately, not rare. It's real work and it takes a finesse that only practice, practice, practice can master. But once you recognize the importance of gatekeepers, and turn them into allies with respect, humor, and compassion, there will be few gates that aren't open to you.

CHAPTER 11

Never Eat Alone

The dynamics of a network are similar to those of a would-be celebrity in Hollywood: Invisibility is a fate far worse than failure. It means that you should always be reaching out to others, over breakfast, lunch, whatever. It means that if one meeting happens to go sour, you have six other engagements lined up just like it the rest of the week.

In building a network, remember: Above all, never, ever disappear.

Keep your social and conference and event calendar full. As an up-and-comer, you must work hard to remain visible and active among your ever-budding network of friends and contacts.

Let me give you an example of what I mean. A few years back, I got the opportunity to travel with then First Lady Hillary Clinton on a C130 troop carrier, crisscrossing the Southwest from one political event to another. She was up at 5 in the morning for breakfast and phone calls back to the East Coast. She gave at least four or five speeches, attended a few cocktail parties where she constantly reached out to scores of individuals, and visited several people's homes. She must have touched 2,000 hands that day

alone. At the end of the night, when most of our entourage struggled to get back on Air Force One, she huddled her staff, sat up
cross-legged, and began to joke and chitchat with them about all
that happened that day. An hour or so of frivolity, and Mrs. Clinton moved on to scheduling the next day. No matter what your
politics, you have to respect that kind of determination and sheer
work ethic. I was shocked by the number of individuals she
remembered by name along the trip. I was having a tough enough
time with remembering everyone's name in our group.

I see examples of this kind of persistence and determination
everywhere. My particular heroes, because of my background, are
those people who came from humble origins. A fellow CEO friend
came from a blue-collar family in the Midwest—his father, like
mine, was a laborer for forty-odd years. He'll tell you he isn't the
smartest guy in the room, he doesn't have the Ivy League pedigree
of his colleagues, and he hasn't climbed the greasy pole by getting
a boost from his family. But today, he is one of the most respected
CEOs in his industry.

His formula is not complicated, but it is rigorous. He talks to at
least fifty people each day. He spends hours a week walking his
company plant talking to employees up and down the ladder. If
you send an e-mail to him or his assistant, you can be sure there
will be a response within hours. He attributes his success to the
blue-collar work ethic and sensibilities he was raised with by his
father. About his more starched white-collar colleagues, he once
told me that while he had learned what these people know, they
would never have an opportunity to learn what he knew.

Now, you have to work *hard* to be successful at reaching out
to others, but that doesn't mean you have to work long. There
is a difference. Some people think building a network requires
eighteen-hour days slogging through meetings and phone calls. If
I'm slogging, or even if it feels like slogging, I'm not doing my
job—at least not well. Or perhaps I'm in the wrong job. Building

a network of friends and colleagues is about building relationships and friendships. It should be fun, not time-consuming.
When your network is set, your goals written down, you'll find
plenty of hours during the day to do what needs to be done.

How do I meet everyone I want to meet during the course of a
week? Someone once remarked cynically, "I'd have to clone myself
to take all the meetings you take."

"Ah, you're onto something," I responded. "I don't clone
myself. I clone the event."

Here's what I mean. A few months ago, I flew into New York for
a two-day business stint. There were a number of people I wanted
to see: an old client and friend of mine who was the former president of Lego and was now trying to figure out what he wanted to do
with the rest of his life, the COO of Broadway Video, with whom I
wanted to discuss a new branded entertainment TV show for one of
my clients, and a close friend that I hadn't seen in too long.

I had two days, three people I wanted to see, and only one
available time slot to see them all. How do you manage a situation
like this?

I "cloned" the dinner and invited all of them to join me. Each
would benefit from knowing the others, and I'd be able to catch
up with all of them and perhaps even get some creative input
about the new TV show. My friend, who has a fantastic sense of
humor, would enjoy the group and add a little levity to what
might have been just a stodgy business meeting.

I asked my friend to join me a half hour in advance at the hotel
I was staying at for a little one-on-one time. And if the details of
the project I was discussing with the COO were private, I might
schedule a little one-on-one time with him after dinner.

The point is I'm constantly looking to include others in whatever I'm doing. It's good for them, good for me, and good for
everyone to broaden their circle of friends. Sometimes I'll take
potential employees for a workout and conduct the interview over

a run. As a makeshift staff meeting, I'll occasionally ask a few employees to share a car ride with me to the airport. I figure out ways to as much as triple my active working day through such multitasking. And, in the process, I'm connecting people from different parts of my "community."

The more new connections you establish, the more opportunities you'll have to make even more new connections. As Robert Metcalfe, the inventor of Ethernet, says: The value of a network grows proportional to the square of the number of its users. In the case of the Internet, every new computer, every new server, and every new user added expands the possibilities for everyone else who's already there. The same principle holds true in growing your web of relationships. The bigger it gets, the more attractive it becomes, and the faster it grows. That's why I say that a network is like a muscle—the more you work it, the bigger it gets.

Such cloning is also a good way to ensure that a meeting or get-together is worthwhile. If I'm meeting someone whom I don't know that well, I might invite someone I do know just to make sure the meeting does not become a waste of time. Mentees, for instance, get a special kick out of sitting in on such meetings—and it can be a great learning opportunity. It gets them face time with me, they get a chance to see business in action, and I make sure our reason for the meeting gets accomplished. In most cases, they end up contributing something to the meeting as well. Don't underestimate young people's ability to find creative new insight.

When you try this sort of thing, pay special attention to the chemistry between people. Do you have a sense of who will get on well with each other? It doesn't mean that everyone has to have the same background and sensibility. In fact, a nice mix of different professions and personalities can be the perfect recipe for a terrific gathering. Trust your instincts. One litmus test I often use is to ask myself if I think I'll have fun. If the answer is yes, that is usually a good sign that the dynamic will work.

Have you taken a colleague to lunch lately? Why not invite him or her out today—and include a few other people from different parts of your company or business network.

Soon, you'll have an ever-expanding web of friends and contacts.

Learn from Your Setbacks

For all his legendary success and greatness as a president, Abraham Lincoln lost all the time. Lincoln experienced numerous business, political, and personal setbacks over his life. But he never let any of his failures discourage him from pursuing his goals.

Lincoln failed in business. He failed as a farmer. He lost running for state legislature. He had a nervous breakdown. He was rejected for a job as a land officer. When he was finally elected to the legislature, he lost the vote to be speaker. He ran for Congress and lost. He ran for and lost a U.S. Senate seat. He ran for vice president and lost. He ran for the Senate and lost again. And, when he was finally elected president, the nation he was elected to lead broke apart. But by this time, all the activities, experiences, and people he came to know in the process helped him set a direction for that country that will stand as one of America's great legacies.

My point is, behind any successful person stands a long string of failures. But toughness and tenacity like Lincoln's can overcome these setbacks. Lincoln knew the only way to gain ground, to move forward, to turn his goals into reality, was to learn from his setbacks, to stay engaged, and press on!

CHAPTER 12

Share Your Passions

I have a confession to make. I've never been to a so-called "networking event" in my life.

If properly organized, these get-togethers in theory *could* work. Most, however, are for the desperate and uninformed. The average attendees are often unemployed and too quick to pass on their résumés to anyone with a free hand—usually the hand of someone else who is unemployed looking to pass on *his* résumé. Imagine a congregation of people with nothing in common except joblessness. That's not exactly a recipe for facilitating close bonds.

When it comes to meeting people, it's not only whom you get to know but also how and where you get to know them.

For example, take the first-class section on an airplane. Flying first class is not something most people can afford, but there's an interesting camaraderie among those front seats that you won't find back in coach. To begin with, there are always a number of movers and shakers up front, in close quarters, for hours at a time. Because they've slapped down an absurd premium for the luxury of getting off the plane a few seconds earlier than the rest of the passengers, fellow first-classers assume you, too, are important, and they often seek to quench their curiosity about who you are and why you're as dumb as they are to pay such an inflated price. I can't tell you how many valuable clients and contacts I've met during a conversation struck up during an in-flight meal. (By the way, this is the only acceptable time to bother your seat mate.)

At a so-called "networking event," the dynamics are just the opposite. People assume you're in the same boat they are—desperate. Credibility is hard to gain. If you're jobless, doesn't it make more sense to hang with the job-givers than fellow job-seekers?

There are better ways, and better places, to spend your time.

Shared interests are the basic building blocks of any relationship. Race, religion, gender, sexual orientation, ethnicity, or business, professional, and personal interests are relational glue. It makes sense, then, that events and activities where you'll thrive are those built around interests you're most passionate about.

Friendship is created out of the *quality* of time spent between two people, not the quantity. There is a misconception that to build a bond, two people need to spend a great deal of time together. This is not the case. Outside your family and work, you probably can count the people you see a great deal of in the course of a month on two hands. Yet, surely, you have more than ten friends. It is what you do together that matters, not how often you meet. That's why you have to pay special attention to where you're most comfortable and what activities you most enjoy.

Usually it's the events and activities you excel at that you're most passionate about. So it makes sense to make these the focus of your efforts. For me, my love of food and exercise has led to the most amazing get-togethers. For others, it may be stamps, baseball cards, politics, or skydiving that brings you together.

The power of shared passion in bringing people together can be seen today in the rising trend of blogs, or Web logs. Blogs are online journals, usually dedicated to an individual's interests, containing commentary and links to relevant news and information.

Popular blogs attract like-minded legions to their sites. The blog-osphere (the community of active bloggers writing on topics that range from spirituality to sports) has grown from a dozen or so Web logs in 1999 to an estimated five *million* today.

When they write the history of the 2004 presidential campaign, an entire chapter could be dedicated to blogs. No other innovation in the last twenty years has influenced electoral politics quite like these impassioned online communities. They've galvanized an unprecedented number of voters into action, raised millions of dollars, and given people an outlet to participate in the political process. It's amazing to think that one person, writing about what or whom they love, could have so much influence or create a community of people so quickly.

When we are truly passionate about something, it's contagious. Our passion draws other people to who we are and what we care about. Others respond by letting *their* guard down. Which is why sharing your passion is important in business.

I can tell more about how someone is likely to react in a business situation from my experience with them at an intimate dinner, or after just one strenuous workout, than I can from any number of in-office meetings. We just naturally loosen up outside the office. Or perhaps it's the venue itself—not to mention the wine over dinner. It's astonishing how much more you can learn about someone when you are both doing something you enjoy.

I have a friend who is the executive vice president of a large bank in Charlotte. His networking hotspot is, of all places, the YMCA. He tells me that at 5 and 6 in the morning, the place is buzzing with exercise fanatics like himself getting in a workout before they go to the office. He scouts the place for entrepreneurs, current customers, and prospects. Then, as he's huffing and puffing on the StairMaster, he answers their questions about investments and loans.

Besides food and exercise, I sometimes take people to church.

That's right, church. I attend a mostly African-American and His-
panic Catholic Church in Los Angeles—St. Agatha's. It's wonderfully "unorthodox." Instead of "passing the peace" in the form of a
simple handshake, a gospel choir belts out uplifting tunes while
the congregants walk around the church hugging each other for
ten minutes. It's an amazing scene. I don't try to foist my beliefs on
anyone; the people I bring along—whether an actor or lawyer or
an atheist or Orthodox Jew—tend to see my invitation as a kind of
personalized gift. It shows them that I think so highly of them that
I'm willing to share such a deeply personal part of my life.

Contrary to popular business wisdom, I don't believe there has
to be a rigid line between our private and public lives. Old-school
business views the expression of emotions and compassion as vulnerability; today's new businesspeople see such attributes as the
glue that binds us. When our relationships are stronger, our businesses and careers are more successful.

Take Bonnie Digrius, a consultant who used to work at the
Gartner Group. Bonnie sends her list of contacts and associates an
annual newsletter that is, well, all about her. She writes of the new
and exciting things she's working on, or about her family. She
wrote about how the death of her father changed her life. You
might think those who received this letter were uncomfortable
with such a public display of emotion. Just the opposite. More and
more people—men, women, colleagues, and strangers alike—
asked to receive Bonnie's letter. They'd write her back and tell her
of similar experiences they'd been through. After a few years, Bonnie had a network that stretched across the nation. She's poured
her heart and passion onto the page and, because of it, she's
received the trust and admiration of hundreds in return.

Make a list of the things you're most passionate about. Use
your passions as a guide to which activities and events you should
be seeking out. Use them to engage new and old contacts. If you
love baseball, for example, take potential and current clients to a

ballgame. It doesn't matter what you do, only that it's something you love doing.

Your passions and the events you build around them will create deeper levels of intimacy. Pay attention to matching the event to the particular relationship you're trying to build. I've got an informal list of activities I use to keep in touch with my business and personal friends. Here are some things I like to do:

1. Fifteen minutes and a cup of coffee. It's quick, it's out of the office, and it's a great way to meet someone new.
2. Conferences. If I'm attending a conference in, say, Seattle, I'll pull out a list of people in the area I know or would like to know better and see if they might like to drop in for a particularly interesting keynote speech or dinner.
3. Invite someone to share a workout or a hobby (golf, chess, stamp collecting, a book club, etc.).
4. A quick early breakfast, lunch, drinks after work, or dinner together. There's nothing like food to break the ice.
5. Invite someone to a special event. For me, a special event such as the theater, a book-signing party, or a concert is made even more special if I bring along a few people who I think might particularly enjoy the occasion.
6. Entertaining at home. I view dinner parties at home as sacred. I like to make these events as intimate as possible. To ensure they stay that way, I generally will invite only one or two people I don't know that well. By dinner's end, I want those people leaving my home feeling as if they've made a whole new set of friends, and that's hard to do if it's a dinner filled with strangers.

Of course, we all need to schedule the appropriate time with friends and family as well, or just to read or relax. While enriching your life to include others whenever and wherever you can, make sure you're not neglecting the key relationships in your life.

When your day is fueled by passion, filled with interesting people to share it with, reaching out will seem less like a challenge or a chore and more like an effortless consequence of the way you work.

CHAPTER 13

Follow Up or Fail

How often do you find yourself standing face-to-face with someone you've met before, but you can't recall their name?

We live in a fast-paced, digital world that bombards us with information. Our inboxes are a constant procession of new and old names demanding our attention. Our brains are in constant overdrive trying to keep track of all the bits and bytes and names that cross our desk each and every day. It's natural that to stay sane, we must forget or ignore most of the data clamoring for a sliver of real estate in our already overcrowded noggins.

In such a world, it's incomprehensible that only a small percentage of us decide to follow up once we've met someone new. I can't say this strongly enough: When you meet someone with whom you want to establish a relationship, take the extra little step to ensure you won't be lost in their mental attic.

Just recently, I was down in Florida giving a speech at an awards ceremony for past and present members of my college fraternity, Sigma Chi. I probably gave my card and e-mail address out to at least a hundred people that night. After the black-tie affair had ended, I retreated to my hotel in the wee hours of the morning and checked my e-mail. There, in my inbox, was a simple gracious note from a young fraternity brother expressing his thanks for the speech, what it meant to him as someone who came from a similar background, and his hopes that someday he and I might sit down for a cup of coffee. Within the next two weeks, well over a hundred people e-mailed or called to express similar sentiments. The follow-up I remember best is the one I got first.

The most memorable gifts I have ever received are those whose value could not be measured in terms of dollars and cents. They are the heartfelt letters, e-mails, and cards I receive from people thanking me for guidance and advice.

Do you want to stand out from the crowd? Then you'll be miles ahead by following up better and smarter than the hordes scrambling for the person's attention. The fact is, most people don't follow up very well, if at all. Good follow-up alone elevates you above 95 percent of your peers. The follow-up is the hammer and nails of your networking tool kit.

In fact, FOLLOW-UP IS THE KEY TO SUCCESS IN ANY FIELD.

Making sure a new acquaintance retains your name (and the favorable impression you've created) is a process you should set in motion right after you've met someone.

Give yourself between twelve and twenty-four hours after you meet someone to follow up. If you meet somebody on a plane, send them an e-mail later that day. If you meet somebody over cocktails, again, send them an e-mail the next morning. For random encounters and chance meetings, e-mail is a fine tool for dropping a quick note to say, "It was a pleasure meeting you. We must keep in touch." In such an e-mail, I like to cite something particular we talked about in the course of our conversation—whether a shared hobby or business interest—that serves as a mental reminder of who I am. When I leave the meeting, I put the name and e-mail address of the new acquaintance in my database and program my PDA or BlackBerry to remind me in a month's time to drop the person another e-mail, just to keep in touch.

Why go to all the trouble of meeting new people if you're not going to work on making them a part of your life?

In the aftermath of a business meeting, I've taken to doing something my classmate at HBS and former COO James Clarke swears by. In his follow-up, he always reiterates the commitments everyone has made, and asks when a second follow-up meeting can be arranged.

When the other person has agreed to do something, whether it's meeting for coffee next time you're in town or signing a major deal, try to get it in writing. It's shouldn't be formulaic or ironclad, just something such as "It was great talking to you over lunch yesterday. I wanted to follow up with some thoughts we discussed yesterday. I believe FerrazziGreenlight can serve the interests of your company, and I've had time to work out the finer details. The next time I'm in town, I'd love to get on your calendar and chat for five or ten minutes."

Nine times out of ten, the person will casually write back accepting your offer to meet again. Then, when the time comes to take that person up on his offer to talk again, you can call him with the force of his e-mail commitment "in writing" behind you. He's already agreed to meet. Now the question is when, and your persistence will assure that happens at some point.

But remember—and this is critical—don't remind them of what they can do for you, but focus on what you might be able to do for them. It's about giving them a reason to want to follow up.

Another effective way to follow up is to clip relevant articles and send them to the people in your network who might be interested. When people do this for me, I'm tremendously appreciative; it shows they're thinking about me and the issues I'm facing.

————

While e-mail is one perfectly acceptable way to follow up, there are other methods to consider. A handwritten thank-you note these days can particularly capture a person's attention. When's the last time you received a handwritten letter? When you get something addressed to you personally, you open it.

The thank-you note is an opportunity to reinforce a perception of continuity in a relationship and create an aura of goodwill. Mention any pertinent information you failed to bring up in your meeting. Emphasize both your desire to meet again and your offer to help.

Here are a few more reminders of what to include in your follow-ups:

- Always express your gratitude.
- Be sure to include an item of interest from your meeting or conversation—a joke or a shared moment of humor.
- Reaffirm whatever commitments you both made—going both ways.
- Be brief and to the point.
- Always address the thank-you note to the person by name.
- Use e-mail *and* snail mail. The combination adds a personalized touch.
- Timeliness is key. Send them as soon as possible after the meeting or interview.
- Many people wait until the holidays to say thank you or reach out. Why wait? Your follow-ups will be timelier, more appropriate, and certainly better remembered.
- Don't forget to follow up with those who have acted as the go-between for you and someone else. Let the original referrer know how the conversation went, and express your appreciation for their help.

Make follow-up a habit. Make it automatic. When you do, the days of struggling to remember people's names—and of other people struggling to remember yours—will be a thing of the past.

CHAPTER 14

Be a Conference Commando

Military strategists know that most battles are won before the first shot is fired. The side that determines where, when, and how an engagement is fought usually gains an insurmountable advantage. And so it is with most successful conferences. Turning a conference into your own turf and setting goals ahead of time is what turns a casual conference attendance into a mission.

Don't just be an attendee; be a conference commando!

Conferences are good for mainly one thing. No, it's not the coffee and cookies at breaks. It's not even pricey business enlightenment. They provide a forum to meet the kind of like-minded people who can help you fulfill your mission and goals. Before deciding to attend a conference, I sometimes informally go so far as using a simple return-on-investment-type thought process. Is the likely return I'll get from the relationships I establish and build equal to or greater than the price of the conference and the time I spend there? If so, I attend. If not, I don't. It's that simple. That may seem like an awfully pragmatic view of conferences, but it works.

Right after we sold YaYa, the new owners instituted a set of cost-cutting policies relative to travel and conferences. I thought the policies were fundamentally off the mark.

The owners saw conferences as boondoggles—pleasant affairs for indulgent executives rather than as revenue generators. To our new parent company, the costs of sending people to a few events each year seemed like an unnecessary expense for a start-up company.

I strongly disagreed and promised to convince them otherwise. I set about recording the actual number of revenue-generating projects that came directly from people I had met at conferences. The owners were stunned when I presented a spreadsheet showing successive deals and how a significant chunk of revenue could be traced back to one conference or another.

Their ill-tempered disposition toward these business get-togethers—and these executives are far from alone in holding such attitudes—stems from an all-too-common misperception that conferences are places to find insight. Wrong. Real, actionable insight mostly comes from experience, books, and other people. Roundtable discussions and keynote speeches can be fun, even inspirational, but rarely is there the time to impart true knowledge.

But there may be no better place to extend your professional network and, on occasion, get deals done. Let me give you an example based on sales. In the old model of selling, 80 percent of a salesperson's time went into setting up meetings, giving a presentation, and trying to close a deal. The other 20 percent was spent developing a relationship with the customer. Today, we focus mostly on relationship selling. Smart salespeople—in fact, smart employees and business owners of all stripes—spend 80 percent of their time building strong relationships with the people they do business with. The slickest PowerPoint presentation can't compete with the development of real affection and trust in capturing the hearts and minds of other people.

Those who use conferences properly have a huge leg up at your average industry gathering. While others quietly sit taking notes, content to sip their free bottled water, these men and women are setting up one-on-one meetings, organizing dinners, and, in general, making each conference an opportunity to meet people who could change their lives.

If these people seem as if they aren't playing by the same rules as their fellow attendees, you're right. They've gone well beyond the traditional, warmed-over advice to Wear Your Badge, Warmly Greet Everyone, Establish Firm Eye Contact, and other common refrains that fail to distinguish them from the rest of the horde.

Yes, there's a guide to getting the most out of a conference. My friend Paul Reddy, a software executive, claims people are either bowling balls or pins at a conference. If you're the ball, you walk (or roll) into a conference, event, or an organization, and you blow it apart. With a dash of bravado and ingenuity, you leave a positive impression in your wake, create friendships, and achieve the goals on your agenda. The pins sit placidly by, waiting for something, anything, to happen to them.

Don't think of your next conference as a business-related retreat. Think of it as a well-coordinated campaign to further your mission. Here are the rules I follow at each and every event I attend:

Help the Organizer (Better Yet, *Be* the Organizer)

Conferences are logistical nightmares. There are a thousand different things that go into pulling off a successful business gathering. The mess that can ensue is an opportunity for you to come in and help out—and become an insider in the process.

Once you're on the inside, you can find out who will be attending and what the hot events will be. And you'll find yourself at all those unlisted dinners and cocktail parties that are thrown for the conference poobahs.

How do you find yourself part of the process? It's not really all that hard. First, review the event's materials, visit its Web site, and find out who the main contact is for putting together the conference. Put in a phone call. The person responsible for these kinds of events is generally overworked and stressed out. I like to call these people a few months ahead of the event and say, "I'm really looking forward to the conference you're putting together. I'm interested in helping make this year be the best year ever, and I'm willing to devote a chunk of my resources—be it time, creativity, or connections—to make this year's event a smash hit. How can I help?"

I guarantee the coordinator will be shocked with delight. I say that because I was once responsible for those stressed-out planners back in my early days as CMO of Deloitte.

Deloitte Consulting was working with Michael Hammer to grow a credible reengineering practice. We thought a conference might be a great way to introduce our relationship with Michael to the market, strengthen our brand, and win a few customers to boot. So we proposed a joint conference hosted by Deloitte and Michael Hammer. We would bring the industry expertise and case studies, and Michael would bring his expertise in reengineering and his understanding of how to run a world-class conference.

It gave me a chance to see the inner workings of how a successful conference is orchestrated and of course build a great relationship with Mike. I became acutely aware of how powerful it was to know, in advance, who would be attending; why some speakers were chosen and some were not; and what the best forums were for networking.

From the outset, our idea was to apply some method to the usual conference madness. A tracking system was put in place that recorded daily our progress against the objectives we set for ourselves. Each Deloitte partner's objective was to meet two people who were assigned to them from the guests we knew would be attending. Each was given one person as a primary target—someone we really wanted to win as a client. The other person was someone we thought Deloitte would benefit from knowing, perhaps a member of the media. The basic goal remained, quite simply, to meet new people.

Because we knew who was attending beforehand, the partners got one-page bios on the people assigned them, listing who they were, what they did, their accomplishments and hobbies, and the potential challenges their company faced that Deloitte might be able to address. This was enough information to make a real connection when the partner finally met the individual.

We also gave the partners a list of ideas of how to actually catch up with their targets and what to say when they met them. At the end of each day, the partners would report whom they met, where, and how the encounter went. If someone had a difficult time meeting their target person, we strategized for the next day, making sure that the partner and the individual they were assigned to would sit at the same dinner table the following evening, or I'd make a point of making the introduction myself, or we'd ask Mike to make an intro in a few cases.

What I had unknowingly created was a unit of conference commandos, prepared in advance with information on who they were to meet, how (we had done research), and where. The results were astounding. The conference was packed. As a result, Deloitte saw an unprecedented amount of business come its way. We have since perfected this art at FerrazziGreenlight, and not only do we advise companies on how to get the most out of their conferences, but also big conference-givers come to us to help them design conferences that will have world-class outcomes for both these companies and their conference attendees.

The key is to work hard to make the conference a success for everyone. At the Hammer conference, all attendees, almost across the board, were shocked by how much business they got done. The right environment was set for networking success.

Of course, Michael Hammer was brilliant, as always, and there was much for all of us to learn from him on content. But everyone's success came from organizing a conference around its real function: an intimate gathering of like-minded professionals in an atmosphere that facilitates profitable relationships.

Listen. Better Yet, *Speak*

Are you someone who thinks becoming a speaker is a big deal? That's true for a lot of people. I'm here to tell you it's not as tough as you might think, but it is also perhaps more important than you can imagine.

Nothing frightens the daylights out of some people like the thought of spending fifteen minutes talking about what they do in front of an audience, even if the audience is made up of generally receptive folks (like family and friends!).

Calm yourself. First, you should know that giving speeches is one of the easiest and most *effective* ways to get yourself, your business, and your ideas seen, heard of, and remembered, and you don't need to be Tony Robbins to find yourself a forum of people willing to hear you out.

How many people find themselves in front of an audience on any given day? The numbers are shocking. There are thousands of forums and events going on—for every imaginable reason—each and every day. All these forums need a warm body to say something the slightest bit inspiring or insightful to their guests. Most speakers, unfortunately, deliver neither.

If you think the people delivering this insight are only those at the top of their respective fields, you're mistaken. So how do you get experience?

Toastmasters International, for instance, provides a forum for the development of speaking skills. With more than 8,000 clubs meeting weekly in groups of up to thirty or forty people, there are a whole lot of speeches, and speakers, being made. On a larger scale, the national speaker circuit is huge. The American Society of Association Executives (ASAE) says the meetings industry is a nearly $83 billion market, with over $56 billion being spent annually on conventions and seminars alone. That ranks conferences—get this!—as the twenty-third-largest contributor to the Gross National Product. The point here is that the opportunity to speak exists everywhere, paid or unpaid. It's fun, it can be profitable, and there's no better way to get yourself known—and get to know others—at an event. Study after study shows that the more speeches one gives, the higher one's income bracket tends to be.

As a speaker at a conference, you have a special status, making meeting people much easier. Attendees expect you to reach out and greet them. They, in turn, give you respect that they don't accord their fellow attendees. Instant credibility and faux-fame is bestowed upon you when you're on a stage (and pretty much any stage, at that).

How do you become a speaker at a conference? First, you need something to say: You need content (which I'll discuss in another chapter). You need to develop a spiel about the niche you occupy. In fact, you can develop a number of different spiels, catering to a number of different audiences (again, I'll get to that later).

If you take the first step and get to know the organizer, landing a speaking gig isn't that tough. In the beginning, it's best to start small. Let me give you an example. A friend of mine left his big firm years ago to start his own consulting business. He needed to establish himself as an expert in the field of branding, and while he was terrified of public speaking, he knew it would be the best way to interact with potential customers and hone his message. He started small, getting to know all the organizers of small, local, industry-specific events. He would ask these people, in return for his help, to give him a room during an off-hour at the end of the event, so he could speak to a small gathering of people that he would organize.

Initially, he wasn't even listed on the conference agenda. He'd meet people throughout the conference and tell them that he was organizing an intimate gathering of professionals interested in talking about their branding issues. The informal atmosphere allowed him to deliver his content without the pressure of a big audience, while at the same time getting valuable feedback from the people that attended. In short order, the rooms he spoke at started getting bigger, his speeches became more refined, and the audience went from intimate to intimidating—though, by then, he had worked through most of his fears.

What if you are at a conference and you're not a speaker? There are other places to distinguish yourself. Remember, you're not there just to learn new things from other people—you're there to meet others and have others meet and remember you.

When sessions open up for questions, try and be among the first people to put your hand in the air. A really well-formed and insightful question is a mini-opportunity to get seen by the entire audience. Be sure to introduce yourself, tell people what company you work for, what you do, and then ask a question that leaves the audience buzzing. Ideally, the question should be related to your expertise so you have something to say when someone comes up and says, "That was an interesting question."

Guerrilla Warfare:
Organize a Conference Within a Conference

True commandos aren't restricted by the agenda that they receive at registration. Who says you can't arrange your own dinner while at the conference, or put together an informal discussion on a particular topic that matters to you?

The dinners at your average event are often a total mess. People's attention is scattershot; everyone is trying to rise above the noise and be polite and engaged with ten different strangers, listen to a keynote address, and get a few mouthfuls of mediocre food all at the same time. It doesn't make for a good setting for conversation.

At times like these, I've been tempted to go back to my room, order room service, and spend the rest of the night in front of my laptop. That, however, would be a terrible lost opportunity.

The alternative is to commandeer the useless hour or two by throwing a dinner of your *own*.

I like to do this at least once during most conferences. Before the event, I'll scout out a nice nearby restaurant and send out pre-invites to a private dinner that I'll host alongside the scheduled affair. You can do this ad hoc during the day or you can send out official invites beforehand. One way I've had big success is sending a fax to the hotel (most conferences have one host hotel where most VIPs will be staying) that the individuals get when they arrive the night before the conference asking them to join a group for dinner or drinks that night. Think about it: no secretaries to screen the message. Likely those people have no plans when they arrive, and even if they do, you will already stand out when you ultimately meet them during the conference, and I assure you they will be grateful for your having thought of them. If the keynote address is being given by someone particularly interesting, I'll turn my own affair into pre- or post-dinner drinks.

Often, creating your own forum is the best way to assure that people you're looking to meet will be in the same place at the same time. Ideally, you'd like to invite a stable of speakers to your dinner, which will provide a star-studded draw to your little event. Remember, even an unknown becomes a mini-star after their talk at an event.

I do this each year at Renaissance Weekend, an annual New Year's weekend gathering for politicians, businesspeople, and other professionals. I send out a funny invite asking a few people if they'd like to play hooky from an official dinner and go to a nice restaurant elsewhere. At Renaissance Weekend, they even have a night designed for going off on your own to do just this. This works best at long three-day conferences. As with college, everyone likes to get off campus. If the conference is in your hometown, be bold enough to invite people to your home for a real treat, as I have always done with the Los Angeles–based Milken Institute Global Conference. This conference is one of the best in the United States for both content and guests. Each year I hold a dinner party at my house the day before the event is set to begin. People generally arrive in town a day early anyway, and a fun, intimate dinner party is always preferable to eating hotel food alone.

Dinner is not the only way to organize a conference within a conference. Long conferences are often filled with social outings—golf, tours, and visits to historic sites. Too often, such events are just plain terrible. Have you ever gone to a museum in a crowd of 400 people? You feel like a herded cow.

There's no reason why you can't take the lead in developing your own personal tour or visit to an out-of-the-way place that convention organizers might not have thought about. An old colleague from Starwood used to do this at winter conferences. An avid skier, he'd research the best skiing in the area—usually some out-of-the-way slopes that no one had taken the time to discover. He'd have no problem attracting a few other skiers who were jazzed about the prospect of some fresh powder.

The more active you become in playing "host" of your own conference within a conference, the better you'll be at helping other people make connections, making you a center of influence. When you meet people at your dinner party or event, don't simply introduce yourself; introduce the folks you meet to other people. If your new acquaintances don't quickly take up the conversation, offer a fact about one guest to another. "Sergio was in charge of Coke's global branding efforts in their heyday. Aren't you looking to refurbish your company's brand, David? You couldn't find a better sounding board than Sergio."

Draft Off a Big Kahuna

If you get to know the most popular man or woman at the conference—the one who knows everyone—you'll be able to hang with them as they circle through the most important people at the conference. Conference organizers, speakers, and name-brand CEOs and professionals attending the event are all worthy kahunas.

Check the convention program for the names of luminaries and key figures. Make those the sessions you attend. Arrive early at events where they'll be speaking. Stand near key entrances or registration tables. Be ready to introduce yourself, or stay behind for a quick chance to meet them.

You must remember to talk with speakers *before* they've hit the stage. Often, that anonymous schlub slurping yogurt at the breakfast table will take on the aura of a celebrity after he's spoken on stage. Find them before they've gained celebrity status, and you have a better chance to connect. Or ask the conference organizer (who has become your buddy anyway) to point them out if you don't know what they look like.

Be an Information Hub

Once you've created an opportunity to meet new people, establish yourself as an "information hub"—a key role of any good networker. How? Go beyond just memorizing the conference's brochure. Identify information the people around you would like to know, and come prepared. This might include information about trade gossip, the best local restaurants, private parties, etc. Pass key information along, or let others know how they can obtain it. This role does not end with the networking event, of course. As an information resource, you're someone always worth knowing.

Master the Deep Bump

The bump is the main weapon in your conference commando arsenal. Reduced to its essence, it is the two minutes you're given with someone you're "bumping into" whom you are looking to meet. Your goal should be to leave the encounter with an invitation to reconnect at a later time.

The bump, like other practices, is nuanced. The perfect bump is one that feels both fast and meaningful at the same time. I call this ideal a "deep bump."

Deep bumps are an effort to quickly make contact, establish enough of a connection to secure the next meeting, and move on. You've just paid a boatload of money to be at this conference (unless you're a speaker, when it's usually free!), and you want to meet as many people as you can in the time that you have. You're not looking to make a best friend. You are looking, however, to make enough of a connection to secure a follow-up.

Creating a connection between any two people necessitates a certain level of intimacy. In two minutes, you need to look deeply into the other person's eyes and heart, listen intently, ask questions that go beyond just business, and reveal a little about yourself in a way that introduces some vulnerability (yes, vulnerability; it's contagious!) into the interaction. All these things come together to create a genuine connection.

Not possible, you exclaim. Ah, but I've seen it done and I do it. The deep bump is not just theoretical mumbo jumbo.

There are some people who need just seconds, rather than minutes, to pull off a deep bump. Former President Bill Clinton, for instance, is the master. I've watched him up close as he works a line of well-wishers and fans (and sometimes, strident opponents). With each person, President Clinton will reach out to shake his or her hand. Most of the time, he'll use two hands or clasp a person's elbow to create instantaneous warmth. He'll make direct eye contact and, in that fleeting moment, ask a personal question or two. I don't know how many times I've heard different people from the same event comment about how incredible it was to be the sole focus of the man's attention. And that's even the Republicans.

The profoundness of that connection doesn't come from the President's desire to impart his opinion or riff on policy. His goal is at once very simple and powerful. The President wants you to like him (so in his own now-famous words, he "feels" what you feel). When he shows in those brief moments that he likes and cares about you, the human response is to reciprocate. He is finely tuned in to the radio station that we each listen to, WIIFM, also known as What's In It For Me? I never once heard Clinton ask for a vote or talk about himself when engaged in these quick, casual encounters. His questions always revolved around what the other person was thinking, what was troubling them.

Most people think a conference is a good time to market their wares. They rush from room to room desperately trying to sell themselves. But a commando knows that you have to get people to like you first. The sales come later—in the follow-up discussions you have after the conference. Now is the time to begin to build trust and a relationship.

Know Your Targets

You're ready to bump. Now you just need someone to bump against.

At each conference, I keep a list of three or four people I'd most like to meet on a folded piece of paper in my jacket pocket. I check off each person as I meet them. Beside their name, I'll jot down what we talked about and make a note about how I'm going to contact them later. And, once you've met with and engaged someone, you find yourself chatting again and again throughout the conference.

You can't, however, rely solely on chance to find them at cocktails or on a break. I usually ask the conference organizer to point to the area where they'll be and I watch where they sit. Most people continue to sit in the same seats throughout the conference.

For example, Barry Diller, the CEO of InterActiveCorp., was someone I'd wanted to meet for years. He's a visionary in commerce and media, with an uncanny ability to foresee, before anyone else, where innovation will turn into profit. He smells money.

Researching one of my conferences, I noticed he was scheduled to speak. I found out when and where and got access to the area where he would have to get on and off the stage. I positioned myself in a place where it would be damn near impossible to get by without giving me a little nudge.

As he walked by, I got his attention. "Mr. Diller, my name is Keith Ferrazzi. I work for Barry Sternlicht as his CMO at Starwood. He's mentioned before that you and I should talk and I thought I'd just make the introduction myself. I know you're busy, but I'm wondering if I can call your office and arrange a time to meet with you when we get back home?" [Pause—to which he responded, "Sure, call my New York office."] "Great, I wanted to talk to you about a number of ideas I have about your business, but I've also admired your career and pioneering work you've done for a long time." That was it. I played my heaviest and hardest card, which was my boss, a fellow visionary entrepreneur for whom Diller held respect. With a name as big as Diller, sometimes the bump can't be as deep as you'd like. Still, with limited time I managed to gain credibility by dropping a familiar and trusted name, show a bit of vulnerability in admitting I admired his career, and suggested I had value to offer with my ideas. That bump went on to realize a job offer and introductions within his company that are now important clients for FerrazziGreenlight.

Your sound-bite introduction will change depending on the circumstances. Generally, it will be a two- or three-sentence opener, tailored to the event, about what you can or want to do for them.

Breaks Are No Time to Take a Break

Breaks are where the real work happens at a conference.

Make sure and stake out the right place. Have you ever noticed how guests gather in the kitchen or some other central place when you have gatherings at home? One warm and centrally located spot is often the center of any party. The same holds true at a business gathering. Determine where most people will gather, or at least pass, and station yourself there. This might be near the food table, the bar, or the reception area.

Be on your game during these times. *U.S. News & World Report* revealed Henry Kissinger's technique for commanding a room: "Enter the room. Step to the right. Survey the room. See who is there. You want other people to see you."

Kissinger knows that great networkers know how to make a memorable first impression. They see a room of people as a playing field. Remember to look sharp. Don't underestimate the importance of dressing well in places where you'll be noticed. And start bumping.

Follow Up

If you didn't think I was a nut before, now it's a certainty. I know I've told you to follow up already, but that's how vitally important I think it is. So here it is again: follow up. After that, follow up again. Then, after you've done that, follow up once more.

I don't like to put it off or it might not get done. How many of you have cards from events that occurred months ago or even longer? That's a lost opportunity. During speeches, I'll sit in the back and write follow-up e-mails to the people I just met at the previous break. Everyone you talked with at the conference needs to get an e-mail reminding them of their commitment to talk again. I also like sending a note to the speakers, even if I didn't get a chance to meet them.

Here's an actual example of one of my follow-up e-mails:

> *Hey Carla,*
>
> *Wow, what a fun time. I didn't expect tequila shots to be a part of the Forbes CIO conference. We definitely have to make this an annual occurrence. Hey, I also wanted to follow up with our discussion on your marketing strategy and your interest in the FerrazziGreenlight loyalty strategy work we've done as a way to help reach your adult women demographic. When can you do a call this week, or at your leisure?*
>
> *Also, I wanted to say that I heard no fewer than three separate people talk about your session and what a great speaker you were. Congrats!*
>
> *Best,*
>
> *Keith*

It's the People, Not the Speakers

You've probably already figured this rule out by now. I don't often find the content of conferences particularly useful. I read a lot. I think about these subjects constantly and talk to a lot of people. By the time I get to a conference, I know the substance of what's going to be said.

Of course, there are exceptions, like when Michael Hammer talked about reengineering and then would magically turn the talk into both a lesson in life and a stand-up comedy routine.

Epiphanies aside, most conference speeches are about one more IBM or Microsoft senior VP talking about his or her process-improvement project. Even when the speaker is interesting, the mentality is the same: It's always about the people.

Don't Be This Person

THE WALLFLOWER: The limp handshake, the position in the far corner of the room, the unassuming demeanor—all signs that this person thinks he or she is there to watch the speakers.

THE ANKLE HUGGER: The ankle hugger is a total codependent and thinks that the first person they meet is their BFF (best friend forever). Out of fear, they shadow their BFF the entire conference. You've spent too much money not to leverage the opportunity to meet many *different* people. So bump! You have a lifetime to build relationships with these people. Collect as many follow-ups as you can.

THE CELEBRITY HOUND: This type of person funnels every bit of their energy into trying to meet the most important person at the event. The problem is, if the person they want to meet truly is the most important person at the conference, that person will be on their guard. And maybe even guarded, literally. A young friend of mine went to see the King of Jordan speak recently and came back ecstatic. He had waited an hour or more, along with 500 other people, for a chance to shake the King's hand. I asked him, "How, exactly, did you benefit from that encounter?"

"I can say I met him," he sheepishly replied. I told him that there were probably at least a handful of dignitaries and members of the King's cabinet in that room whom no one knew or wanted to know. Wouldn't it have been better for my young friend to actually have had a conversation with one of them, instead of a handshake with someone who will not remember him beyond the handshake? Maybe he could have struck up a relationship. Instead, he got a photo and a handshake.

THE SMARMY EYE DARTER: Nothing will give you a bad rap in less time. Be Bill Clinton instead. If you spend only thirty seconds with someone, make it thirty seconds of warmth and sincerity. Nothing will give you a good rap in less time.

THE CARD DISPENSER/AMASSER: This guy passes his card out like it had the cure for cancer written on its back. Frankly, cards are overrated. If you perform the bump successfully, and extract a promise for a future meeting, a piece of paper is irrelevant. This person gloats over the number of "contacts" he's made. In reality, he's created nothing more valuable than a phone book with people's names and numbers to cold-call.

CHAPTER 15

Connecting with Connectors

It has become part of our accepted wisdom that six degrees is all that separates us from anyone else in the world. How can that be? Because some of those degrees (people) know many, many more people than the rest of us.

Call them super-connectors. We all know at least one person like this individual, who seems to know everybody and who everybody seems to know. You'll find a disproportionate amount of super-connectors as headhunters, lobbyists, fundraisers, politicians, journalists, and public relations specialists, because such positions require these folks' innate abilities. I am going to argue that such people should be the cornerstones to any flourishing network.

What Michael Jordan was to the basketball court, or Tiger Woods is to golf, these people can be to your network. So who are they, really, and how can you get them to become prized members of your circle of associates and friends?

In his bestselling book *The Tipping Point*, Malcolm Gladwell cites a classic 1974 study by sociologist Mark Granovetter that surveyed how a group of men in Newton, Massachusetts, found their current job. The study, appropriately titled "Getting a Job," has become a seminal work in its field, and its findings have been confirmed over and over again.

Granovetter discovered that 56 percent of those surveyed found their current job through a personal connection. Only 19 percent used what we consider traditional job-searching routes, like newspaper job listings and executive recruiters. Roughly 10 percent applied directly to an employer and obtained the job.

My point? Personal contacts are the key to opening doors—not such a revolutionary idea. What is surprising, however, is that of those personal connections that reaped dividends for those in the study, only 17 percent saw their personal contact often—as much as they would if they were good friends—and 55 percent saw their contact only occasionally. And get this, 28 percent barely met with their contact at all.

In other words, it's not necessarily strong contacts, like family and close friends, that prove the most powerful; to the contrary, often the most important people in our network are those who are acquaintances.

As a result of the study, Granovetter immortalized the phrase "the strength of weak ties" by showing persuasively that when it comes to finding out about new jobs—or, for that matter, new information or new ideas—"weak ties" are generally *more* important than those you consider strong. Why is that? Think about it. Many of your closest friends and contacts go to the same parties, generally do the same work, and exist in roughly the same world as you do. That's why they seldom know information that you don't already know.

Your weak ties, on the other hand, generally occupy a very different world than you do. They're hanging out with different people, often in different worlds, with access to a whole inventory of knowledge and information unavailable to you and your close friends.

Mom was wrong—it does pay to talk to strangers. As Malcolm Gladwell wrote, "Acquaintances, in short, represent a source of social power, and the more acquaintances you have, the more powerful you are."

Throughout this book, I try to emphasize that what's most important is developing deep and trusting relationships, not superficial contacts. Despite Granovetter's research, I believe friendships are the foundation for a truly powerful network. For most of us, cultivating a lengthy list of mere acquaintances on top of the effort devoted to your circle of friends is just too draining. The thought of being obligated to another hundred or so people—sending birthday cards, dinner invites, and all that stuff that we do for those close to us—seems outlandishly taxing.

Only, for some, it's not. These people are super-connectors. People like me who maintain contact with thousands of people. The key, however, is not only that we know thousands of people but that we know thousands of people in many different worlds, and we know them well enough to give them a call. Once you become friendly with a super-connector, you're only two degrees away from the thousands of different people we know.

A social psychologist by the name of Dr. Stanley Milgram proved this idea in a 1967 study. He ran an experiment that set out to show that our big, impersonal world is actually quite small and friendly.

It was Milgram's experiment that created the notion of "six degrees of separation." In the experiment, he sent a package to a few hundred randomly selected people in Nebraska with the instructions that they forward the package to an anonymous stockbroker in Boston whom they did not know. Each person could send the packet only to someone whom they knew on a first-name basis, and who they thought was more likely to know the stockbroker than they were themselves. About a third of the letters reached their destination, after an average of only six mailings.

What was surprising was that when all those chains of people were analyzed, Milgram found that a majority of the letters passed through the hands of the same three Nebraskans. The finding drives home the point that if you want access to the social power of acquaintances, it helps to know a few super-connectors.

Connectors can be found in every imaginable profession, but I'm going to focus on seven professions where they most commonly congregate. Each of these kinds of connectors provides me with a link to an entire world of people, ideas, and information that, in a very significant way, has made my own life a little more fun, helped my career along, or made the businesses I worked for more successful.

1. Restaurateurs

Fifty-seventh Street isn't exactly lower Manhattan, but it was downtown to Jimmy Rodriguez, the nightlife impresario who made the Bronx hip for the A-list with his first eatery. Jimmy's Downtown, his second restaurant, lured the same set of celebrities, politicians, and athletes looking for good food and good times.

When I was in New York, it was my spot. The scene was exclusive without being pompous: soft light, a gleaming onyx bar, and a pumping R&B soundtrack makes the place feel like a hip country club. Jimmy would fly around tables hooking you up with free appetizers and introducing you to people he thought you might want to meet.

It was like a private club, without membership dues.

My memories of Jimmy were of a true-blue connector. In fact, it's a requisite for most people who own restaurants. When I was in Chicago, it was Gordon's Restaurant, and in L.A., it is Wolfgang Puck. The success of their enterprise depends on a core group of regulars who see the restaurant as a home away from home.

And it's quite easy to get to know a restaurateur. The smart ones will go out of their way to make your experience delightful. All you have to do is reach out and go there often enough.

When in a new city, I generally ask people to give me a list of a few of the hottest (and most established) restaurants. I like to call ahead and ask to speak with the owner (though the maître d' will do) and tell them that I go out regularly, sometimes in large parties, and I'm looking for a new place to entertain, a lot!

If you don't go out as often as I do, find one or two restaurants that you enjoy and frequent them when you do go out. Become a regular. Make a point of meeting the staff. When you're entertaining for work, bring others there. When you have to cater an event, use them.

Once you get to know the owner, it'll become like your very own restaurant—a place that has the patina of exclusivity and cachet a private club imparts with all the warmth and comfort of your own home.

With some advance planning and a little loyalty, a restaurateur will not only share the bounty of his kitchen with you but introduce you to his roster of other clients as well.

2. Headhunters

Recruiters. Job-placement counselors. Search executives. They are like gatekeepers. Instead of answering to one executive, however, the really successful ones may answer to hundreds of executives in the field in which they recruit.

Headhunters are professional matchmakers, earning their wage by introducing job candidates to companies that are hiring. Should you get the job, the headhunter gets a sizable commission, typically a percentage of the successful candidate's first year's compensation.

As a result, headhunters are an interesting blend of salesman and socialite. To find candidates, headhunters often place job ads.

They also contact likely candidates directly, perhaps on the referral of a friend or colleague. In the industries in which they specialize, they become invaluable resources of names and information.

The sweet spot for a headhunter revolves around two issues. You're either hiring them to do a search or you're helping them do a search on behalf of someone else. If you're in the market for a job, let as many search firms as are willing hit the phones for you.

I keep a file of headhunters: who they are and what they're looking for. And I return every call from them, helping to tap my network to find people for their jobs. I know they'll help me with access to some of their clients when I need their help. After all, they are in the networking business!

Can anyone contact a headhunter? To be honest, headhunters prefer to be the one contacting you. But if you're careful about not trying to sell yourself before you offer up the network of contacts you can provide to them, they'll be receptive. In the early years of my career, when I was not in the position of hiring them and didn't know people who were using search consultants, I would ask pointedly, "What searches are you working on? How can I help you find people?"

The other advice in this area is to act as a pseudo-headhunter yourself, always on the lookout to connect job-hunters and job-seekers or consultants and companies. When you help people land a new gig, they'll be inclined to remember you if they hear of a new position opening. Moreover, if you help, say, a vendor of yours land a new client, they'll usually be more open to negotiating prices on your next project. Helping others find good employees is a real currency.

3. Lobbyists

Well informed, persuasive, and self-confident, lobbyists are generally impressive networkers.

By virtue of their job, they are intimately familiar with the ways of large organizations and how local and national government work. They are almost uniformly passionate people whose goal is to sway politicians to vote on legislation in a way that favors the interest they represent.

How do they work? Lobbyists will often host cocktail parties and dinner get-togethers, allowing them to interact with politicians—and their opponents—in a casual atmosphere. Their more grass-roots efforts involve long hours spent on the phone and in writing letters, trying to rouse the community to get involved behind an issue. All of which makes them a rather easy group to please. Can you hold an event for them? Volunteer your services? Refer other volunteers to their cause? Introduce them to potential clients?

Lobbyists tend to bump up against a lot of people who it might be helpful to know, including those who are powerful and successful.

4. Fundraisers

"Follow the money" are words fundraisers live by. They know where it is, what it will take to get it, and most important, who's most likely to give it away. As a result, fundraisers, whether they work for a political organization, university, or nonprofit group, tend to know absolutely everybody. And while they have the unenviable job of trying to convince people every day to part with their well-earned money, they are almost always incredibly well liked. It's a selfless job often done for the best of reasons, and most people recognize that anyone who has a good friend who is a fundraiser has an open door to a whole new world of contacts and opportunities.

5. Public relations people

PR people spend their whole day calling, cajoling, pressuring, and begging journalists to cover their clients. The relationship between media and PR is an uneasy one, but at the end of the day, necessity brings them together like long-lost cousins.

A good friend who works in PR can be your entrée into the world of media and, sometimes, celebrity. Elana Weiss, who co-leads the PR firm I used called The Rose Group, introduced me to Arianna Huffington (through someone she knew in Arianna's office), the noted author and political columnist. Arianna has since become a friend and confidante and one of the dazzling lights at my dinner parties in L.A.

6. Politicians

Politicians at every level are inveterate networkers. They have to be. They shake hands, kiss babies, give speeches, and go to dinners, all in the name of gaining the trust of enough people to get elected. The stature of politicians is derived from their political power rather than their wealth. Anything you can do to help them gain power with voters, or exercise power in office, will go a long way to ensuring you a place in their inner circle.

What can a politician do for you? Local city hall politicians can be key to working through the thicket of local governmental bureaucracy. And politicians at any level, if successful, are celebrities—and their networks reflect that.

How can you reach out? Join your local Chamber of Commerce. Local executives, businesspeople, and entrepreneurs generally populate the Chamber. In every community, there are plenty of young politicos looking to climb the political ladder. Early on, before their rise to prominence, you can engender a lot of loyalty and trust by supporting their goals and chipping in when they decide to run for office.

7. Journalists

Journalists are powerful (the right exposure can make a company or turn a nobody into a somebody), needy (they're always looking for a story), and relatively unknown (few have achieved enough celebrity to make them inaccessible).

For years, since I was back at Deloitte, I've called on journalists at different magazines, taking them to dinners and pumping them full of good story ideas. I now know people in top positions at almost every major business magazine in the country. Which is one of the reasons why in less than a year after I took over YaYa, with barely a shred of revenue to its name, the company—and, more important, the idea YaYa was trying to sell—appeared in publications like *Forbes,* the *Wall Street Journal,* CNN, CNBC, *Brand Week, Newsweek,* the *New York Times* . . . the list goes on.

These are seven different professions tailor-made for super-connectors. Reach out to some. And there are others—lawyers, brokers, etc. Become a part of their network and have them become a part of yours. Cut the umbilical cord to the folks around the office water cooler. Mix it up. Hunt out people who look and act and sound nothing like you do. Seek out ideas from people you don't ordinarily talk to who inhabit professional worlds you don't ordinarily travel in.

In one word: Connect. In four better words: Connect with the connectors.

CONNECTORS' HALL OF FAME PROFILE
Paul Revere (1734–1818)

Understanding Paul Revere's legacy to the world of networking is as simple as grasping the following: Some people are *much* more well connected than others.

If you moved to a small town and wished, for some reason, to meet everyone in town, what would you do? Go door-to-door, greeting one resident at a time? Or would you try to find one plugged-in resident who could open all the doors for you?

The answer is clear.

Today, that plugged-in townie might be, say, the high school principal, the Little League commissioner, or the church pastor. But in Paul Revere's day—think of the 1770s in the Boston metro area—the most plugged-in people were like Revere, the owner of a silversmith shop in the city's North End, businessmen and merchants who dealt with individuals at every level of Boston society and culture.

Revere was also an extremely social individual: He formed several clubs of his own and joined many others. As a teenager, he and six friends formed a society of church bell ringers; as an adult, he joined the North Caucus Club, a society founded by Samuel Adams's father to choose candidates for local government. In 1774, when British troops began to seize munitions, Revere formed yet another club, of sorts, responsible for monitoring the movements of British troops. In addition, Revere belonged to the Masonic Lodge of St. Andrew, through which he was friendly with revolutionary activists such as James Otis and Dr. Joseph Warren.

All of which helps to explain why Revere, among all Bostonians in the year preceding the Revolution, served as courier for the Boston Committee of Correspondence and the Massachusetts Committee of Safety, riding express to the Continental Congress in Philadelphia. It was also he who spread the word of the Boston Tea Party to New York and Philadelphia. Revere, in short, was a man who knew not only people—he knew gossip, he knew rumors, he knew news, and he knew it from every level of Boston society.

In April 1775, Revere caught wind of British orders to capture rebel leaders and forcibly disarm the colonists. So Revere and his fellow rebels devised a warning system: Two lanterns shining from the steeple of Boston's Old North Church (the city's tallest building) indicated that the British troops were advancing on Boston by sea; one candle indicated a land advance. Either way, the rebels in Boston and its surrounding suburbs would know when and where to flee and take up arms.

We all know the "one if by land, two if by sea" part of this story. What's less known is that Revere's networking savvy is what allowed *him*—and maybe only him—to be the one entrusted with illuminating the church steeple.

The church, as it happened, was Anglican; the rector strongly supported the Crown. But Revere knew the vestryman, John Pulling, through the North Caucus Club. And through his shop, he knew the sexton, Robert Newman, who had a key to the building.

Revere's connections were crucial to him that fateful night. After lighting the lanterns, Revere needed to reach Lexington, to warn rebel leaders Sam Adams and John Hancock. First, two acquaintances rowed Revere across the Charles River, to Charlestown; there, a horse was waiting for Revere, lent to him by another pal, Deacon John Larkin.

Chased by Redcoats, Revere was diverted north of Lexington, to the town of Medford. Because he knew the head of Medford's military, Revere rode to his house and warned him. With the militiaman's help, Revere alerted the town of Medford before heading to Lexington.

Most of us know the Lexington part of the story. Less known is that on the same night that Revere made his midnight ride, a man named William Dawes went galloping off in the other direction to muster the militias to the west of Boston. Revere's ride stirred up an army, while something like three people showed up from the towns Dawes visited. Why? Revere was a connector: He knew everybody, and so was able to storm into one village after another, banging on all the right doors and calling out all the right people by name.

Historians say Revere was blessed with an "uncanny genius for being at the center of events." But it doesn't take genius for that—just involvement and active interest in your community and a friendship (or two) with a connector.

CHAPTER 16

Expanding Your Circle

The most efficient way to enlarge and tap the full potential of your circle of friends is, quite simply, to connect your circle with someone else's. I don't think of a network of people as a "net," into which you wrangle contacts like a school of struggling cod. Again, it's like the Internet, an interconnecting series of links in which each link works collaboratively to strengthen and expand the overall community.

Such collaboration means seeing each person in your network as a partner. Like a business in which cofounders take responsibility for different parts of the company, networking partners help each other, and by extension their respective networks, by taking responsibility for that part of the web that is theirs and providing access to it as needed. In other words, they exchange networks. The boundaries of any network are fluid and constantly open.

Let me give you an example of what I mean from my own life. One Saturday afternoon, I went to join my friend Tad and his wife Caroline at the Hotel Bel-Air in Los Angeles. Tad introduced me to Lisa, the manager of the hotel, who cuts a striking pose: tall, blond, articulate, charming, funny, and casual all at the same time.

"If between the two of you there's someone in L.A. you don't know, I'll be very surprised," Tad told us. In his eyes, we were both master networkers. Lisa was, as many in the hospitality business are, a super-connector.

Within ten minutes of meeting each other, we knew we were going to be great friends. Lisa and I spoke the same language.

Lisa had heard about the dinner parties I regularly threw for business. Your guests should be staying at the Bel-Air during their L.A. jaunts, she told me. I, in turn, looked around the Bel-Air and thought how memorable it would be to hold some of my events in such swanky surroundings. Could Lisa and I form a social partnership?

So I made a simple suggestion.

"Lisa, let's share a few months of dinner parties. You hold a dinner party at the Bel-Air and give me half the invite list. Then I'll hold one of my dinner parties and give you half of the list. We'll split the tab for each event, saving each of us a bundle of money, and together we'll meet a lot of new, exciting people. By cohosting the events, we'll make them that much more successful."

Lisa agreed, and our dinner parties were a huge success. The unique mix of people from the worlds of business and entertainment was fun and interesting. Not only did we introduce our friends to an entirely new group of people, but the dynamic at the parties was exhilarating.

Politicians, the inveterate masters of networking, have exchanged their networks in this fashion for years. They have what are called "host committees," groups of people hailing from different social worlds who are loyal to a specific politician and charged with introducing their candidate to their respective circle of friends. A typical well-established politician will have a host committee of doctors, lawyers, insurance professionals, college kids, and so on. Each committee is made up of well-connected people in their respective worlds who organize parties and events granting the politician access to all their friends. To my mind, it offers a great template for people looking to expand their own network.

Are there worlds you want more access to? If so, see if you can find a central figure within that world to act as your own one-person host committee. In a business context, say you plan on selling a new product that your company is introducing several months down the line, and most of your customers will be lawyers. Go to your personal lawyer, tell him about the product, and ask him or her if they'd be willing to come to a dinner with a few of their lawyer friends that you'd like to host. Tell them that not only will they get an early look at this fabulous new product, but they'll have an opportunity to meet your friends, who could become potential clients. They'll become responsible for holding events that will usher you into their group of friends. You'll become responsible for doing the same for them. This is exactly what I am doing at FerrazziGreenlight Training & Development as we roll out our training course "Relationships for Revenue Growth" into the legal profession. This training and development has been successfully taught at consulting firms, financial services companies, and to software sales forces and many others. But who better to capitalize from relationship selling than lawyers?

This kind of partnering works wonderfully. But the underlying dynamic at work has to be mutual benefit. It should be a win-win for all involved.

If you are sharing someone else's circle of friends, be sure that you adequately acknowledge the person who ushered you into this new world, and do so in all the subsequent connections that they helped foster.

Never forget the person who brought you to the dance. I once mistakenly invited a brand-new friend to a party without inviting the person who introduced us. It was a terrible mistake, and an unfortunate lapse in judgment on my part. Trust is integral to an exchange of networks that demands treating the other person's contacts with the utmost respect.

As your community grows, partnering becomes more of a necessity. It becomes a matter of efficiency. One contact holds the key to maintaining all the other relationships in his or her network. He or she is the gatekeeper to a whole new world. You can meet dozens, even hundreds of other people through your relationship with one other key connector.

Two quick rules of thumb:

1. You and the person you are sharing contacts with must be equal partners that give as much as they get.
2. You must be able to trust your partners because, after all, you're vouching for them and their behavior with your network is a reflection on you.

A word of caution—never give any one person complete access to your entire list of contacts. This is not a free-for-all. You should be aware of who in your network is interested in being contacted and how. Exchanging contacts should take place around specific events, functions, or causes. Consider carefully how your partner wants to use your network and how you expect to use his. In this way, you'll be more helpful to the other person, which is the kind of genuine reciprocity that makes partnering, and the world, work.

CHAPTER 17

The Art of Small Talk

We all have what it takes to charm everyone around us—colleagues, strangers, friends, the boss. But having it and knowing how to work it is the difference between going through life in the shadows and commanding center stage wherever you happen to be.

So you weren't born with that essential ingredient of charm, the gift of gab. So what? Few are.

We've all struggled with that ancient fear of walking into a room full of complete strangers and having nothing to say. Instead of looking out at a sea of potential new friends and associates, we see terrifying obstacles to the wet bar. It happens at business meetings, conferences, PTA meetings, and in just about every forum where being social matters. That's why small talk is so important. That's also why, for those of us without a knack for small talk, situations such as these that can help us meet so many others are also the situations that make us feel the most naked and uneasy.

And in this area, technology hasn't helped one bit. Wallflowers see e-mail and instant messaging as a nifty escape hatch from having to interact with others. The truth is, however, that these new modes of communication aren't particularly good for creating new relationships. The digital medium is all about speed and brevity. It may make communication efficient, but it's not effective when it comes to making friends.

Yet some are able to negotiate social situations with relative ease. How do they do it?

The answer, most people assume, is that the ability to make successful small talk is somehow innate, is something you're born with. While comforting, this assumption is entirely untrue. Conversation is an acquired skill. If you have the determination and the proper information, just like any other skill, it can be learned.

The problem is that so much of the information out there is flat-out wrong. I know too many CEOs who take pride in their terse, bottom-line behavior. They proudly assert their disinterest in "playing the game"; they revel in their inability to be anything but gruff.

But the fact is that small talk—the kind that happens between two people who don't know each other—is the most important talk we do. Language is the most direct and effective method for communicating our objectives. When playwrights and screenwriters develop characters for their work, the first thing they establish is motivation. What does the character want? What is he or she after? What are his or her desires? The answers dictate what that character will and won't say in dialogue. That exercise is not particular to the dramatic world; it's a reflection of how we humans are hardwired. We use words not only to articulate and make concrete our own deepest desires, but also to enlist others in quenching those desires.

About ten years ago, Thomas Harrell, a professor of applied psychology at Stanford University Graduate School of Business, set out to identify the traits of its most successful alumni. Studying a group of MBAs a decade after their graduation, he found that grade-point average had no bearing on success. The one trait that was common among the class's most accomplished graduates was "verbal fluency." Those that had built businesses and climbed the corporate ladder with amazing speed were those who could confidently make conversation with anyone in any situation. Investors, customers, and bosses posed no more of a threat than colleagues, secretaries, and friends. In front of an audience, at a dinner, or in a cab, these people knew how to talk.

As Harrell's study confirmed, the more successfully you use language, the faster you can get ahead in life.

So what should your objective be in making small talk? Good question. The goal is simple: Start a conversation, keep it going, create a bond, and leave with the other person thinking, "I dig that person," or whatever other generational variation of that phrase you want to use.

A lot has been said about how one should go about doing that. But in my opinion, the experts have gotten wrong the one thing that works the best. The first thing small-talk experts tend to do is place rules around what can and can't be said. They claim that when you first meet a person, you should avoid unpleasant, overly personal, and highly controversial issues.

Wrong! Don't listen to these people! Nothing has contributed more to the development of boring chitchatters everywhere. The notion that everyone can be everything to everybody at all times is completely off the mark. Personally, I'd rather be interested in what someone was saying, even if I disagreed, than be catatonic any day.

When it comes to making an impression, differentiation is the name of the game. Confound expectation. Shake it up. How? There's one guaranteed way to stand out in the professional world: Be yourself. I believe that vulnerability—yes, vulnerability—is one of the most underappreciated assets in business today.

Too many people confuse secrecy with importance. Business schools teach us to keep everything close to our vest. But the world has changed. Power, today, comes from sharing information, not withholding it. More than ever, the lines demarcating the personal and the professional have blurred. We're an open-source society, and that calls for open-source behavior. And as a rule, not many secrets are worth the energy required to keep them secret.

Being up front with people confers respect; it pays them the compliment of candor. The issues we all care most about are the issues we all want to talk about most. Of course, this isn't a call to be confrontational or disrespectful. It's a call to be honest, open, and vulnerable enough to genuinely allow other people into your life so that they can be vulnerable in return.

How many negotiations would have ended better if both parties involved were simply honest and forthright about their needs? Even when there is disagreement, I've found people will respect you more for putting your cards on the table.

Whether at the negotiating table or at the dinner table, our penchant for inhibition creates a psychological barrier that separates us from those we'd like to know better. When we leave a formal, hesitant, and uncomfortable conversation where we've held back our true selves, we console ourselves by dismissing the encounter, or more often the person, by thinking, "We had nothing in common anyway."

But the truth is everyone has something in common with every other person. And you won't find those similarities if you don't open up and expose your interests and concerns, allowing others to do likewise.

This has some comforting implications.

Once you know heartfelt candor is more effective than canned quips in starting a meaningful conversation, the idea of "breaking the ice" becomes easy. Too many of us believe "breaking the ice" means coming up with a brilliant, witty, or extravagantly insightful remark. But few among us are Jay Leno or David Letterman. When you realize the best icebreaker is a few words from the heart, the act of starting a conversation becomes far less daunting.

Again and again I'm surprised by the power of the vulnerability principle in the art of making small talk. Recently I attended a Conference Board meeting, an annual gathering for executives in marketing and communications. As is the custom, participants gather for a dinner the night before the event.

That night, sitting around the table were the heads of marketing for companies like Wal-Mart, Cigna, Lockheed, Eli Lilly, eBay, and Nissan. All of them were people who managed significant marketing budgets. Their importance to my business was significant. This was an occasion that called for my being at my best.

Problem was, I left my best somewhere over Pittsburgh on the flight there. The soundtrack of my life that night was the "Blues." Hours before, I had received the final and definitive e-mail that confirmed my worst fears: I was single again. I had just experienced the end of a traumatic and emotionally draining breakup. I was in no mood to talk.

Sherry, the woman I was sitting beside, whom I had just met, had no idea I wasn't being myself. As the conversation raged on at the dinner table, I realized I was doing all the things I tell people never to do. I was hiding behind polite, inconsequential questions about nothing in particular.

Here we were, Sherry and I, looking at each other and talking, but really saying nothing. It was clear we both couldn't wait for the check.

At some point, I recognized how absurd I was behaving. I've always told people I believe that every conversation you have is an invitation to risk revealing the real you. What's the worst that can happen? They don't respond in kind. So what. They probably weren't worth knowing in the first place. But if the risk pays off, well, now you've just turned a potentially dull exchange into something interesting or even perhaps personally insightful—and more times than not, a real relationship is formed.

It was at that point that I just came out and said what I was feeling. "You know, Sherry, I've got to apologize. We don't know each other very well, but I tend to be a whole lot more fun than I'm being this evening. It's been a tough day. I just had a board meeting where my board members put me through the wringer. More important, I just suffered a pretty difficult breakup and it's still got me down." Just like that, the rabbit was out of the hat. A risky opening, a flash of vulnerability, a moment of truth, and the dynamics of our conversation changed instantly.

Sure, she could have felt uncomfortable with such a personal admission. Instead, it put her at ease. "Oh my, that's no problem. Trust me, I understand. Everybody goes through it. Let me tell you about *my* divorce."

We became engaged in ways we hadn't expected. Sherry's shoulders relaxed. Her face loosened. She opened up. I felt drawn into the conversation for the first time that night. She went on to tell me about her painful divorce and all the things she had gone through in the months after it. All of a sudden, the discussion went into the emotional ramifications of breakups and how challenging they can be. For both of us, it turned out to be a cathartic moment. More than that, Sherry gave me some wonderful advice.

What happened next surprised even me. Upon hearing our conversation, several normally buttoned-up members of the group stopped their conversation and were drawn to ours. The entire table bonded over the very common trials and tribulations of marriage and relationships: men, women, gay, straight, it didn't matter. People who had been pensive and withdrawn were suddenly giving personal testimonies while the rest of us joined in supportive stories of our own. By evening's end, we were laughing and talking intimately; it turned into one incredible dinner. Today, I really look forward to seeing my friends at this annual event. They are important people to me—yes, some of them have become customers, but more of them are real friends I feel I can count on.

The message here is that we can go through life, particularly conferences and other professional gatherings, making shallow, run-of-the-mill conversation with strangers that remain strangers. Or we can put a little of ourselves, our real selves, on the line, give people a glimpse of our humanity, and create the opportunity for a deeper connection. We have a choice.

These days, I rarely blanch at the chance to introduce topics of conversation that some consider off-limits. Spirituality, romance, politics—these are some of the issues that make life worth living.

Of course, there are always fail-safe conversation starters suitable for every business function: How did you get started in your business? What do you enjoy most about your profession? Tell me about some of the challenges of your job? But safety—whether in conversation, business, or life—generally produces "safe" (read: boring) results.

The real winners—those with astounding careers, warm relationships, and unstoppable charisma—are those people who put it all out there and don't waste a bunch of time and energy trying to be something (or someone) they're not. Charm is simply a matter of being yourself. Your uniqueness is your power. We are all *born* with innate winning traits to be a masterful small talker.

The best way to become good at small talk is not to talk small at all. That's the art; here is some of the science:

Learn the Power of Nonverbal Cues

You're at a meeting when you turn to the person standing next to you. She turns to face you, and within a fraction of a second your mind makes a thousand computations. In that instant, you're trying to figure out whether you should run, fight, or be friendly. What you're doing, anthropologists say, is thinking like a caveman.

Deep in our genetic code, we are conditioned to be afraid of strangers. Will they eat us or feed us? That's why we form first impressions so quickly; we have to decide whether or not it is safe to approach.

You have about ten seconds before a person decides, subconsciously, whether they like you or not. In that short period of time we don't exchange a lot of words; our judgment is mostly based on nonverbal communication.

How do you get someone who doesn't know you to feel comfortable talking?

This is not the time to play hard-to-get, keep a distance, or play mysterious. These all-too-common reactions may work for the likes of Marlon Brando, but for the rest us, such poses register as "keep away!" in our prehistoric minds. Instead, we should take the initiative in creating the impression we want to give. People are wowed by social decisiveness when it's offered with compassion and warmth. How another person perceives you is determined by a number of things you do before you utter your first word.

- First, give the person a hearty smile. It says, "I'm approachable."

- Maintain a good balance of eye contact. If you maintain an unblinking stare 100 percent of the time, that qualifies as leering. That's plain scary. If you keep eye contact less than 70 percent of the time, you'll seem disinterested and rude. Somewhere in between is the balance you're looking for.

- Unfold your arms and relax. Crossing your arms can make you appear defensive or closed. It also signals tension. Relax! People will pick up on your body language and react accordingly.

- Nod your head and lean in, but without invading the other person's space. You just want to show that you're engaged and interested.

- Learn to touch people. Touching is a powerful act. Most people convey their friendly intentions by shaking hands; some go further by shaking with two hands. My favorite way to break through the distance between me and the person I'm trying to establish a bond with is to touch the other person's elbow. It conveys just the right amount of intimacy, and as such, is a favorite of politicians. It's not too close to the chest, which we protect, but it's slightly more personal than a hand.

Be Sincere

Whether you spend five seconds or five hours with a new contact or acquaintance, make the time count. In Los Angeles, where I live, eye darters are a party staple. They're constantly looking to and fro in an attempt to ferret out the most important person in the room. Frankly, it's a disgusting habit, and one that's sure to put off those around you.

The surest way to become special in others' eyes is to make *them* feel special. The correlate, of course, is equally true: Make people feel insignificant and your significance to them shall certainly diminish.

Develop Conversational Currency

When meeting someone new, be prepared to have something to say. Keep up with current events. Cultivate some niche interest. A single narrow specialty (cooking, golf, stamps) for which you have passion will have surprising expansive powers.

After business school, I indulged my passion for food and took a few months off taking courses at Le Cordon Bleu Culinary School in London. Back then, I thought it was a frivolous expenditure of my time. But my knowledge and passion for cooking that came from that experience has come into play time and again in casual conversations. Even people who aren't that interested in food enjoy hearing my funny and sometimes embarrassing stories about learning my way around a French kitchen in London. What you talk about is ultimately less important than how. It's edifying and interesting to hear someone talk about something they have a great interest in. Which means you can also talk about other people's passions. My COO at YaYa, James Clarke, for example, climbed Mt. Everest while performing his duties virtually for all but the week he was summiting. The astounding stories he has told me about the experience are now excellent conversation fodder.

Just remember not to monopolize the conversation or go into long-winded stories. Share your passion, but don't preach it.

Adjust Your Johari Window

The Johari Window is a model, invented by two American psychologists, that provides insight into how much people reveal of themselves. Some people are introverted, revealing little; they keep their window relatively closed. Other people are extroverted, revealing a great deal and keeping their windows open. These tendencies also fluctuate in different environments. In new and strange situations, with people we are unfamiliar with, our window remains small; we reveal little and expect others to do the same. If, on the other hand, the climate is safe and trusting with others that are similar to us, we share more of ourselves. Our windows open wider.

Successful communication depends, according to the model, on the degree to which we can align ourselves and our windows to match those we interact with.

Greg Seal, one of my earliest mentors who recruited me to Deloitte, brought this idea to my attention, and I'm forever grateful. As a brash, outspoken young guy, my window was wide open. Whether I was trying to sell consulting services to a shy CEO of an engineering company or working with that company's rowdy sales staff, my brash, outspoken style remained constant. Back then it wasn't clear to me why, for instance, the sales staff came out of meeting with me jazzed and the CEO couldn't wait for me to leave his office. When Greg introduced the idea of the Johari Window, and the need to adjust how open or closed that window was depending on with whom you were speaking, it made perfect sense. Greg remained true to himself no matter whom he spoke with, but he delivered his message in a tone and style that fit that person best.

Every person's Johari Window can be more or less open depending on the circumstances. And different professions— from those that demand a lot of interpersonal skills, like sales, to those that, like accounting, are generally more solitary—attract people whose windows share similar tendencies. A computer programmer's window, for example, may not open wide unless he or she is around peers. A strong marketing person's window, on the other hand, tends to be open regardless of the environment.

The key is knowing that in conducting small talk, we should be aware of the different styles at play and adapt to the person we're talking with. I know I can be gregarious and fun and outspoken when meeting with the FerrazziGreenlight Training & Development staff. In a meeting with my loyalty-management strategy consultants, who are much more analytical, I ratchet down the excitement and focus on being more deliberate and precise. If we address someone with the wrong style, the window may close shut with nothing revealed. No connection is made.

Throughout my day, I come into contact with hundreds of different people, each with their own distinct communication style. The concept of the Johari Window has helped me become conscious of my need to adapt my conversational approach to each person I want to connect with.

One helpful technique I use is to try and envision myself as a mirror to the person with whom I'm speaking. What's the cadence of their speech? How loudly do they talk? What's their body language? By adjusting your behavior to mirror the person you are talking to, he'll automatically feel more comfortable. This doesn't mean, of course, that you should be disingenuous. Rather, it shows that you're particularly sensitive to other people's emotional temperaments. You're just tweaking your style to ensure that the windows remain wide open.

Make a Graceful Exit

How do you conclude a conversation? During meetings and social gatherings, I'm often quite blunt. I'll mention something meaningful that was said in the course of our conversation and say, "There are so many wonderful people here tonight; I'd feel remiss if I didn't at least try and get to know a few more of them. Would you excuse me for a second?" People generally understand, and appreciate the honesty. There's also always the drink option. I'll say: "I'm going to get another drink. Would you like one?" If they say no, I don't have an obligation to come back. If they say yes, I'll be sure to enter into another conversation on my way to the bar. When I return with a drink, I'll say, "I just ran into some people you should meet. Come on over."

Until We Meet Again

In order to establish a lasting connection, small talk needs to end on an invitation to continue the relationship. Be complimentary and establish a verbal agreement to meet again, even if it's not business. "You really seem to know your wines. I've enjoyed tapping your wisdom; we should get together sometime to talk about wine. We can both bring one of our more interesting bottles."

Learn to Listen

As William James pointed out, "The deepest principle in human nature is the craving to be appreciated."

You should be governed by the idea that one should seek first to understand, then to be understood. We're often so worried about what we're going to say next that we don't hear what's being said to us now.

There are few ways to signal to your listener that you are interested and listening actively. Take the initiative and be the first person to say hello. This demonstrates confidence and immediately shows your interest in the other person. When the conversation starts, don't interrupt. Show empathy and understanding by nodding your head and involving your whole body in engaging the person you're talking with. Ask questions that demonstrate (sincerely) you believe the other person's opinion is particularly worth seeking out. Focus on their triumphs. Laugh at their jokes. And always, always, remember the other person's name. Nothing is sweeter to someone's ears than their own name. At the moment of introduction, I visually attach a person's name to their face. Seconds later, I'll repeat the person's name to make sure I got it, and then again periodically throughout the conversation.

If All Else Fails, Five Words That Never Do

"You're wonderful. Tell me more."

CONNECTORS' HALL OF FAME PROFILE
Dale Carnegie (1888–1955)

"Learning to 'small talk' is vital."

The late professor Thomas Harrell of Stanford's Graduate School of Business loved researching the traits of alumni. His chief finding, as you now know, is that successful graduates are social, communicative, and outgoing. "Getting-along skills," more than anything else, determined who got ahead.

And that's why the legacy of Dale Carnegie—the first person to *sell* small talk as a corporate skill—remains intact, nearly seven decades after the 1936 release of his bestseller *How to Win Friends and Influence People*.

For Carnegie, too, small talk became a means for self-advancement.

Born in 1888, the son of a Missouri pig farmer who struggled all his life, Carnegie grew up ashamed of being poor. The feeling never quite wore off, and, as a young man, he contemplated suicide. When he was twenty-four, and struggling for subsistence in New York City, Carnegie offered to teach night classes in public speaking at the 125th Street YMCA. Fewer than ten students attended his first class. For weeks, Carnegie shared with his students the skills he'd learned as a standout high school debater and as a student at Missouri State Teachers College. He taught people how to shirk shyness, boost self-confidence, and ease worry, using ideas that amount, then and now, to common sense. Remember people's names. Be a good listener. Don't criticize, condemn, or complain.

After his first several classes, Carnegie ran out of stories to tell. So he asked his students to stand up and talk about their own experiences—and offered feedback on their performances. It was then that he realized that as students overcame their fear of taking the floor, and became more comfortable talking openly about themselves, their self-confidence rose accordingly.

In Carnegie's classes, businessmen, salesmen, and other professionals found a place devoted to affordable, commonsensical self-improvement. By 1916, Carnegie's course was so successful that he needed to train, for the first time, official "Dale Carnegie Course" instructors. By 1920, Carnegie had published *Public Speaking*, an official text that he used to launch Carnegie courses in Boston, Philadelphia, and Baltimore.

And it's possible none of it would've happened had not Carnegie encouraged his initial classes to open up and to share *their* stories. It's no wonder Carnegie never failed to stress listening as a crucial networking skill. In an age when computers and e-mail take the personal touch out of doing business, Carnegie's homespun logic remains as relevant as ever. People, after all, are still people, and who couldn't use a reminder of lessons like:

- "Become genuinely interested in other people."
- "Be a good listener. Encourage others to talk about themselves."
- "Let the other person do a great deal of the talking."
- "Smile."
- "Talk in terms of the other person's interests."
- "Give honest and sincere appreciation."

Though he successfully applied the fundamentals of smart smalltalking to his own life, Carnegie was reluctant—at first—to share his secrets in book form. The course cost $75, and Carnegie wasn't keen on giving away its content. But Leon Shimkin, an editor at Simon & Schuster, was a passionate graduate of Carnegie's classes. Shimkin finally convinced Carnegie, to the benefit of us all, to write a book. "Perhaps by practicing the very sort of flattery and persistence that Mr. Carnegie himself advocated and admired—Mr. Shimkin won him over," wrote Edwin McDowell in the *New York Times* in 1986.

For Shimkin, and millions more like him, Carnegie emboldened us with the belief that we can learn to get along better with other people—and achieve great success—no matter who we are or how poor we were.

Turning Connections into Compatriots

CHAPTER 18

Health, Wealth, and Children

W hat do you really want? Side by side, those five words may be the most universally resonant in the English language.

As I discussed in the chapter "What's Your Mission?" the answer to "What do you really want?" determines all that you do and all the people who help you accomplish it. It provides the blueprint for all your efforts to reach out and connect with others. Likewise, when you understand someone else's mission, you hold the key to opening the door to what matters most to them. Knowing that will help you create deep, long-lasting bonds.

In my initial conversation with someone I'm just getting to know, whether it's a new mentee or simply a new business contact, I try to find out what motivations drive that person. It often comes down to one of three things: making money, finding love, or changing the world. You laugh—most people do when confronted with the reality of their deepest desires.

Get comfortable with that reality. Learning to become a connector means in some sense learning to become an armchair therapist. As you continue down this path, you'll become a keen observer of the human psyche. You'll have to learn what makes people tick and how best to satisfy whatever tick that may be. It means calling something BS when you see people being less than honest with themselves.

The most successful relationship builders are, indeed, a nifty amalgam of financial guru, sex therapist, and all-around do-gooder.

Connecting is a philosophy of life, a worldview. Its guiding principle is that people, all people, every person you meet, is an opportunity to help and be helped. Why do I place so much importance on mutual dependence? For starters, because, as a matter of necessity, we are all social beings. Our strength comes from what we do and know cumulatively. The fact is, no one gets ahead in this world without a lot of help.

Eliminating things like intimidation and manipulation, there is only one way to get anybody to do anything. Do you know what it is?

This is far from a trivial question. Business is, after all, the ability to motivate a group of individuals to move an idea from concept to reality; to take a theory and make it a practice; to gain the buy-in of your employees and colleagues; to encourage others to execute your plans.

If you're still not sure what the answer is, take heart; many people don't. There are hundreds of new books published each year grappling with how to engender loyalty and motivation. Most arrive at the wrong answer.

They get it wrong because of the assumptions they make. It's in vogue for people to exclaim: Everything is new! Everything is different! Business has changed! The answers, people suggest, must be found in technology or new forms of leadership or funky organizational theories. But is there anything really new or different about people? Not really.

The principles of how to deal with other people are the ones Dale Carnegie espoused over sixty years ago that have proven to be universal and timeless.

The only way to get people to do anything is to recognize their importance and thereby make them feel important. Every person's deepest lifelong desire is to be significant and to be recognized.

What better way is there to show appreciation and to lavish praise on others than to take an interest in who they are and what their mission is?

There is an added nuance to discovering what matters to people. Helping someone accomplish his or her deepest desires is critical not only to forming a bond with someone but to keeping that bond strong and growing. Loyalty may be the forgotten virtue of the modern age, but it remains the hallmark of any strong relationship and a value many companies are working hard to bring into their day-to-day practices.

Loyalty, to me, means staying true to someone (or something, like a brand or a customer segment) through thick and thin. Loyalty is a marathon rather than a sprint. As any good brand manager knows, you don't win customer loyalty quickly. It has to be earned. How?

Let me tell you a story about Michael Milken: yes, the financial and deal-making guru but also a man who is a philanthropist and deeply insightful human behaviorist. Through Entertainment Media Ventures (EMV), Mike was an investor in the start-up company I joined after Starwood. And, during my recruitment as CEO, I made it clear to him and my friend Sandy Climan, who led EMV, that a big motivation of taking the job would be to learn from Mike while running the company. I had already gotten to know Mike independently a few years back while acting as an advisor to DuPont, when the company was starting a consumer soy-milk joint venture. Mike was someone I had always wanted to meet—one of my early aspirational contacts. I had discovered through some articles I had read about him that he had a great deal of interest in soy and its curative effects. He had suffered a bout with prostate cancer, which he turned into a passion for health care and the importance of preventative medicine. To Mike, diet was an integral component in that mix, and it became a personal and philanthropic passion.

From the beginning of my tenure as CEO, I sought to build the company and further my relationship with Mike. He, in turn, took me under his wing and opened his world to me.

If he was going to New York for one of his many CapCure fundraisers, which support scientific research to find cures for prostate cancer, or traveling to someplace to give out recognition and money to exceptional teachers through the Milken Family Foundation, I would try to catch a ride. My only goal was to watch how he worked and perhaps glean a few insights in the process. I made it a point to identify customers or prospects at whatever destination city he was going to, so it was time well spent for YaYa as well.

Most of the time, we would sit quietly working. He would plow through one of the ten bags of reading he lugs with him wherever he goes, and I, of course, would be pounding away on my computer, e-mailing and connecting with abandon for YaYa revenue generation and business development. There was much to be learned in simply watching what he read and how he thought or reflected.

On one trip in particular, Mike and I began to talk about people's passions, what really mattered to people. It was then that I received profound insight about people and loyalty. You see, Mike, in addition to having a brilliant quantitative mind, is also a relationship artist.

I have seen him spend hours talking to people you'd never expect him to take an interest in: secretaries, the very old and the very young, the powerful and the powerless. He loves people, their stories, and how they view the world. When I mentioned that to him, I was reminded of what Ralph Waldo Emerson once said: "Every man I meet is my superior in some way. In that, I learn of him." Everyone had something to teach him.

This focus on people was the reason so many of them showed so much loyalty to him. I feel that same loyalty. I asked how so many people became so invested in their relationship with him. What did he know that others didn't? Mike paused for a moment, as he does when he particularly likes (or dislikes) a question. Then he smiled.

"Keith," he said, "there are three things in this world that engender deep emotional bonds between people. They are health, wealth, and children."

There are a lot of things we can do for other people: give good advice, help them wash their car, or help them move. But health, wealth, and children affect us in ways other acts of kindness do not.

When you help someone through a health issue, positively impact someone's personal wealth, or take a sincere interest in their children, you engender life-bonding loyalty.

Mike's experience was, in fact, backed by research. Psychologist Abraham Maslow created a theory outlining human beings' hierarchy of needs. We all have the same needs, Maslow believed, and our more basic needs must be satisfied before our higher needs can be addressed.

The highest human need, said Maslow, is for self-actualization— the desire to become the best you can be. Dale Carnegie astutely recognized this. But Maslow argues we can't attend to our highest needs until we attend to those at the bottom of the pyramid, like the necessities of subsistence, security, and sex. It is within this lower group—where health, wealth, and children reside—that Mike was saying loyalty is created. In addressing those three fundamental issues, you accomplish two things: 1) You help someone fulfill those needs they most need met, and 2) You allow them the opportunity to move up the pyramid of needs to tackle some of their higher desires.

I reflected on my own experience and found he was absolutely right.

Recently, a friend of mine was diagnosed with prostate cancer. Because of my relationship with the CapCure foundation, I knew the lead doctor there. I gave him a call to see if he could spend some time with my friend. Another friend, Mehmet Oz, the wunderkind who directs the Cardiovascular Institute at Columbia University and is a founder and director of the Complementary Medicine Program at NewYork-Presbyterian Hospital, is always taking the calls of people I send his way.

I know intimately how in a time of anxiety a reassuring expert is worth all the wealth in the world. Throughout my father's heart-related illness, a family friend named Arlene Treskovich, who worked for one of the best heart doctors in Pittsburgh, gave us access to medical advice few blue-collar Pittsburgh families can afford. She was just doing what she was taught; her mother, Marge, had worked at the Latrobe Hospital and used to make sure that any member of our family or friends of our family who were hospitalized were treated like royalty, even if it was just an extra Jell-O from the kitchen when it was closed. To this day, I would do anything Arlene asked of me.

Sometimes, all it requires is taking an interest and providing emotional support. Let me give you an example. Robin Richards was the founding president of music portal MP3.com and built one of the highest-profile Internet companies in the world. He skillfully navigated MP3.com through a very difficult period before selling it to Vivendi Universal, which subsequently hired him as a key executive. I met Robin around this time because he was leading a negotiation to buy our company.

The deal ultimately fell through, but during the process, I learned Robin had a young child who had suffered from a terrible form of cancer. When he shared this deeply painful and private piece of information over dinner with me, the dynamics that so often attend a negotiation flew out the window. We discussed our shared experiences and I introduced him to Mike, who was equally passionate about finding a cure for this form of cancer. Robin and I are still good friends to this day, and I know we would both bend over backward for the other.

Have you helped someone lose weight by passing on a good diet? Have you found a particular vitamin or supplement that has helped you and passed it on to others? These may seem like little things. But with these three issues, health and diet included, the little things mean everything.

When it came to wealth, I thought of the many men and women whom I've helped find jobs. While it's not the same as making someone millions through innovative financing instruments, as Mike had done for many people, a job significantly altered these friends' economic situation. If someone I know is looking for a job, I reach out through my network for leads. If they've already found a job they're interested in, I call the decision maker. Sometimes I'll simply help someone revise his or her résumé, or act as a reference. Whatever I can do. And I do the same for businesses. For the restaurants I frequent, for example, I make it my mission to send as much business their way as possible. I work hard to funnel customers to all my contacts who are consultants, vendors, and suppliers of all stripes. I know they are good, I trust them, and I want others to benefit from their expertise as well.

People's children mean everything to them. I take it upon myself to mentor kids. It's fun, it's helpful, and teaching is the finest method I know for learning. The loyalty I've gained from placing a person's child in an internship, whether at my company or a friend's company, is immeasurable.

Take my experience with Jack Valenti, the former Chairman and Chief Executive Officer of the Motion Picture Association. Texas born, Harvard educated, Valenti has led several lives: a wartime bomber pilot, advertising agency founder, political consultant, White House Special Assistant, and movie industry leader. He knows everyone; more important, every one who knows him has loads of respect for the man (in an industry not keen on doling out respect to anyone).

Valenti had been an aspirational contact of mine for some time. I never sought him out, but he was somebody I knew would be very interesting, a hardworking Italian guy who worked his way up from nothing. I figured we had plenty in common.

Our first encounter was pure serendipity. I attended a luncheon for cabinet members at the Democratic National Convention in Los Angeles during President Clinton's last year of office. I spotted Jack among the attendees. When we all sat down for lunch, I made sure he and I were sitting next to each other.

Our conversation that afternoon was good, entertaining, and polite. I had no mission or purpose. I hoped it might, someday, form the basis for something more substantive.

Not long after, a friend called me, knowing I was passionate about mentoring. "You know, Jack Valenti's son is looking for work in your industry. You might want to meet with him and give him some advice."

Jack's son is a very bright chip off the old block, both charming and smart. I gave him some advice, introduced him to some people within the industry that he should know, and that was it.

Several months later, at the Yale CEO conference, I saw Jack again.

"Jack," I said, "I'm sure you don't remember me. There's no reason you should. We sat together for lunch once at a Democratic convention. But I met with your son a few months ago to give him some career advice. I was wondering how he is doing?"

Jack dropped everything he was doing and couldn't have been more interested. He peppered me with questions about his son and what the best tack was to enter my industry.

I followed up our encounter a day later with a dinner invitation, along with an array of political and entertainment honchos he could meet.

"Sure, I'd love to come to dinner if my schedule allows," he told me. "But more important, I'd like to get together for lunch with you, me, and my son."

Jack probably wasn't that interested in my dinner invitation. Who knows? But he was interested in the welfare of his son. Jack regards my dinner invitations with a lot more excitement than he would have if I had not had the chance to give his son some simple and sound advice.

Too many people think an invitation alone is enough to engender loyalty. Back in my days at Deloitte, and I see it today in my consulting practice, a lot of people felt that taking clients and prospects out to a fancy dinner, a ballgame, or a show was the way to build loyalty. I've fallen into that trap myself. In the beginning of a relationship, those kinds of outings are merely forums that allow you to connect strongly enough with the other person to help them address the issues that matter to them most. However, we've encouraged some of our biggest Fortune 100 clients to begin to invite their clients and prospects into their executives' homes to have dinner, meet the family, and understand how they can really help their clients as individuals.

But remember, if you're going to deal with people's most important issues, give those issues the commitment that they deserve. If not, your best intentions will backfire. Hell hath no fury like a person for whom you've promised the most intimate of help and delivered none.

Can you walk the talk? It's easy for someone to say, "I care about people. I believe in helping and being helped. I believe that helping people become healthy or make money or raise successful children is paramount in life." Many people say those things—but then you see their actions, you hear about them from their own networks, and you discover they really don't believe any of it. You can be sure your network will broadcast your true colors very quickly and with lasting effects to all its members.

Where do you start? You start with the philosophy, the worldview, that every human is an opportunity to help and be helped. The rest—whether it means helping with someone's health, wealth, children, or any other unsatisfied desires—follows from that.

CHAPTER 19

Social Arbitrage

Some people become power brokers through sheer intimidation and force of will; others, generally with far better results, learn to become indispensable to the people around them.

I still remember the advice that made me aware of these two routes to power. Greg Seal pulled me into his office one day not long after I had been hired at Deloitte, sat me down, and said, "Stop driving yourself—and everyone else—crazy thinking about how to make yourself successful. Start thinking about how you're going to make everyone around you successful."

From the moment I had arrived at Deloitte, I was a man on a mission. I wanted to work more hours, meet more partners, be on the biggest projects solving the biggest problems—and I wanted to do it all *now*, because I was desperate to make a name for myself. In the wake of my ambition, a whole lot of people didn't like me. And at Deloitte, as in all organizations, it isn't easy getting things done when your peers dislike you.

That you'd anger and abuse some people on your way to the top used to be accepted practice. Michael Korda's 1975 book on the secrets to becoming a corporate chieftain, *Power! How to Get*

It, How to Use It, advised that "master players . . . attempt to chan-
nel as much information as they can into their own hands, then
withhold it from as many people as possible." But if thirty years
ago power was attained through a monopoly of information (and
a whole lot of angry people), today the system is more akin to
social arbitrage: a constant and open exchange of favors and intel-
ligence, as Greg had so wisely advised.

How does this work? Think of it as a game. When someone
mentions a problem, try to think of solutions. The solutions come
from my experience and knowledge, and my tool kit of friends and
associates. For example, if I'm in a conversation and the other person mentions they're looking to buy a house in Los Angeles, the first
thing I think is "How can my network help?" And there's no time to
linger. Mid-conversation, I'll pull out my cell phone and locate
someone who can help my companion buy a home. As I'm dialing,
I might say something like, "You need to meet this Realtor I know
named Betty. No one knows the Los Angeles area better. Here's her
phone number, but hold on—" Now Betty is on the line. "Hi, Betty,
it's so nice to hear your voice. It has been too long. Listen, I'm standing here with a friend who is in need of your wisdom. I just gave
him your number and wanted to tell you personally he'd be calling."
The connection is made, the work is done, and whatever happens
next, both parties are pleased by my efforts on their behalf.

This is social arbitrage at work. And the first key is, don't wait
to be asked. Just do it.

Let me give you another example, an interaction I had with
Hank Bernbaum, the CEO of High Sierra, a small bag manufac-
turer out of Chicago. Hank had seen a short profile on me and my
marketing expertise in the magazine *Fast Company*. He called me
out of the blue and said, "The article on you was excellent."

Already, he had my attention.

"We're a tiny company," he said, "and we're terrible at marketing. We've got the best duffels and bags in America, but no one

knows it. Our revenue and market size is a quarter of what it should be. Can you help?"

He added, "By the way, we don't have a lot of money to burn."

I usually love taking these calls when time allows, because I'm able to play confidante, counselor, or even concierge, for so many different people. I'm constantly introducing two people from different parts of my life who might benefit from knowing each other. It's a sort of ongoing puzzle, matching up the right people and the right opportunities. Once you, too, start to see the world this way, it opens up exciting opportunities. It's both rewarding and fun. Hank needed some consulting help and his bags needed exposure. I called Peter, a consultant who had worked with me at Starwood Hotels, a terrific marketing guy and someone who loved the outdoors. A perfect fit. Then I called another friend who is head of marketing at Reebok. Their bags never sold as well as their other products, and I thought the two might benefit from sharing insights and experiences. I even "cloned" a meeting I had with a marketing executive at Reebok, and brought Hank along to make face-to-face introductions.

Then I asked Hank if he'd ever had any publicity. He hadn't. I sent a couple of Hank's totes to Alan Webber, the editor of *Fast Company*. A few months later, the magazine did a piece on High Sierra products after Alan had his writers evaluate a particularly innovative travel bag we had sent.

Hank was ecstatic. But then I added one more thing: "Hank, the calls I'm making on your behalf, you need to be doing this for yourself. Do you belong to the Executive Club in Chicago?"

"I've been thinking about it," he said. "Why?"

"You've got to stop thinking of yourself and your company as an island. You need to meet people. There are a lot of CEOs and smart people in the Executive Club who could've done what I'm doing for you, only a few years ago. You need to be making these connections."

Soon after, Hank started networking locally with other executives. Hank's products are superb; what he needed was the network. However, it's not just he and I who have prospered. My former colleague, Peter, the outdoorsy marketer from Starwood, used the experience to build the confidence he needed to ultimately go out on his own. He now has a thriving consulting firm in New York. The CMO at Reebok? He was grateful for an introduction that might help him boost his bag business. What started with one man and a problem, ended with several people and many solutions.

My point? Real power comes from being indispensable. Indispensability comes from being a switchboard, parceling out as much information, contacts, and goodwill to as many people—in as many different worlds—as possible

It's a sort of career karma. How much you give to the people you come into contact with determines how much you'll receive in return. In other words, if you want to make friends and get things done, you have to put yourself out to do things for other people—things that require time, energy, and consideration.

Successfully connecting with others is never about simply getting what you want. It's about getting what you want and making sure that people who are important to you get what they want first. Often, that means fixing up people who would otherwise never have an opportunity to meet.

The best sort of connecting occurs when you can bring together two people from entirely different worlds. The strength of your network derives as much from the diversity of your relationships as it does from their quality or quantity.

Most of us know the people within our own professional and social group, and little more. Through other connectors, and on your own, I would urge you to make a point of knowing as many people from as many different professions and social groups as possible. The ability to bridge different worlds, and even different people within the same profession, is a key attribute in managers who are paid better and promoted faster, according to an influential study conducted by Ron Burt, a professor at the University of Chicago Graduate School of Business.

"People who have contacts in separate groups have a competitive advantage because we live in a system of bureaucracies, and bureaucracies create walls," says Burt. "Individual managers with entrepreneurial networks move information faster, are highly mobile relative to bureaucracy, and create solutions better adapted to the needs of the organization."

His research goes a long way toward answering that persistently nagging question: Is it what you know or who you know that leads to success? For Burt, it's both. Who you know determines how effectively you can apply what you know. Getting things done, and climbing the walls of your company, require having the right relationships.

I've always been well aware of this idea. At Deloitte, I got to know the CMOs of our largest competition. At Starwood, I quickly became familiar with the industry influencers. When I became CEO of YaYa, I set out to meet the leadership in the media and computer games industry. What I didn't realize was that all along I was setting the groundwork for the success of Ferrazzi-Greenlight at the same time. No matter what the job, if I was going to push my company's product into an important brand position among those who mattered, I needed to be able to converse with the players inside and outside the industry who could help me make that happen. One of the ways I achieved this was by helping *them* get to know one another—which they, too, knew was beneficial for their business. I was surprised, for instance, that the heads of marketing for the big consulting firms didn't know one another.

Maybe you're thinking to yourself, "But I don't know any executives or key people in my industry! And why would they want to get to know me anyway?" Not a problem. Performing social arbitrage when your financial and relational resources are thin is actually not too big a hurdle. The solution is knowledge, one of the most valuable currencies in social arbitrage. Knowledge is free—it can be found in books, in articles, on the Internet, pretty much everywhere, and it's precious to everyone.

The ability to distribute knowledge in a network is a fairly easy skill to learn. So easy, in fact, you should get started today. Identify some of the leading thinkers and writers in your industry. Do these figures have any new books on the market? Look at what's hot on the nonfiction *New York Times* bestseller list. Or for business bestsellers, check out the *Wall Street Journal*'s list in the Personal Journal section on Friday. Buy the book, read it, and take some notes summarizing the Big Idea, a few of its interesting studies or anecdotes, and why it's relevant to the people you're thinking about passing your knowledge on to. You've just created your own Big Idea of the Month Cliffs Notes (or whatever snazzy title you choose). Now pick a few people, some whom you know well and some you don't, and e-mail them your work. All you have to say is "Here are some cool ideas I think you'd like to be on top of."

Presto! You're now a knowledge broker. After you get the swing of it, you might want to send out a monthly Big Idea Cliffs Notes e-mail. Turn it into a newsletter. If one month you don't have the time, you could forward some particularly helpful article you read. Or, if the book is particularly interesting and you really want to make an impression, send the book itself.

It's easy enough to make knowledge brokering a habit. Let's say, for instance, someone mentions over lunch or in the minutes before the start of a meeting that they are having a hard time dealing with their teenage son or daughter. You should hear "problem." As a practitioner of social arbitrage, you think "need to find a solution." If you don't have any personal advice, the solution will come from asking yourself, "How can my network of friends and contacts help? Which one of my friends has teenagers?" It probably won't take long before you come up with someone you know, maybe your own parents, who handled their own teenage kids in a constructive manner. Get on the phone and ask them if they have any advice, or if they used any books or articles to help them through the process. Now pass it on.

Or let's say you're a real estate agent but you aspire to be a clothing designer. I don't know too much about clothes, but as with just about any subject, I'm sure others do (one of those people has almost certainly written a book about it). Do a search on Amazon.com, and find something that seems helpful to someone looking to become a clothing designer. Then send the aspiring clothing designer a link or even the book itself, or broker a direct conversation—that would be real value.

Yes, this kind of reaching out takes time and a certain thoughtfulness. But that is exactly why it's so appreciated. Facilitating all those connections, all that knowledge, and ultimately all that happiness is what being a truly modern-day "power broker" is all about.

To paraphrase Dale Carnegie: You can be more successful in two months by becoming really interested in other people's success than you can in two years trying to get other people interested in your own success.

CONNECTORS' HALL OF FAME PROFILE

Vernon Jordan

"Make yourself indispensable to others."

Vernon Jordan, dealmaker extraordinaire, former Clinton advisor, and Washington super-lawyer, currently sits on ten corporate boards, including American Express, Dow Jones, Revlon, and Xerox. He's the Senior Managing Director for Lazard, an international investment bank, and also a high-ranked senior counsel at the Washington, D.C., law firm of Akin Gump. *Fortune* ranked him ninth on its list of the most powerful black executives.

According to *Time* magazine, Jordan earns a seven-figure income from a "law practice that requires him to file no brief and visit no courtroom, because his billable hours tend to be logged in posh restaurants, on cellular phones . . . making a deft introduction here, nudging a legislative position there, ironing out an indelicate situation before it makes the papers." He doesn't just talk a good game. He makes things happen.

It's hard enough, in this life, to hold down just one job in a high-powered organization. But Jordan has made himself so valuable—so coveted—to so many employers that he actually works for several at once—and none of them seem to mind his vocational polygamy.

Along the way, Jordan has become one of Washington's most networked individuals, a man who seems to have friends and influence in every quarter and province. He's connected Lou Gerstner with IBM. He approached Colin Powell about replacing Warren Christopher as Secretary of State. He helped James Wolfensohn become President of the World Bank.

How has he done it?

Jordan has used social arbitrage to make himself indispensable—he is, in every sense of the word, a modern-day power broker. But he wasn't always at the vortex of everything that happens in Washington. He didn't even live full-time in Washington until Akin Gump hired him in 1982. By the time he arrived there, he'd done enough in his career—having built up several decades of contacts made and favors done—to know that, before long, he'd become a man of influence in his new town. Akin Gump knew it too, which is one reason they hired him: "I knew he would fit into the Washington legal community and come to be a dominant figure in it," said Robert Strauss, a senior partner. "This is a town built on the use of power and on relationships, and Vernon is about as good a people person as I know."

Jordan became a household name to all Americans in the 1990s because of his relationship with Bill Clinton. But long before then, Jordan was well known to the black community.

In the '60s, Jordan was an active civil rights lawyer in Atlanta. Later, he became a field secretary for the NAACP, fighting for school integration and registering black Georgians to vote. In 1964, Jordan left the NAACP to head the Southern Regional Council's Voter Education Project (VEP). His role was to find volunteers who could organize voter drives, and to raise money for the project. Raising money compelled Jordan to travel throughout the South, pitching wealthy foundations on why they should grant money to the VEP. It was this position that allowed Jordan to gain respect as a man who could fight for the cause from *within* the establishment. His Rolodex began to expand as he forged connections with both the heads of foundations and the VEP supervisors in Washington, D.C.

Jordan first ingratiated himself to the Fortune 500 community when, in 1966, he was invited to President Johnson's White House conference on civil rights, which was attended by hundreds of CEOs. For the remainder of the '60s and '70s, he traveled as a plugged-in member of both corporate and civil rights circles. His involvement in one circle made him all the more valuable to the other. Favors done and friends made in one circle could be leveraged to do favors and make friends in the other.

Jordan's full-time jobs allowed him to keep one foot in each world. In 1970, he became executive director of the United Negro College Fund. In 1972, he became president of the National Urban League, a pro-business civil rights organization—a job he held for ten years. Both posts allowed Jordan to gracefully expand his personal network, to the point where, in 1982, Akin Gump paid him quite a hefty price for his services. "Vernon did not come cheap," said Strauss. "But I told him: 'We'll carry you for a few years until you figure out what it's all about here, then you will carry us for a long time after that.'"

Jordan's career is a wonderful example of the opportunity that comes from bringing different people together from different worlds and different organizations to do good things. When Jordan became a public figure during the Clinton-Lewinsky scandal, he was challenged on his claim that it was normal for him to help a virtual stranger like Monica Lewinsky find a job. His network once again came to his aid. Washington attorney Leslie Thornton detailed in the *Wall Street Journal* how Jordan had gone out of his way to help her and others. She revealed what many young black and white professionals had long known privately: Jordan had been opening doors for people of all colors and creeds for decades.

CHAPTER 20

Pinging—All the Time

If 80 percent of success is, as Woody Allen once said, just showing up, then 80 percent of building and maintaining relationships is just staying in touch.

I call it "pinging." It's a quick, casual greeting, and it can be done in any number of creative ways. Once you develop your own style, you'll find it easier to stay in touch with more people than you ever dreamed of in less time than you ever imagined.

Yes, there's grunt work involved. Pinging takes effort. That's the tough part. You have to keep pinging and pinging and pinging and never stop. You have to feed the fire of your network or it will wither or die.

How many times have you asked yourself, "What's his face . . . Ya know, that guy . . ." Or "I know her, I just can't remember her name . . ." We all face that situation all too often, to my mind. Every time I hear those statements uttered, I sense a network or community of contacts withering.

These days we're overwhelmed with so much information that our minds can prioritize only the most recent data. What does it take to break through the white noise of information overload? Becoming front and center in someone's mental Rolodex is contingent on one invaluable little concept: repetition.

- People you're contacting to create a new relationship need to see or hear your name in at least three modes of communication—by, say, an e-mail, a phone call, and a face-to-face encounter—before there is substantive recognition.

- Once you have gained some early recognition, you need to nurture a developing relationship with a phone call or e-mail at least once a month.

- If you want to transform a contact into a friend, you need a minimum of two face-to-face meetings out of the office.

- Maintaining a secondary relationship requires two to three pings a year.

Using the above rules of thumb should give you an idea of what it'll take to keep your own network humming. I make dozens of phone calls a day. Most of them are simply quick hellos that I leave on a friend's voice mail. I also send e-mail constantly. Using a BlackBerry, I've found I can do the majority of my pinging while in trains, planes, and automobiles. I remember—or at least my PDA remembers—personal events like birthdays and anniversaries, and I make a special point of reaching out to people during these times.

When it comes to relationship maintenance, you have to be on your game 24/7, 365 days a year.

There's no doubt you have to bring a certain vigor to this part of the system. But hey, this is just my way of doing things. You'll figure out your own way. The governing principle here is repetition; find a way to ensure that you'll contact people regularly without putting too much strain on your schedule.

One way I've found to make maintaining my network of contacts, colleagues, and friends easier is to create a rating system for the network that corresponds to how often I reach out. First, I divide my network into five general categories: Under "Personal," I include my good friends and social acquaintances. Because I'm generally in contact with these people organically, I don't include them on a contact list. The relationship is established, and when we talk, it's as if we'd been in touch every day. "Customers" and "Prospects" are self-explanatory. "Important Business Associates" is reserved for people I'm actively involved with professionally. I'm either doing business with them currently or hoping to do business with them. This is the mission-critical category. Under "Aspirational Contacts," I list people I'd like to get to know, or I've met briefly (which is anyone from your boss's boss to a worthy celebrity) and would like to establish a better relationship with.

After reading the chapter on taking names, you've probably already begun to segment and categorize your network in a way that works for you—there is no standard method here. Create a segmentation that works for you and your objectives. This is a good habit and one that deserves repeating. All successful people are planners. They think on paper. Failing to plan, as they say, is planning to fail. And a plan is a list of activities and names.

The next step is to print out your master list of contacts that contains all the people in your network under the categories you've placed them in. The question now is How often do you contact each person on the list? I use a pretty simple system, but there's no reason you can't improve upon it. I'll go down my master list and add the numbers 1, 2, or 3 next to each name.

A "1" gets contacted at least each month. This means I'm actively involved with the person, whether it's a friend or a new business associate. With new relationships, a "1" generally means I have yet to solidify the relationship with at least three different forms of communication. Each time I reach out to a person, I like to include a very short note next to their name telling me the last time I contacted them and how. If last month I sent an e-mail saying hello to a potential customer rated "1," this month I'll give a call. Also, contacts designated "1" I add to my cell phone's speed dial. (How I love thee, speed dial, let me count the ways! It allows me quick reference and an easy way to get in touch fast.) If I have a free moment in a cab, I'll just go down the speed dial and make several calls to keep in touch with people I've not spoken to recently.

A "2" rating indicates my "touch base" people. These are either casual acquaintances or people whom I already know well. They get a quarterly call or e-mail. I try to include these people in mass e-mails about my business. And like the rest of my network, they get either an annual holiday card or birthday call.

Those people rated "3" are people I don't know well, who, because of time and circumstance, I'm unable to devote any significant energy to pinging. These people are strictly acquaintances, people I've met in passing, but who have found their way into my address book. I hope to reach this group, in some way, at least once a year. The surprising thing about this category is that, because you don't know the person all that well when you do reach out with a card or e-mail, the reaction is wonderful. Most people are delighted, and their curiosity piqued, when someone they don't know all that well sends them a note, however short.

The third step, as I mentioned in the chapter on taking names, is segmenting your network into call lists. In time, your master list will become too unwieldy to work from directly. Your call lists will save you time and keep your efforts focused. They can be organized by your number ratings, by geography, by industry, and so on. It's totally flexible. If I'm flying to New York, for example, I'll print out a "New York list" and make a few calls to my "1s" when I got off the plane. "Hi, Jan. Just landed in New York and it made me think of you. No time to meet this trip, but I just wanted to touch base." This New York list also proves very helpful a week in advance of the trip in trying to fill in those extra slots of time I may have in my schedule.

Where do I find the time? Again, you find time everywhere. I ping in the cab, or in my car. I ping in the bathroom (BlackBerry only). When I'm bored at a conference, I ping via e-mail. I've developed the habit of saving every e-mail I send and receive. I put each e-mail, when I receive it, in one of my categories, and Outlook records whether I've returned the e-mail or not. Then I just open up those files and respond, pinging away. I make a habit of reviewing my master list at the end of the week and cross-checking it with the activities and travel plans I have for the following week. In this way, I stay up-to-date and have my trusty lists at my side all week long.

Another time-saver is to pay close attention when you place your phone calls. There are times, amusingly enough, when I call in order NOT to get through. Sometimes you don't have time for an in-depth conversation; you just want to drop a line and say hello. I try and take mental notes of people's phone habits if I want to simply leave a message, I'll call when I know they're not around. Calling their office really early or late usually does the trick.

The important thing is that you build the concept of pinging into your workflow. Some organizations go so far as to make pinging integral to their organizational processes. I'm told that the consulting firm McKinsey and Company actually has a rule of thumb that one hundred days after a new CEO takes charge of a company, McKinsey assigns one of their consultants to call and see how McKinsey might help. One hundred days is, McKinsey figures, just enough time for the new CEO to feel that he or she knows what the issues and problems are, but not enough time to have gotten his or her arms around the solutions.

With pinging gaining credibility as an important business practice, it shouldn't surprise you that some ingenious new software has been developed to make it easier. Plaxo is a neat new program that I've found really helpful. The software this company has developed keeps people connected by solving the common but frustrating problem of out-of-date contact information. The software goes into your database of contacts, pulls out everybody with an e-mail address, sends the record that you have of them, and asks them to update it. When they do so, it sends you back an e-mail stating their new information. Automated pinging!

I do it every six months or so and have become a true devotee. Not long ago, I did a Plaxo update. A few days later, I got an e-mail from a former prospect I'd lost contact with who wrote, "We talked a year ago. Nothing came of it. Now might be a better time to talk." The e-mail turned into a two-million-dollar account.

The medium and message of a ping runs the gamut. There is the "I just called to say I care" ping that I use for closer contacts. Essentially, I want to convey the message, "Hey, it has been too long since we've spoken and I wanted you to know that I miss you, that you are important to me." And then there are the more professional versions of the above. But always try to make any message as personal as possible.

For people important to my career or business, I tend to favor the value-add ping. Here I'm trying to provide something of value in my communication, recognizing when someone I know gets a promotion, or the company he or she runs has a good financial quarter, or he or she has a child. I also like to send relevant articles, short notes of advice, or other small tokens that convey that I am thinking of them and am eager to help.

Get creative. I have one friend who carries a digital camera wherever he goes. When he returns from a conference or work-related travels, he pings the people he met with a quick hello and a picture attached. It's a great idea that has worked very well for him. I've got another friend who uses music in a similar manner. When he meets someone new, he asks the person what kind of music he or she enjoys. This guy has a growing digital music library that's off the charts, and he's always on top of the latest grooves. When he pings, he might write, "It was a pleasure meeting you the other day. You mentioned your love of jazz. It just so happens that I have a rare recording of Miles Davis. I thought you'd get a kick out of it. Let me know what you think."

Once you've cultivated a contact with a new associate or friend, nurture it by pinging. It's the Miracle-Gro for your blooming garden of friends and associates.

The Pinging Staple: Birthdays

Standard advice on acknowledging the events in people's lives suggests sending Christmas or Chanukah cards. The holidays, in my opinion, are *not* the best time to focus your pinging energies. Why? Because it's hard to differentiate yourself from the other 150 people doing the same thing.

My personal favorite pinging occasion remains birthdays, the neglected stepchild of life's celebrated moments. As you get older, the people around you start forgetting your big day (mostly because they think they want to forget their own). Mom might not call a day late, but your brother or sister will. Your friends will figure, "Why remind the poor guy he's getting up there in age?" Before long, that residual disappointment turns into resentment, and the resentment turns into apathy. Or at least the appearance of apathy.

"Nah, birthdays aren't my thing," I hear people say all the time. You persuasively tell your family, "Don't do anything big, but if you do something, make it small."

Well, I don't believe it. I'm onto your game, friend. You care, and so does everybody else.

We've been conditioned since childhood, despite our best efforts to be "Birthday Scrooges" in adult life, that that day is all about you. It is *your* day, and it has been since you were a kid. And even when you're seventy years old, deep down inside, despite all your protestations, a little recognition of that seventy-year-old life feels good even if you don't get a big red wagon anymore.

Don't kid yourself—EVERYONE CARES ABOUT HIS OR HER BIRTHDAY!

I was in New York some years back and up popped a reminder on my Palm: "Birthday—Kent Blosil." Kent was the man who successfully got past my gatekeeper. When I met Kent that day, and I received his contact information, I asked for his birth date, as I try to do with everyone. It's not intrusive, and most people forget the moment after they tell me.

Kent was a Mormon. Born in Salt Lake City, Utah, he had upward of ten brothers and sisters. With such a large family, you'd think the man's phone would be ringing off the hook on his birthday.

I hadn't spoken to him for over a year. It was a busy day for me, and I didn't see the reminder until close to 3:00 P.M. that afternoon. Generally, I like to make birthday calls in the early morning. This way I get someone's voice mail, and when they come in to work that morning, they're greeted with my rendition of "Happy Birthday." I can't tell you how many New York City cabdrivers must think I'm an utter lunatic.

So when Kent actually picked up his phone that afternoon, my personal Pavarotti of "Happy Birthday" greeted him. No greetings. No niceties. I just let it rip.

Normally, I get laughter and a grateful "Thanks." This time, after I had finished, the phone went silent. "Kent, you there? It's your birthday, right?" Nothing. Not a word. I thought I'd made a jerk out of myself and missed the day or something.

"Kent?"

Finally he stammers out, "Yeah." He was choked up, audibly holding back tears.

"You all right?"

"You remembered my birthday?" he said. People are always shocked by this.

"You know, Keith, this year none of my brothers or sisters or family . . . well, nobody remembered my birthday. Nobody remembered," he said. "Thank you so much."

He never forgot. People never do.

CHAPTER 21

Find Anchor Tenants and Feed Them

W hen I was an insolvent student working my way through business school, my apartment wasn't what you'd call a spotless designer residence. Minimal, yes. A bit grungy, definitely. Still, it never stopped me from throwing outrageously fun dinner parties where I enjoyed the company of good friends—and a few strangers.

It was in those days that I learned how powerful the art of throwing dinner parties could be in creating wonderful memories and strengthening relationships in the process. Today I can safely say my strongest links have been forged at the table. The companionable effects of breaking bread—not to mention drinking a few glasses of wine—bring people together.

In those early years, my 400-square-foot, one-bedroom apartment opposite the football field, with a kitchen table that could barely seat two adults, held wild get-togethers for four, six, even fifteen guests. The mix was always a diverse medley of professors, students, Boston locals, and, sometimes, a person I met in line while checking out groceries. I never thought twice about some of the minor inconveniences those impoverished days bestowed on my events, like forcing my guests to eat with plates in their laps.

For all the sheer delight and good times a dinner party can impart, it seems our fast-food culture has diminished our centuries-old belief in the power of a shared meal in your own home to comfort, nurture, and connect people. Some people seem to think it's too hard, too time-consuming. The only image they have of a dinner party is of those grandly ornate occasions once glamorized by Martha Stewart, a friend by the way. Maybe those female-hosted TV shows are, perhaps, another reason why men, in particular, have forgotten the virtues of hosting a simple dinner gathering. They think it's feminine. But trust me, guys, you can serve a fine meal in your home and still be masculine—and, if you're single, it will do a world of good for your dating lives.

Nearly once a month an array of different people from different worlds gathers at my home in Los Angeles or hotel suite in New York or a friend's home in San Francisco to have fun, talk business, and meet new people. But I learned the art of throwing these events back in my dingy Cambridge apartment.

Before my dinner parties had any cachet, I had to develop a deliberate strategy for attracting a good mix of people that would expand my social horizons and get a reputation that would keep people coming back.

You, me, every one of us—we have an established peer set. But if you only have dinner parties with the same people, your circle of relationships will never grow. At the same time, we're confronted with a small obstacle. Randomly inviting strangers, especially strangers who hold a level of prestige and experience above your own peer set, is rarely effective. These people want to hang around people of their own background, experience, or social status.

Parents tend to stay away from their children's gatherings unless they expect other parents to be in attendance as well. In college, juniors and seniors avoid the parties populated solely by freshmen and sophomores. In the adult world, it's no different. Go to any cafeteria at any major corporation in the country. You'll generally find each strata of the organization—from the administrative staff on up to the executive suite—congregating in their own cliques to eat their lunches.

To overcome this herd mentality and pull people into my dinner parties that would otherwise not come, I developed a helpful little concept I call the "anchor tenant."

Every individual within a particular peer set has a bridge to someone outside his or her own group of friends. We all have, to some degree or another, developed relationships with older, wiser, more experienced people; they may be our mentors, our parents' friends, our teachers, our rabbis and reverends, our bosses.

I call them anchor tenants; their value comes from the simple fact that they are, in relation to one's core group of friends, different. They know different people, have experienced different things, and thus, have much to teach.

Identifying and inviting an anchor tenant to your dinner party isn't hard. Someone you know probably has access and is close enough to such an individual that an invitation will be well received. You'll discover who these people are by paying attention to your friends' stories and taking notice of the one or two names that continually pop up. They tend to be the names of people who have had a positive influence on your friends' lives. And it stands to reason that they can have the same effect on you.

Once you've identified a person outside your social circle and successfully invited him or her to a dinner, here's an added little nuance that pays terrific dividends. Landing an anchor tenant isn't about entertaining your dinner-party regulars. They'll come no matter what. But an anchor allows you to reach out beyond your circle in subsequent invitations and pull in people who wouldn't otherwise attend. To put it in terms of the company cafeteria, now that you have the CEO eating lunch at the manager's table, other executives will jump at the opportunity to eat at the table, too.

Frankly, anyone who can add a little electricity to your dinner party is an anchor tenant. Journalists, I've found, are terrific anchor guests. They aren't particularly well paid (which makes them suckers for free meals), their profession has a good deal of intrigue, they are always on the lookout for good material and see such dinners as a potential venue for new ideas, they're generally good conversationalists, and many folks enjoy an opportunity to get their ideas heard by someone who might publicize them to a larger audience. Artists and actors, famous or not, fall into the same category. On those occasions when you can't land as big a fish as you might have liked, you can try to pull in a person with proximity to power: a political consultant to an interesting politician, the COO of an interesting company under an interesting CEO, and so on. In these cases, it's about brand association.

Once you've landed an anchor tenant, finding the right mix of people is critical. For me, the invitation list needs to be a mix of professional folks I want to do business with today, contacts I aspire to do business with down the road, and those I call "light attractors"—guests who are energetic, interesting, and willing to speak their mind. Of course, a local celebrity or two never hurts. And it goes without saying that you should have your friends and family present, as well.

Political columnist Arianna Huffington is one of my favorite dinner guests. She's gracious, fun, and always outspoken. How did I land her? Through an intro from my friend Elana Weiss, who knew someone in Arianna's office, I sent her an e-mail. I told her I was a big admirer and that I threw these very fun dinner parties in Los Angeles and she'd undoubtedly make them better. She showed up only for cocktails at first, had a great time, and has become a regular and a dear friend.

While these kinds of dinners can often cinch an important business deal, be careful not to include too many business associates on the invite list or business agendas in the discussion. Talking about budgets and other management mumbo jumbo all the time will ensure a dull evening. These events are about building relationships.

Six to ten guests, I've found, is the optimal number to invite to a dinner. I usually invite fourteen now, but that's after a lot of practice. I also invite an extra six or so people to pop in before or come after for drinks and dessert. This group should be closer friends who won't get offended for not being at the main event but will appreciate being part of the group nonetheless. Generally, when you invite someone to dinner, you get a 20 to 30 percent acceptance rate because of scheduling difficulties. When someone says they cannot come because of another dinner or engagement, I often suggest they come before the dinner for drinks and appetizers, or even after, for dessert and drinks.

These "bonus guests" will arrive a little before dinner has concluded. I'll have folding chairs at the ready so they can pull up next to the dinner table, have dessert, and chat with the guests. Just when most dinner parties tend to slip and people begin to look at their watches thinking about what time they have to get up in the morning, the energy level spikes with a whole new group. Suddenly, the dinner turns raucous again.

At about this time, the music that's been playing on the stereo gives way to a live piano player. I don't announce this. From the dining room or deck where I serve dinner, guests slowly pick up on the fact that the music coming from the living room has changed. Sometimes it's not only the piano. I may hire a singer, invite a bunch of young vocalists to come show off, or do a bit more research and find out if there are some local alumni who used to be part of Yale's renowned singing group, the Whiffenpoofs. For a reasonable fee, the kids are happy to belt out a few old tunes for an old alumnus.

As dessert is being served, the Poofs start singing. The afterparty guests arrive, and now the night is swinging. Some people stay at the table, while others adjourn to the living room to sing along and hang out. The next thing I know, it's one or two in the morning and I'm closing down another successful event.

If you like to eat and you enjoy the company of others, you can pull off your own version of a dinner party that will work beautifully whatever the setting.

My friend Jim Brehm is one of the most elegant designers in New York. He had a beautiful studio apartment downtown where he used to host a party every other Thursday. By the way, Thursdays are wonderful days for dinner parties. It doesn't cut into people's weekend plans and yet folks are willing to go a little late knowing that they have only one day left in the work week.

I marveled at Jim's ability to make simplicity so elegant. I found the same quality in Jim's architecture and designs. His studio had a long bench covered in velvet along one wall and a few black leather cubes to sit on. We'd be served champagne. Light jazz music would play in the background. The dinner guests tended to be a fascinating mix of artists and writers and musicians.

To eat, we'd walk five steps to a small simple wooden table with no tablecloth, adorned with two silver candles. The chairs were fold-out. Each plate had a big bowl of homemade chili on it and a torn-off piece of fresh bread. For dessert, he would serve ice cream and more champagne. It was simply perfect, and perfectly simple.

Anyone can throw a dinner party. Let me give you an example—my former business manager, Mark Ramsay. I first met Mark when he was an accountant for another business manager who specialized in entertainment clients. He was an unhappy camper back then, and he wanted to break out on his own. After mustering enough courage, at the age of twenty-five, he opened his own operation. I became his first client.

Mark became a regular at my dinner parties in New York. As a client and a friend, Mark would return the favor by inviting me out to dinner or to see a show. After a few years, however,

I asked Mark, "So what's up with not having me over to your home for dinner?" A meal at someone's home, after all, is what I enjoy most.

His answer was all too common, especially among the younger people I mentor. He told me, "I could never do a dinner party like yours. I don't have that kind of money and I live in a run-down studio. I don't even have a dining table."

"Dining table! Who needs a dining table?" I said.

With that, I convinced Mark to give it a try. I told him I'd be his anchor guest and suggested that he invite four others for dinner. I told him to get some simple wine, but plenty of it. For appetizers, set out chips and salsa, or dip with vegetables. Buy a foldable round tabletop that one can easily find and place it on the coffee table. Voilà!—you've got yourself a grand dining table.

For food, I told him, forget about cooking. Get some salads and a roasted chicken from the deli. For dessert, buy some cookies and ice cream, and keep the wine flowing.

The party was a huge success. Mark invited a potential client, me, and a friend I brought along. All four of us are now his clients.

You see, there's only one real rule to these get-togethers: Have fun. All right, there are a few other rules that might help you along the way. Among them:

1. Create a theme.

There is no reason that a small dinner party should not have a theme. One simple idea can help you pull the food and atmosphere together. You can build a party around anything, really. It could be your mother's meatloaf recipe, a holiday, black tie (used rarely, as we want people to be totally comfortable), vegan food, specific music—whatever you like. People will get jazzed when they know you're being creative.

I remember one example of a theme being put to good use that comes from an article I read years ago in the *Washington Post,* about a woman named Perdita Huston. When President Carter appointed Huston regional director of the Peace Corps for North Africa, the Near East, Asia, and the Pacific in 1978, she started her weekly For Women Only dinner parties.

The dinner parties filled a void for Huston, who explained how she came up with the idea. "Because of the size of the region I administered for the Peace Corps, I was obliged to do much traveling.

"When I wasn't out of town on Peace Corps business, I thought it important to be at home with my son, Pierre, who was then seven years old. Also, because of my travels, I began losing touch with many of my friends, but instead of trying to see people one-on-one in restaurant situations, I devised this scheme of giving weekly dinner parties.

"Right about that same time, I also came to realize there were a lot of women in my situation: single women in high-level jobs whose professional lives were presenting certain problems and often overwhelming their private lives. In many ways, the women in the Carter administration were pioneers who needed supportive networking, so I decided to limit my guests to women only.

"What I did was simply expand my Sunday cooking to include preparations for a Monday-night meal for twelve. I would often make couscous or a lamb-based soup, which is used during Ramadan in Algeria to break the fast at sundown. It's called chorba, which means soup; in fact, it's called The Soup. It's very spicy and good enough to be an entire meal. Often I would just prepare a huge tureen of it along with hot bread and a big salad. Desserts were simply fruit and cheese.

"The response to my Monday-night For Women Only dinner was really overwhelming," she continued. "I always used my finest china and crystal and silver candlesticks. In other words, I treated these occasions the way most hostesses treat conventional male/female dinner parties.

"Our dinner-table conversations are unusually candid. We talk—or argue—about U.S. foreign policy or discuss problems common to women in management positions, such as how to combat stereotypes or sexism in the workplace.

"We get a lot of feedback from each other and, because of our experience, can suggest various people to see, organizations to contact, or strategies to develop. Because they are so supportive, these dinners have become very important to many of us."

Huston's weekly parties became an institution in the Washington, D.C., area where she lived. It brought like-minded women together who bonded and supported one another through the similar trials and tribulations each was going through. There's no reason you can't do the same thing. Creating a theme around a point of commonality—be it race, religion, gender, occupation, or anything else—can infuse your get-togethers with added purpose, and help you attract others.

2. Use invitations.

While I'm all for slapdash impromptu parties, the dinner parties that will be most successful will be those you've devoted some time and energy to. Whether by phone, e-mail, or handwritten note, be sure to get your invites out early—at least a month in advance—so people can have a chance to plan accordingly—and so you'll know who is and who is not coming.

3. Don't be a kitchen slave.

There's no sense in a party being all work. If you can't hire a caterer, either cook all the food ahead of time or just use takeout. If the food is good and the presentation snazzy, your guests will be impressed.

These days, I usually opt for a caterer. But you can have a similarly elegant party for much less if you're willing to get creative and spend some time preparing. The key to low-budget dinner parties is to keep it simple. Make one large dish, like a stew or chili that can be prepared a day or two ahead of time. Serve it with great bread and salad. That's all you need.

Well, maybe not ALL you need. My other expense is alcohol. I love—love!—great wine. I always go a little overboard with the vino. And really, could God have blessed us with a better social lubricant? It amounts to the finest party favor ever created. But again, everyone has their own predilections, and I'm sure you can pull off a perfectly fabulous dinner party with just soda.

4. Create atmosphere.

Make sure to spend an hour or two gussying up your place. Nothing expensive or out of the ordinary, mind you. Candles, flowers, dim lighting, and music set a good mood. Add a nice centerpiece to the dinner table. Get a young family member to walk around serving drinks if you don't have a bartender or waiter. The point is to give your guests all the signals they need to understand that it's time to enjoy.

5. Forget being formal.

Most dinner parties don't call for anything fancy. Follow the KISS principle (Keep It Simple, Silly). Good food. Good people. Lots of wine. Good conversation. That's a successful dinner party. I always underdress just so no one else feels they did. Jeans and a jacket are my standard fare, but you judge for yourself.

6. Don't seat couples together.

The essence of a good dinner party lies in seating everyone properly. If you seat couples together, things can get boring. Mix and match, putting people together who don't know each other but perhaps share an interest of some kind. I like to set placeholders where I want people to sit. Each placeholder is a simple card with the guest's name on it. If I have the time, I love to put an interesting question or joke on the back of the card that guests can use to break the ice with one another. Or you can go out and buy funny greeting cards just to make things interesting.

7. Relax.

Guests take their cues from the host—if you're having fun, odds are that they will, too. The night of the party, your job is to enjoy all the fruits of your labor. That's an order.

Trading Up and Giving Back

CHAPTER 22

Be Interesting

I remember when being a marketer was simpler. Essentially, marketers were expected to create an ad, get it to the consumer through one of the few available media sources, and then sit back and wait.

Those days are good and gone. The way the world speaks and listens has changed radically. And the tools we use to communicate are changing at a similar pace. As access to consumers grows, so does consumer power. They can choose from hordes of entertainment venues, use software tools to filter out unwanted messages, and shoot down surviving messages with a heightened sense of cynicism. It's just not as easy to be heard. Brand loyalty is tougher to achieve. Conventional advertising and marketing just won't cut it—and neither will traditional thinking among those who want to get their message across. The CMO of today and tomorrow must be a strategist, a technologist, creative, and always focused on the sales and financial return on his marketing investments. Not a lot of individuals, consulting firms, or agencies combine all those traits. As a result, the life of the CMO is a lonely one, and the life of the CEO who expects all this is too often a frustrated one.

My growing sense of these changes, along with conversations with respected marketers, is the main reason I founded Ferrazzi-Greenlight, to focus on marketing strategies and programs that push the marketing spend closer to actual sales. To count less on big broadcast advertising and more on building personalized loyalty between clients and their customers. That might mean creating a loyalty program for a retailer similar to what we operated at Starwood Hotels. Or designing an infomercial for a complex new product launch. Or facilitating an "ambassador's program" for a large engineering firm that targeted just 500 customers, prospects, and influencers in the United States.

I hope it's not a surprise that I see effective marketing as just building relationships with customers and prospective customers.

Let me translate this macro trend to a very personal scene that repeats itself over and over again when I give lectures at colleges. It will take place just before or after I've given my talk. A student will muster the nerve to approach me, and admiring as I am of such initiative, I'll be very receptive. Then, remarkably, nothing will be said beyond, "Hi, I'm so-and-so and your talk was great." Perhaps I'll ask what they got out of it or how they see what I talked about playing out around them in the world. Too often, my attempts are met with comments like "Oh, I don't know," or "I just think what you said was great. I'm not sure I could ever do all that . . ."

Oh, wow, I'd think, it was fantastic talking with you, but I've got some bathroom tiles that need cleaning. Not to be too rough here, but how can you talk to someone when they have nothing to say? How can you offer your company or your network anything of value if you have not thought about how you want to stand out and differentiate yourself in building that relationship?

Marketers and networkers alike take heed: Be interesting! All that you've read thus far doesn't relieve you of the responsibility of being someone worth talking to, and even better, worth talking about. Virtually everyone new you meet in a situation is asking themselves a variation on one question: "Would I want to spend an hour eating lunch with this person?"

Consultants call it the airport question. In the lengthy interview process that that industry has become famous for—a peppering of complicated case studies and logic-testing puzzles—the one question consultants use to choose one person over a pool of equally talented candidates is the one question they ask only of themselves: "If I were trapped in John F. Kennedy Airport for a few hours [and all travel-weary consultants inevitably spend too much time in airports], would I want to spend it with this person?"

Have you mentioned in conversation your large jazz collection, or the time you spent in the Ivory Coast, or your contrarian views on some political debate? Squeeze a little time into your schedule to keep up with what's going on in the world. Pay attention to interesting tidbits you hear, and work to remember them so that you can pass them on to people you meet. Get a daily subscription to the *New York Times* or the *Wall Street Journal*. Remember, people don't only hire people they like, they hire people that they think can make them and their companies better. That means someone with an expanded view of the world. It means you need to be aware of your intellectual property, and what you have to say that others might benefit from. It shows you're interested and involved in the world around you.

What happens when you don't have a platform of ideas to defend? When you're running for office, you lose an election.

In my sophomore year at Yale, I ran for New Haven City Council. The party in New Haven wanted an outspoken, presentable candidate to run against the less-than-exciting opposing candidate. I had been known through my involvement in the Political Union as a very young chairman, having started one of the first fraternities on campus (Sigma Chi), and therefore had some name recognition. When offered the opportunity, I jumped at it. I didn't have a thought as to what I had to offer or why New Haven might want me as its representative. This was more ego than fore-thought.

To this day, my loss in that election sticks in my craw. I actually refused to dig in and really campaign, to learn the local issues. My opponent, Joel Ratner, developed a deep local platform and took to the streets and dining halls. I shied away from that level of engagement, expecting that my dynamic style would carry the day.

Joel was emboldened by his ideas, and his passion galvanized voters. I, on the other hand, just thought it would be cool to run for an elected office. After all, I was recruited. I didn't seek the office, and I told the party up front that my studies and other lead-ership responsibilities had to come first.

Well, my defeat was embarrassing, and it was my own fault. The experience taught me an important lesson. No matter what organization I represented or what professional avenue I pursued in the future, all my efforts had to be powered by a deep passion and a set of beliefs that went well beyond my own personal bene-fit. To move others, you have to speak beyond yourself. Boldly putting yourself out there was one thing, and a good thing, but that wasn't enough. There was a difference between getting atten-tion and getting attention for your desire to change the world. Congratulations, Joel, I hear you did a great job. The better man clearly won in that race.

Be a Person of Content: Have a Unique Point of View

Being interesting isn't just about learning how to become a good conversationalist. Don't get me wrong, that is important, but you need a well-thought-out point of view. I honestly hope from now on you'll be a newspaper-reading maniac ready to engage the topics of the day with anyone you meet. But being interesting and having content are very different. The former involves talking intelligently about politics, sports, travel, science, or whatever you'll need as a ticket of admission to any conversation. Content involves a much more specialized form of knowledge. It's knowing what you have that most others do not. It's your differentiation. It's your expertise. It's the message that will make your brand unique, attracting others to become a part of your network.

Being known is just notoriety. But being known for something is entirely different. That's respect. You have to believe in something, as Joel Ratner did, for people to believe in you.

Once I learned my lesson, I wasn't going to repeat it. I was not just going to be another generalist. I was going to have a unique point of view, an expertise. My first job out of college at Imperial Chemical Industries, I mastered the ins and outs of Total Quality Management. Later, when I worked at Deloitte, reengineering was my hook. At Starwood, I pushed for direct marketing. Later, I mastered interactive marketing. Today, I've wrapped all my experiences into a set of beliefs around the radically changing dynamics of marketing overall and its evolution toward relationship marketing: moving marketing dollars closer to sales.

In every job and at every stage in my career, I had some expertise, some content that differentiated me from others and made me unique, made me more valuable in my relationships with others and the company I worked for. It created precious opportunities for me to gain credibility and visibility in my field. Content is a cause, an idea, trend, or skill—the unique subject matter on which you are the authority.

What will set you apart from everybody else is the relentlessness you bring to learning and presenting and selling your content. Take, for example, my experience when I was hired as CEO of YaYa. The company's board was aware of how I had used reengineering to heighten the market's perception of Deloitte, and how, at Starwood, the idea of changing the way the hospitality industry branded itself generated a wave of publicity. They knew that the ability to capture a buzz-worthy message and get it into the crowded marketplace of ideas would prove crucial for a new company whose product was totally untested. This seemed right for me. I was a "market maker": someone who could create excitement and belief around YaYa's point of view. The problem was coming up with the credible and unique point of view that people were ready to buy. That was our challenge, or the company would fail.

One of our first goals when I came to YaYa was to find a hook that could transform the company's current lack of sales while also generating broader intrigue in the marketplace, and really create a market. I started, as I always do, by immersing myself in the subject. I became a voracious reader and would spend hours late at night checking out a variety of articles, analyst reports, books, and Web sites. I talked to CEOs, journalists, and consultants who specialized in the interactive advertising industry, games industry, and training world.

This stage can be quite frustrating. There's a huge learning curve to get up to speed. Suddenly you're confronted with a miasma of numbers, data points, differing opinions, and a boatload of disparate new information. On some occasions, as was the case with TQM and reengineering, you can acquire content by simply appropriating another person's innovative ideas and become a leader in distributing and applying those ideas. On other occasions, as with YaYa, we had to develop the content from scratch. That meant taking all the disparate dots of information and connecting them in a way others had not.

There should be no mystique around dot connecting among those who are continually at the forefront of business innovation. Remember those wise words of Mark McCormack in his book *What They Don't Teach You at Harvard Business School*: "Creativity in business is often nothing more than making connections that everyone else has almost thought of. You don't have to reinvent the wheel, just attach it to a new wagon."

As my immersion process continued, I became more and more frustrated that the marketing and training field was not taking advantage of the two powerful new mediums that YaYa was based on—the Internet and video games. As I learned more about marketing and training online, I drew analogies to other new mediums that changed the landscape. I reminded marketers that when we first transitioned from radio to television, all we did was put a camera in front of a radio announcer and call it advertising. It took a while to settle into the medium and its new rules. Here again, with the Internet, we were applying old models to a new environment. The Net was all about interactivity and community building, where concepts or just jokes were spread around the world in moments. And yet marketers were just taking old advertising ideas, like billboards and bumper stickers, and putting them online in the form of banner ads. That those ads weren't successful should have come as no surprise. Training had a similar argument. Would you rather engage in learning in a fun interactive environment or the traditional and stale forms of training that employees were being force-fed today? Which would be more effective?

Then you had the games world in general. The startling numbers suggested an untapped phenomenon. In 1999, games revenues surpassed movie box-office revenues. And the demographic of online gamers was changing radically as content was branching out to cater to adults and women. The average age of online gamers is now thirty-five, 49 percent of whom are women. I also learned of a German company that developed a cool turkey-shoot game for Johnnie Walker that got so many downloads, the prime minister commented that the game had become a drain on national productivity. Still, no one thought of games as anything but niche entertainment.

With the information at hand, I now had to connect the dots and find that new wagon. This is actually the fun part. You start in a fantasy world with no limitations or constraints. Instead of bashing my head against the wall trying harder and harder to solve a specific problem, I like to ask the question: "If I could use some magical potion in this situation, what could I do with all this new information?" Such fantasizing doesn't have to be, and often shouldn't be, a solitary endeavor. I get other interested parties—employees, colleagues, and insiders—to help me create wild scenarios and ask seemingly absurd questions. I did this with a small group, and we threw out each and every fantastical idea that came to us. By fantasizing, using the magic potion, and including a group of people to riff without rules, we were able to use our creativity to find a way forward.

These fantasy sessions were productive. We started to imagine how games might be applied to more than just leisure and entertainment. We started to question assumptions such as what business we were in (was it entertainment, marketing, or services?), what product we should offer (was it games, advertising, training, consulting, enabling technology?), and who our real customers could be (geeky adolescents, adults, Fortune 500 companies?). We started to visualize how we might connect the gaming medium—which had a large and growing demographic of users—and the Internet medium—which had a large and growing group of companies trying to figure out how best to use it to interact with their customers.

As an entrepreneur or an employee, you have the creative abilities to make similar connections in your own industry. How do I know? Because everyone has them! Your abilities may be stored away or infrequently used, but they are there. The question is, how do you put them to work for you? We went to work to crack this nut.

The results were significant. We realized there was an opportunity to not just sell games or sell advertising onto game sites but to create interactive games online to be used as a powerful and new immersive form of advertising. When people redefined YaYa as a marketing company rather than a video-game company, we realized our customers weren't the end users; our real customers were the companies who wanted access to the end users. The shift in focus allowed us to see games less as a product than a medium itself, able to deliver any kind of message one wanted to send. You could use games to train and educate employees, as advertising vehicles, in brand-awareness campaigns, in direct one-to-one marketing, as a means for collecting data on the preferences of customers, and so on. Where television eventually turned to commercials to replace the on-air radio personality, games could replace banner ads on the Internet.

And thus the unique point of view for YaYa was born. We began to trumpet advergaming and edutainment as the next powerful communications medium, an untapped marketing segment perfect for product placements, branded gaming events, custom games-related training for businesses, and on and on. It wasn't long before I was not only attending games conferences but also speaking at them.

Once a resonating pitch is perfected, getting attention is less of a problem. Journalists are hungry for ideas. Getting access to them is often as simple as calling the magazine or newspaper they work for, which can be found on their Web sites, and asking to speak with the reporter that covers your beat. I've never met a journalist with a gatekeeper. Moreover, I've never had my calls go unreturned after leaving a message that said, "I've got the inside scoop on how the gaming industry is going to revolutionize marketing. I've appreciated your work for a long time now; I believe you are the right person to break this story."

I've been leaving those kinds of messages on reporters' voice mail for years, and reporters are hugely appreciative. Most of the time, the story doesn't even involve my company or me. I'm just building the credibility I'll need when the day comes to make my own pitch. Which is probably why, today, I know people in top positions at almost every major business magazine in the country.

I've had fellow CEOs who view, say, the *Wall Street Journal* or *Forbes* as impenetrable institutions; they shake their head in wonderment at how over and over again, no matter where I'm at or what organization I represent, I never fail to get press. The answer is that I understand and give them what they need: great stories.

However, I've also had a lot of help. Once I had developed YaYa's unique point of view, for example, I brought it to the ad agencies. It was interactive agency KPE that brought YaYa and advergaming to market. They were the agency to "discover" us and what we were doing. And then the big games companies got involved. I went to the most progressive guys I knew, people like Bobby Kotick, the CEO of Activision who, in a partnership with the Nielsen Company, put his company's influence and money behind measuring how effective games were as a medium for advertisers. Bobby and I would be on CNN or CNBC back-to-back plugging each other's ideas.

"Keith, what's your secret? Bribes, blackmail—come on, just tell me," one CEO friend jokingly asked after YaYa appeared in a major spread in *Fortune,* while his own company, which was four times larger than YaYa, and several years older, had barely made it into its own newsletter.

So I told him: "Create a story about your company and the ideas it embodies that readers will care about. That's your content. Then share it. Have you ever picked up the phone and actually talked to a reporter about why you think what you do is so special? You cannot outsource this to PR; journalists deal with thousands of PR people a day. Who's going to be more passionate and more informed than you? You're the expert on what you do."

They Can't Outsource Content Creators

We've seen how content helped transform a company into a recognizable brand. But what if YOU are the brand? What's your content? What hooks are you selling? The same process we used to figure out how to make YaYa interesting to the marketplace can be applied to making you interesting to your network and beyond.

A unique point of view is one of the only ways to ensure that today, tomorrow, and a year from now you'll have a job.

It used to be that two arms, two legs, and an MBA were a one-way ticket to the executive office. That's barely the price of entry these days. In America's information economy, we frame our competitive advantage in terms of knowledge and innovation. That means today's market values creativity over mere competence and expertise over general knowledge. If what you do can be done by anyone, there will always be someone willing to do it for less. Witness all those jobs moving offshore to Bangladesh and Bangalore. The one thing no one has figured out how to outsource is the creation of ideas. You can't replace people who day in and day out offer the kind of content or unique ways of thinking that promise their company an edge.

Content creators have always been in high demand. They get promotions. They're responsible for the Big Ideas. They're regularly asked to speak at conferences and are featured in newspapers and magazines. Everyone within their company—and many within their industry—knows their name. They are the celebrities of their little worlds, and their fame comes from always seeming to be one step ahead.

So how did they get that way? The easiest route is by expertise.

As I look back on my career, the recipe seems straightforward: I'd latch on to the latest, most cutting-edge idea in the business world. I'd immerse myself in it, getting to know all the thought leaders pushing the idea and all the literature available. I'd then distill that into a message about the idea's broader impact to others and how it could be applied in the industry I worked in. That was the content. Becoming an expert was the easy part. I simply did what experts do: I taught, wrote, and spoke about my expertise.

At ICI, my first job after college, I talked my way into a management-training program by convincing the interviewer to take on a liberal arts major as an experiment. Every trainee who had ever been hired prior to that had some fancy degree in chemical engineering, material sciences, or something technical like that.

There was no way I was going to advance at ICI based on my engineering expertise. In my first few months of the program, however, I noticed that Total Quality Management was all the rage, one of those consultant-driven business trends that light the business world on fire every few years.

In my free time, I studied all the texts that were available. A few months into my job, I volunteered my "expertise," citing my background in organizational behavior (from my total of two undergraduate courses I had taken!). With one stroke, I became one of ICI's three go-to guys when it came to TQM. The thing is, I only really became an expert once I started trying to teach the discipline within the company. I would go on to parlay my experience into giving speeches, writing articles, and connecting with some of the top business minds in the country. After a short period, I even persuaded the industrial giant ICI to craft a new position for me within a newly forming group as one of the leaders of TQM in North America.

There's no better way to learn something, and become an expert at it, than to have to teach it. Some of the best CEOs I know refuse to turn away business even when it might call for skills or experience that their company doesn't have. These CEOs see such a scenario as an opportunity. "We can do that," they'll say. In the process, both the CEO and their employees learn skills they need. They jump at trying something new and they get the job done. In fact, after reading this book, there's no reason you couldn't put together a course on relationship building or content creation at your local community college. You'll learn in preparation, and gain even more interacting with students.

In short, forget your job title and forget your job description (for the moment, at least). Starting today, you've got to figure out what exceptional expertise you're going to master that will provide real value to your network and your company.

How do you start?

Well, there's the easy way and then there's the hard way, and I've done both. As I did at ICI and Deloitte, you can find someone who has already connected the dots and become an expert of their content. That's the easy way.

The hard way is connecting the dots on your own. The bad news is there's no concrete blueprint or step-by-step guide for this process. The good news is that creating content is not an act of divine inspiration or something reserved for the brilliant. Though I imagine both brilliance and inspiration could come in handy, I don't claim either in abundance. Instead, I've relied on some guidelines, a few habits, and a couple of techniques that have proven wonderfully useful.

Here are ten tips on helping you on your way toward becoming an expert:

1. Get out in front and analyze the trends and opportunities on the cutting edge.

Foresight gives you and your company the flexibility to adapt to change. Creativity allows you to take advantage of it. Today, where innovation has become more important than production, not moving forward means going backward. Early adaptors, trend-spotters, knowledge brokers, change agents, and all those who know where their industry is heading and what next big ideas are coming down the pike have become the stars of the business world.

Identify the people in your industries who always seem to be out in front, and use all the relationship skills you've acquired to connect with them. Take them to lunch. Read their newsletters. In fact, read everything you can. Online, there are hundreds of individuals distilling information, analyzing it, and making prognostications. These armchair analysts are the eyes and ears of innovation. Now get online and read, read, read. Subscribe to magazines, buy books, and talk to the smartest people you can find. Eventually, all this knowledge will build on itself, and you'll start making connections others aren't.

2. Ask seemingly stupid questions.

If you ask questions that are like no other, you get results that are unlike any that the world has seen. How many people have the courage to ask those questions? The answer: all the people responsible for the greatest innovations. "Don't you think having all your MP3s on a little Walkman-like device would be cool?" Thus, the iPod. "Why can't we view our pictures immediately?" Thus, the instant photographic industry. "People sure like burgers and fries. Why not give it to them quickly?" Thus, McDonald's and the fast-food industry.

The power of innocence in business is wonderfully depicted in a scene from the movie *Big*, where Tom Hanks plays a kid transformed into an adult. In one poignant moment, Hanks is sitting in on an executive meeting at a major toy company, and one vice president is PowerPointing his way through a presentation about a new toy. All the numbers work. All the graphs point to a successful product launch. And yet Hanks's childlike innocence prompts him to say, "I don't get it." In actually playing with the toy, as he had, all the graphs and numbers didn't matter: The toy simply wasn't fun. Sometimes the numbers do lie. Sometimes all the PowerPoint presentations in the world won't provide cover for a company that has forgotten to ask the most basic of questions.

For years, the people running the companies that produced games believed they were in the entertainment business. I asked, "What if we're really in the marketing business?"

3. Know yourself and your talents.

I had no chance competing with the science geeks at ICI. In developing an expertise that highlighted my strengths, I was able to overcome my weaknesses. The trick is not to work obsessively on the skills and talents you lack, but to focus and cultivate your strengths so that your weaknesses matter less. I'd apply the 80/20 rule in that you should spend some time getting better at your weaknesses but really focus on building your strengths.

4. Always learn.

You have to learn more to earn more. All content-creators are readers or at least deep questioners or conversationalists. They're also sticklers when it comes to self-development. Your program of self-development should include reading books and magazines, listening to educational tapes, attending three to five conferences a year, taking a course or two, and developing relationships with the leaders in your field.

5. Stay healthy.

Research has discovered that at midafternoon, due to sleep deprivation, the average corporate executive today has the alertness level of a seventy-year-old. You think that executive is being creative or connecting the dots? Not a chance. Sounds hokey, but you have to take care of yourself—your body, mind, and spirit—to be at your best. As hectic as my schedule can get, I never miss a workout (five times a week). I try to take a five-day vacation every other month (I do check e-mails and catch up on reading). I go on a spirituality retreat once a month, even if it's a one-day local meditation retreat. And I do something spiritual each week—usually church. That gives me energy to allow me to keep my otherwise twenty-four-hour schedule.

6. Expose yourself to unusual experiences.

When management guru Peter Drucker was asked for one thing that would make a person better in business, he responded, "Learn to play the violin." Different experiences give rise to different tools. Find out what your kids are interested in and why. Stimulate your creativity. Learn about things that are out of the mainstream. Travel to weird and exotic places. Knowing one's own industry and one's native markets is not enough to compete in the future. Take a deep and boundless curiosity about things outside your own profession and comfort zone.

7. Don't get discouraged.

My first e-mail to the CEO of ICI regarding TQM was never returned. To this day, I face rejection on a regular basis. If you're going to be creative, cutting edge, out of the mainstream, you'd better get used to rockin' the boat. And guess what—when you're rockin' the boat, there will always be people who will try and push you off. That's the bet you have to take. Deeply committed professionals need to know the score: Passion keeps you going through the rough times come hell or high water, and both will come. There will be continual changes and challenges requiring you to be persistent and committed. Focus on the results and keep your eyes open for what is happening on the edges of your industry.

8. Know the new technology.

No industry moves quicker or places more emphasis on innovation. You don't need to be a "techno geek," but you do need to understand the impact of technology on your business and be able to leverage it to your benefit. Adopt a techno geek, or at least hire or sire one.

9. Develop a niche.

Successful small businesses that gain renown establish themselves within a carefully selected market niche that they can realistically hope to dominate. Individuals can do the same thing. Think of several areas where your company underperforms and choose to focus on the one area that is least attended to.

A former mentee of mine, for example, works for a growing start-up that offers a new kind of pet product. Not long after he was hired, he noted that one of the countless issues the start-up was struggling with was pricey postal rates that were cutting into the company's margins. Frankly, that's not the kind of issue that registers very high up on the totem pole of priorities for a start-up, but then again, this mentee wasn't very high up either.

He took it upon himself to research the problem by calling the official responsible for small business at UPS, FedEx, and others. A few weeks later, he sent a detailed memo to the CEO about how the company could reduce its postal costs. The CEO was delighted. The mentee's niche expertise in mail branded the young man as a valuable up-and-comer in the company, and these days, he's developing expertise in issues much farther up the totem pole.

10. Follow the money.

Creativity is worthless if it can't be applied. The bottom line for your content has to be: This will make us more money. The lifeblood of any company is sales and cash flow. All great ideas are meaningless in business until someone pays for it.

CONNECTORS' HALL OF FAME PROFILE

Dalai Lama

"Use your content to tell stories that move people."

Known as a world leader, holy man, diplomat, hero, and the
Tibetan Ghandi, the Dalai Lama simply prefers to be recognized as
"a simple Buddhist monk—no more, no less."

On his great ascent toward world renown ever since his escape
from his homeland in Tibet—fleeing the occupying armies of China
in the late 1950s—this unique national figure has captured the
public imagination, raised millions of dollars, and rallied celebrities, politicians, and laymen alike to his cause of reclaiming his
homeland.

What can the aspiring connector learn from this deeply modest
man?

The answer: Powerful content communicated in a compelling
story can energize your network to help you achieve your mission.

Because here's the thing with the spiritual leader of the Tibetan
people: Folks give him money, love, and support even though he's
peddling neither product nor service. Folks pay him, big time, even
though he makes no promises about a bountiful return on investment. Folks pay just to hear him speak about life in general, or the
struggles of Tibet, his non-nation nation.

You may have thought that a degree in business, or better yet an
MBA, was needed to become a leader or person with content. Not
true. The Dalai Lama doesn't have a single degree. He does, however, deliver a simple but profound message of world peace and
compassion packaged in colorful stories and anecdotes—a message that earned him the Nobel Peace Prize in 1989.

Now you might be thinking: "Wait a minute. There's no way you
can compare my white-collar pursuit to connect—and the stories *I'd*
be telling to win friends and influence people—to the stories that
the Dalai Lama has to share. I eat three meals a day. He's been
without a country since the Fifties."

And you'd be correct. Your story *won't* be as compelling as his.
But your story*telling* can be. Here's how:

In telling a gripping story, the Dalai Lama understands that the message must be both simple and universal. Journalist Chris Colin, in speculating why the Dalai Lama's cause is so popular, wrote, "Perhaps the clarity of the atrocity resonates in the West, where few international disputes seem so cut and dried . . . Here, in a nation nostalgic for the seemingly black-and-white struggles of the comparatively simpler past, the 'Free Tibet' cause has wings."

Though he is one of the most learned scholars of one of the most complex of all the world's philosophies, the Dalai Lama is sure not only to present his cause in a clear, simple-to-understand vision, but he also goes to great lengths to show how the cause relates to us all.

The most gripping stories are those concerning identity—who we are, where we've come from, and where we are going. They tap into something common to all people. The Dalai Lama tells us that to be concerned with the Tibetan people is to be concerned with yourself. "The more we care for the happiness of others," he says, "the greater our own sense of well-being becomes." In this way, he shows how the basic concerns of all people—happiness based on contentment, appeasement of suffering, and the forging of meaningful relationships—can act as the foundation for universal ethics in today's world. Thus, he appeals to his cause by appealing to everyone's cause.

That doesn't mean your business, your résumé, or whatever content you're trying to pitch has to actually *be* oversimplified or overly universal. But you should figure out how to spin your yarn in a fashion that a) is simple to understand, and b) everybody can relate to. Another way to think about this is to ask yourself, "How does my content help others answer who they are, where they are from, and where they are going?"

On some level, it's still baffling why anyone gives money to the Tibetan cause. For the Tibetan cause, arguably, is a lost one; after four decades, China still shows no signs of reversing itself.

And still, the Dalai Lama persuades people to donate their money and energy. How does he do it? One thing he does is use facts and historical examples within his stories to stoke our passions. He does not, as a businessperson might do with graphs and analysis, attempt to logically convince us of his position. He makes us feel his position. For example, check out this Q&A, from a 1997 interview in *Mother Jones*:

Q: What do you think it will take for China to change its policy toward Tibet?

Dalai Lama: It will take two things: first, a Chinese leadership that looks forward instead of backward, that looks toward integration with the world and cares about both world opinion and the will of [China's] own democracy movement; second, a group of world leaders that listens to the concerns of their own people with regard to Tibet, and speaks firmly to the Chinese about the urgent need of working out a solution based on truth and justice. We do not have these two things today, and so the process of bringing peace to Tibet is stalled.

But we must not lose our trust in the power of truth. Everything is always changing in the world. Look at South Africa, the former Soviet Union, and the Middle East. They still have many problems, setbacks as well as breakthroughs, but basically changes have happened that were considered unthinkable a decade ago.

What truly moves us as human beings, what prompts us into action, is emotion. Despite the odds, the Dalai Lama makes us believe that the seemingly impossible is, in fact, possible. In your own stories, use emotion to convince your doubters that underdogs sometimes win and Goliaths sometimes crumble.

Follow the example of this simple Buddhist monk who channels his charm and warmth into compelling stories that energize a diverse swath of people into action. In this new era of brands, in an economy that values emotions over numbers, storytellers will have the edge. As Michael Hattersley wrote in a *Harvard Business Review* article, "Too often, we make the mistake of thinking of business as a matter of pure rational calculation, something that in a few years computers will handle better than humans. One hears this in conference room and corridor: 'What do the numbers indicate?' 'Just give me the facts.' 'Let's weigh the evidence and make the right decision.' And yet, truth to tell, few talents are more important to managerial success than knowing how to tell a good story."

So forget bullet points and slide shows. When you've figured out what your content is, tell an inspiring story that will propel your friends and associates into action with spirit and fearlessness, motivated and mobilized by your simple but profound story-telling.

CHAPTER 23

Build Your Brand

Regardless of age, regardless of position, regardless of the business we happen to be in, all of us need to understand the importance of branding. We are CEOs of our own companies: Me Inc. To be in business today, our most important job is to be head marketer for the brand called You.

—Tom Peters

As a marketing professional, I'm keenly aware that perception drives reality and that we are all, in some sense, brands. I know how all my choices—what I wear, my conversational style, my hobbies—fashion a distinctive identity.

Image and identity have become increasingly important in our new economic order. With the digital sea swelling in sameness and overwhelmed in information, a powerful brand—built not on a product but on a personal message—has become a competitive advantage.

Your content will become the guiding star of your brand, helping to integrate all your connecting efforts around a uniform and powerful mission. Good personal brands do three highly significant things for your network of contacts: They provide a credible, distinctive, and trustworthy identity. They project a compelling message. They attract more and more people to you and your cause, as you'll stand out in an increasingly cluttered world. As a result, you will find it easier than ever to win new friends and have more of a say in what you do and where you work.

If I were to say, "Swoosh," what comes to mind? I'd be shocked if most people didn't respond, "Nike." After exposing consumers to the Nike swoosh for two decades, and infusing the symbol with all the athletic grandeur we now associate with the symbol, the company has trained us to think "Nike" whenever we see that simple little symbol.

Powerful stuff, don't you think?

Within a network, your brand can do something similar. It establishes your worth. It takes your mission and content and broadcasts it to the world. It articulates what you have to offer, why you're unique, and gives a distinct reason for others to connect with you.

Branding guru and all-star business consultant Tom Peters instructs in his customary bravado to "create your own micro-equivalent of the Nike swoosh." He wants to bring Madison Avenue to your cubicle, holding out the branding success of Michael Jordan and Oprah Winfrey as a template for every Willy Lohman wanting to become Willy Gates.

How have we gone from pitching products to pitching ourselves?

Peters insists that we live in a "World Turned Upside Down." The conventions of the past are meaningless. Rules are irrelevant. The lines have blurred between new and old economy, Hollywood, huge corporations, and simply huge, incorporated individuals.

It's what Peters calls the "white-collar revolution." A confluence of factors—including a streamlining of business processes, technology that replaces jobs, an increase in outsourcing to foreign countries, and an age of entrepreneurialism where more and more people see themselves as free agents—are combining in such a way that Peters predicts over 90 percent of all white-collar jobs will be radically different or won't exist at all in ten to fifteen years. He says, "You must think of your job, your department, your division as a self-contained 'Inc.' You must do WOW projects."

In terms of branding, then, the bottom line for everyone comes down to a choice: to be distinct or extinct.

"I'm sick to death of hearing, 'I'd like to, but they won't let me,'" Peters preaches, hitting his iconoclastic stride. "Be the CEO of your own life. Raise hell. Let the chips fall where they may. It'll never be easier to change jobs than it is today." Yes! Yes! Yes!

Few things infuriate me more than when people say they're helpless, or even indifferent, to distinguishing themselves from their peers and colleagues. I remember giving advice to an extremely smart young guy named Kevin, who was working at the consultancy PriceWaterhouseCoopers. In the course of our discussion, he told me he wasn't happy with what he was doing or how his career was playing out. He was, he told me, just another anonymous number cruncher with no alternatives given the staid environment there.

"Wrong!" I told him. "You have alternatives, you're just not creating them for yourself. You have to start taking ownership of managing your career. You have to start making an effort to change your brand from anonymous number cruncher to slightly famous difference maker."

When I made some suggestions on how he might go about doing this, he said, "That sort of thing can't be done at a big consulting company." I thought my head was going to explode. I think he probably thought so, too.

"Kevin, that's just self-defeating crap. From the first day I joined Deloitte—that's a pretty large consulting firm, right?—I went out of my way to take on projects no one wanted and initiated projects no one had thought of doing. I e-mailed my boss, and sometimes my boss's boss, ideas. And I did it almost every day. What was the worst thing that could happen? I'd get fired from a job I didn't like anyway. Alternatively, I'd make the effort to create the job—regardless of where it was—that I thought would make me happy."

FerrazziGreenlight's training-and-development division does a lot of training at professional schools and new-hire training for big companies. In our training, we try again and again to hammer home the message that your career is yours and yours alone to manage. Every job I've ever had, I've made an effort to brand myself as an innovator, a thinker, a salesman, and someone who could get stuff done. When I was just a management trainee at ICI, my first job out of college, I sent a set of recommendations to the CEO. So he never responded. But I never stopped sending those e-mails.

It's just silly to think you can't impact people's personal and professional expectations of who you are. By making the effort, you can break the glass ceiling by expanding people's view of your capability.

Peters tells his own story of an airline stewardess who suggested that her airline put one olive in their martinis rather than two. The suggestion went on to save the company over $40,000 a year and the stewardess was—instantly—branded. Today, she's probably a vice president.

The novelist Milan Kundera once reflected that flirting is the promise of sex with no guarantee. A successful brand, then, is the promise *and* guarantee of a mind-shattering experience each and every time. It's the e-mail you always read because of who it's from. It's the employee who always gets the cool projects.

To become a brand, you've got to become relentlessly focused on what you do that adds value. And I promise you can add value to whatever job you're doing now. Can you do what you do faster and more efficiently? If so, why not document what it would take to do so and offer it to your boss as something all employees might do? Do you initiate new projects on your own and in your spare time? Do you search out ways to save or make your company more money?

You can't do all that if you're solely concerned with minimizing risk, respecting the chain of command, and following your job description to the letter. There's no room for yes-men in this pursuit. Those with the gumption to make their work special will be the ones to establish a thriving brand.

You can't do meaningful work that makes a difference unless you're devoted to learning, growing, and stretching your skills. If you want others to redefine what you do and who you are within organizational boundaries, then you have to be able to redefine yourself. That means going above and beyond what's called for. It means seeing your résumé as a dynamic, changing document every year. It means using your contacts inside and outside your network to deliver each project you're assigned with inspired performance. Peters calls this the pursuit of WOW in everything you do.

There are a whole lot of road maps out there these days to self-incorporated wow-ness. But the maps often rely more on intuition than navigation. The key generally comes down to a few simple things: Shake things up! Find your value! Obsess on your image! Turn everything into an opportunity to build your brand.

So how do you create an identity for a brilliant career? How do you become the swoosh of your company? Of your network? Here are three steps to get you on the road to becoming the next Oprah Winfrey:

Develop a Personal Branding Message (PBM)

A brand is nothing less than everything everyone thinks of when they see or hear your name. The best brands, like the most interesting people, have a distinct message.

Your PBM comes from your content/unique value proposition, as we discussed in the last chapter, and a process of self-evaluation. It involves finding out what's really in a name—your name. It calls for you to identify your uniqueness and how you can put that uniqueness to work. It's not a specific task so much as the cultivation of a mind-set.

What do you want people to think when they hear or read your name? What product or service can you best provide? Take your skills, combine them with your passions, and find out where in the market, or within your own company, they can best be applied.

Your message is always an offshoot of your mission and your content. After you've sat down and figured out who you want to be, and you've written goals in some version of ninety-day, one-year, and three-year increments, you can build a brand perception that supports all this.

Your positioning message should include a list of words that you want people to use when referring to you. Writing those words down are a big first step in having others believe them. Ask your most trusted friends what words they would use to describe you, for good and for bad. Ask them what are the most important skills and attributes you bring to the table.

When I was once hungry to become chief executive officer at a Fortune 500 company, my PBM read as follows: "Keith Ferrazzi is one of the most innovative and bottom line–focused marketers and CEOs in the world. His string of dramatic 'firsts' have followed every position he has held. His passion gives off a light that he carries wherever he goes."

Package the Brand

Most people's judgments and impressions are based on visuals—everything other than the words you speak that communicates to others what you're about. For everyone in every field—let's be real—looks count, so you'd better look polished and professional.

There is one general, overarching caveat in this step: Stand out! Style matters. Whether you like it or not, clothing, letterheads, hairstyles, business cards, office space, and conversational style are noticed—big time. The design of your brand is critical. Buy some new clothes. Take an honest look at how you present yourself. Ask others how they see you. How do you wish to be seen?

The bottom line is you have to craft an appearance to the outside world that will enhance the impression you want to make. "Everyone sees what you appear to be," observed Machiavelli, "few really know what you are."

When I was younger, I used to wear bow ties. I felt that it was a signature that people would not quickly forget, and it worked. "You were the guy who spoke at the conference last year wearing the bow tie," I'd hear over and over again. Over time, I was able to give up that signature, as my message and delivery became my brand and I didn't think the bow tie corresponded to my evolving image of someone on the cutting edge of ideas.

Why not create a personal Web site? A Web site is a terrific and cheap marketing tool for your brand, and a great way to force you to clearly articulate who you are. With a good-looking site, you look as polished and professional as any major corporation on the Internet.

This may sound trivial, but it's not. Little choices make big impressions.

Broadcast Your Brand

You've got to become your own PR firm, as I'll talk about in the next chapter. Take on the projects no one wants at work. Never ask for more pay until after you've been doing the job successfully and become invaluable. Get on convention panels. Write articles for trade journals and company newsletters. Send e-mails filled with creative ideas to your CEO. Design your own Me, Inc. brochure.

The world is your stage. Your message is your "play." The character you portray is your brand. Look the part; live the part.

CHAPTER 24

Broadcast Your Brand

Now you have your "content," and the beginnings of a brand. You're getting good, really good. That's how you've become an authority in your company. But your job is not done. If the rest of the world isn't familiar with how good you are, you and your company are only gaining part of the benefit. The fact is, you've got to extend your reach and level of outside recognition. That's how you'll become an authority not just in your company but in your industry.

It comes in part from visibility. I'm not suggesting you stand on your local street corner with a sign on a sandwich board exclaiming, "Put me on TV!" Though come to think of it . . . well, let's hold off for now. I've got some suggestions on high-stakes self-promotion that will make your effort becoming known a little bit easier, sans the public embarrassment. And I'm no stranger to embarrassment. I've taken a few knocks to learn the right and wrong ways to let others know about what I do.

You don't have to look far to see why increased visibility might be important for your career, and for extending your network of colleagues and friends. Take, for example, self-promoting phenom Donald Trump. How many other real estate moguls do you know offhand? Right—I can't name anyone else either. Why is the "The Donald" considered the ultimate dealmaker? Probably because he's called himself that a million times over in any number of articles and television interviews and now a highly rated TV show. Because he has a book entitled *The Art of the Deal*.

But his self-promotion is not just ego (though by how much, I'm not quite sure); it makes plenty of business sense, too. His buzz-worthy brand now has a value unto itself. Buildings with his name on it are more valuable and bring in higher rental fees. When The Donald went bankrupt, banks that would have otherwise foreclosed on any other struggling mogul gave Trump leeway, not only because they knew he was good at what he did but because they knew his name alone would go a long way in helping him recover from his setbacks. Trump is a talented developer, but then so are a lot of other people. The difference? He promotes himself.

The fact is that those people who are known beyond the walls of their own cubicle have a greater value. They find jobs more easily. They usually rise up the corporate ladder faster. Their networks begin to grow without much heavy lifting.

I can hear the groans of discomfort already stirring. You may be thinking, "I'm shy. I don't like to talk about myself. Isn't modesty a virtue?" Well, I can assure you that if you hide your accomplishments, they'll remain hidden. If you don't promote yourself, however graciously, no one else will.

Like it or not, your success is determined as much by how well others know your work as by the quality of your work. Luckily, there are hundreds of new channels and mediums for you to get the word out.

So how do you promote Brand You?

Every day, you read or hear about companies in newspapers, magazines, on television, and on the Web. Most of the time the article or story is about celebrity CEOs and big companies. It's not because they are more deserving of the press than you or me. It's the result of well-planned and strategic public relations. Big companies have PR machines working for them to shape and control their image (though not always successfully).

Smaller companies and individuals have to do it themselves. But by using some pluck and a strategy of your own, access to the media is not as difficult as you may think. Journalists do less sleuthing for their stories than you'd imagine. They get a majority of their stories from people that have sought them out, and not the other way around. And like everyone else in any profession, they tend to follow the herd. Which means once you get written about, other reporters will come calling. Assigned you as a subject, they'll do a quick Google search, and presto: They'll find you are an already cited source and will seek you out to cite you again.

One article creates visibility, which in turn will put you in front of other journalists, creating the possibility of more articles and visibility. A journalist's deadlines make magazine and newspaper work the art of the possible, not the perfect.

The key is to view the exposure of your brand as a PR campaign. How are you going to get your message out there? How are you going to make sure that the message gets out the way you want it to get out? Sure, your network is a good start. Everyone you meet and everyone you talk to should know what you do, why you're doing it, and how you can do it for him or her. But why not broadcast that same message to a thousand networks across the country?

Now we're talking.

As I mentioned before, when I became CEO of YaYa, it was a company with virtually no revenue, and clearly no recognized market. We had visionary founders, Jeremy Milken and Seth Gerson, but we needed a market.

There was, however, one company with a similar product. I'm going to call them Big Boy Software. They had created a software tool that facilitated the actual creation of high-end games. They too were trying to find their business model and generate revenue. Both of us were in a race to become the established brand in the new market we were creating.

Soon after we defined the advergaming space, Big Boy saw how YaYa was picking up steam (and generating operating revenue) selling games to big brands. They followed suit, positioning themselves as competitors to YaYa. The main difference between them and us was that they had way, way more money. They had raised a huge amount of capital that put our resources to shame. There is no need to go into the comparative details of who was a better company (I'm a little biased, of course). But the fact remains, they had tons of resources and we did not—at all.

So how did YaYa become the market leader?

The answer is, we created buzz: that powerful, widespread phenomenon that can determine the future of individuals, companies, and movies alike. Buzz is the riddle every enterprising person is trying to solve. It's a grassroots, word-of-mouth force that can turn a low-budget flick about a witch into a multimillion-dollar blockbuster. (Ever hear of *The Blair Witch Project*?) You feel its energy in Internet chat rooms, at the gym, on the street, and all of it is stoked by a media hungry for the inside scoop. Buzz is marketing on steroids.

Here's an example of how well it works: Remember Napster? One day it was a clever software idea hatched in some kid's dorm room allowing users online to link up and share MP3 music files. Six months later, it was a Silicon Valley start-up, the source of a major lawsuit, playing bandwidth havoc with servers around the country. Even when it was shut down, the name had enough buzz to be bought for something like $50 million.

Advertising or a life-empowering endorsement by Oprah had nothing to do with it. Napster was, well, cool. And as a result of buzz, it was very famous.

As a marketer, over the years, I have developed an idea of how buzz is created. One way is to generate what I call "catalytic moments." When you watch a big football game, have you noticed how the tide of a game will suddenly turn in favor of one team or the other? It starts with a huge play, and in many cases is followed by more key plays. Buzz is like that. It needs a situation, a pivotal moment, an inside scoop, a crazy giveaway—something that will get the crowd whispering. Unfortunately, YaYa was too young and poor for such a strategy.

Another way is to report compelling news by leveraging the power of the media to get your brand sizzling. The Jesse Ventura for Governor of Minnesota campaign is a perfect example. Significantly outspent by two major competitors, Ventura gained valuable media exposure by persuading the media to report on things like his creative use of advertising and a G.I. Joe–like action figure. Similarly, I look for compelling stories that create buzz within the news media.

That's where feeding the "influentials" comes into play. Influentials are what marketing wonks call those people who can ignite brand buzz. They are the small segment of the population that will adopt a cool product early on and infect everyone else with the bug. They are also the celebrities and experts whose word is gospel. It's imperative that you identify those people and get your brand in front of them.

I mentioned the KPE agency before. They were just what I was looking for. An interactive marketing and technology consultancy on the cutting edge, KPE had taken an early interest in the new space we were creating. They were a recognized name among Fortune 1000 companies known for spotting the newest trends. Happily, their head of strategy was Matt Ringel, whom I had gotten to know from our mutual interest in the nonprofit devoted to preserving objects and places of historical significance, called "Save America's Treasures."

I reached out to Matt and proposed that he lead an effort to write an article introducing this space to the market. I knew that a white paper (research documents that consulting companies put out on hot topics of the day) introducing us and the technology from an unbiased perspective would be far more effective and lead to more credibility than anything we could do ourselves. I worked with Matt and his right hand, Jane Chen, for weeks on the paper, giving them examples from YaYa, getting clients to speak with them, introducing methodologies and insights that we had gained through our experience. I had gone to analysts before this who were interested in the space and were now willing to speak to Matt about what we were doing as well.

I was giving KPE another opportunity to look cutting edge and take a leadership position in the space, while in return, just by dint of the access I was giving KPE, I bet that YaYa would be the primary example in the case study. Great things came from the article, including the new name for the space, which we called (thanks to the creativity of Jane Chen) "Advergaming." The name alone had buzz.

One lesson we learned from the experience is that your PR campaign has to be realistic. More often than not, you will have to start small. You'll be forced to focus on your local paper, high school and college newsletters, or industry trade journals. Or perhaps just a white paper listed on some consulting company's Web site. The point is to light the fire.

When the white paper was completed, it received amazing publicity thanks to KPE's PR engine (which, unlike us, they could afford), and we indeed came out as the instant leader of the space. As an interesting side note, I subsequently recruited both Matt and Jane into YaYa (I wanted the founders of advergaming in my organization).

It took less than a year for us to appear on the cover of *BrandWeek,* in the marketplace section of the *Wall Street Journal,* in the technology section of the *New York Times,* in a feature for *Forbes* . . . the list goes on. I was consistently on every panel with the competition (generally I was invited for free while "the boys" paid for the opportunity). While money can certainly be a substitute for good PR, it's hard to have enough of it to offset the credibility one gets from just one article in *Forbes* or the *New York Times.*

The competition, on the other hand, got little press and failed to create a distinct message. It all goes back to your content. Once you have it, you can begin to mold it in a way that will capture attention. You need to impart a sense of urgency and make the message timely. Reporters continually ask, "But why is it important NOW?" If you can't answer that sufficiently, your article will wait.

In YaYa's case, I highlighted how the games industry is the fastest-growing segment of the entertainment business and how surprisingly no one had figured out how to tap into that growth for anything other than pure fun and leisure. That isn't always enough. I had written a piece for the *Wall Street Journal*'s weekly column called the Manager's Journal. The editor liked the piece but kept pushing it back so he could publish other pieces that were timelier. So I began to rewrite the intros to my piece each week, to relate to something that was in the news at the time. In short order, the article finally saw the light of day.

Once you light a fire and get the buzz going, you want to get your story in front of journalists. The misconception is that you have to "work" the press. But overeager PR professionals, who don't know the meaning of "No," are working reporters hourly. Journalists get fed up with people who are nitwits and pitch articles without substance. The media is like any other business. They have a job to do. If you can help them do their job better, or easier, they're going to love you.

You have to start today building relationships with the media before you have a story you'd like them to write. Send them information. Meet them for coffee. Call regularly to stay in touch. Give them inside scoops on your industry. Establish yourself as a willing and accessible source of information, and offer to be interviewed for print, radio, or TV. Never say, "No comment."

To illustrate: I remember the first time I, as the newly minted project leader of Deloitte's reengineering efforts, sat with one of *Fortune*'s top journalists, Tom Stewart. My PR firm introduced Tom and me, and I came ready to impress. I had read every piece he had written in the last five years. I playfully gibed him about obscure predictions he had made years ago in other articles, and was prepared to thoughtfully discuss his most recent column. I wanted to be as useful as possible, giving him access to trends, ideas, and all the contacts at my disposal. I did the same thing for other journalists at other major newspapers and magazines.

Tom and I had a blast. Tom's energy and intellectual curiosity was contagious. I suppose I had something to offer him as well, because he readily took my next lunch offer and the next after that.

It was more than just mutual admiration. I was prepared to act, sound, and feel like an expert. When I didn't know something, I was sure to pass him on to the person who did. If you are constantly apologizing with "Well, I am not the expert," people will believe you and wonder why you wasted their time.

I never did ask Tom for anything in particular. We'd meet a few times a year and I'd try to be as helpful as possible. Sure, I remember the first time I saw one of my ideas in his column months after we had discussed it, and lo and behold, a competitor firm was quoted rather than Deloitte. I went through the roof. My instinct was to call him immediately and express my unhappiness. But, instead, I held back and simply invited him for another lunch.

Is such a thing too time-consuming? Not if you're convinced it behooves your company's efforts and if you enjoy the interaction. When I was at Deloitte and would show up on TV, I *was* Deloitte. When I was in *Forbes,* it was the company that reaped the benefits in business development.

Over time, the hours you put in developing relationships with journalists will pay off, as it did for me with Tom, both personally and professionally. Deloitte's name eventually started to pop up with increasing frequency in the pages of *Fortune,* because our stories were being heard by someone who could retell them. I never asked Tom for an article, but giving him good ideas in our lunches certainly didn't hurt. Today, Tom is the editor-in-chief of the *Harvard Business Review,* and I'm planning to take him to lunch soon to hear out a few more ideas. Remember, though, you can't force-feed or pressure a good journalist. Any attempt to do so will surely end your professional relationship. The best journalists are almost always also the most ethical.

In traversing the media landscape, be aware that there are also some land mines. Sometimes what media wants to write, and the story you think they should write, is a very different thing.

I learned this the hard way. One day I got a call from the well-known reporter Hal Lancaster, who was writing a column about managing one's career for the *Wall Street Journal.* The story appeared Tuesday, November 19, 1996. I know the exact date because I had the article framed so I would never forget the lesson I learned.

When Hal called, I was ecstatic. He was a famous reporter for a prestigious newspaper asking about what I did. I was a relative kid at Deloitte. Well, that wasn't exactly the slant of the story, but my excitement got the best of me. Hal said he was doing a piece on the changing nature of work. He had a hypothesis that the end of the reengineering movement was having a major impact on those who had led reengineering projects and those who had been affected by the projects.

Rather than listen more closely to his angle, I tried to impress upon him what I thought the real story was about. Big mistake! If a reporter calls you, states his story and the angle he's taking, you can be sure you'll be used as an example to buttress his angle. Rare is the occasion that a journalist will hear you out and say, "Oh my God, you're right! I'm going about it all wrong." Rarely—I meant never. But back then, I thought I'd set Hal straight. He, however, ended up straightening me out.

I took a lot of time with Hal explaining how I had been on the normal partner track leading Deloitte's reengineering effort, but now that the trend was ending, I was transitioning into an exciting special project involving marketing. "I'm going to change the way traditional consulting companies market themselves."

He pushed past my excitement. "Do you feel displaced in the post-reengineering world?" he wanted to know. Sure, I conceded, there was some change involved, but certainly nothing traumatic. He wanted me to say I felt aimless. But my new gig excited me. I considered it a huge step up.

The day the story appeared, I ran to the newsstand to get the paper. There, blaring out for everyone to see, was the heading "A demotion does not have to mean the end of a fulfilling career." Right above the fold in BIG BOLD letters was my name: "Mr. Ferrazzi says the change was difficult, but he has embraced the assignment as an opportunity."

He was implying I was demoted!

I got slammed. Oh, and the ribbing I got from my boss, Pat Loconto. "So, I heard you were demoted and no one reports to you. That's terrific! It will save us tons on HR costs, starting with that raise of yours."

Be careful. Listen to the reporter when he or she says, "I'm doing a story about displaced workers . . ." No matter what YOU say, that's the story he'll write.

Now that you know a little more about the lay of the land, it's time to get yourself buzzing. Here's an action plan for creating a PR strategy for Brand You:

You Are Your Own Best PR Representative

You must manage your own media. Public relations companies are facilitators and act as leverage. I've been represented for years. The best ones can be strategic partners, but ultimately the press always wants to talk to the big guy—you, not a PR rep. Most of the biggest articles about me came from my own contacts. Yes, a PR firm can help you generate those contacts, but early in your career you won't need them and you probably won't be able to afford them.

Who better than you to tell your story with credibility and passion? Start making calls to the reporters who cover your industry. Have lunch with them. If something timely occurs around your content, send a press release. There's no secret behind press releases. They're nothing more than two or three paragraphs describing what's memorable about your story. *It is that easy.*

Remember, media folks are just plain fun. They tend to be interesting and smart, and they're paid to be up to speed on everything that is going on in the world. And they need you as much as you need them. They may not need your exact story at the exact time you want, but with a little stick-to-itiveness, they'll come around.

Know the Media Landscape

Nothing infuriates reporters and editors more, I'm told, than to get a pitch from someone who clearly has no idea what their publication is about or who their audience is. Remember, media is a business, and the companies who are in the media are looking for ratings or to sell more issues. The only way they can do that well is by serving their specific audience. "Listen, I'm a devoted reader of this magazine," I'll tell editors while mentioning a few recent articles I've enjoyed. "I've got a story for you that I know your audience will be interested in, as I've been thinking about it for a long time." That's not a line, either. Before I call journalists, I'll spend time reading their articles, figuring out what they cover, and what kinds of stories their publications like to run.

Work the Angles

There are no new stories, it has been said, only old stories told in new ways. To make your pitch sound fresh and original, find an innovative slant. What's your slant? Anything that screams, "Now!" Let's say you're opening a pet store. To a magazine devoted to entrepreneurs, perhaps you play up how your store is one recent example of the entrepreneurial boom in the opening of local retail stores. Suggest why this is happening and what the magazine's readers could learn. Selling it to your local newspaper is easy. What caused you to switch careers? What is particular to your situation that highlights something going on within your community? And don't forget catalytic moments. Maybe you sell a rare animal no one else does. Or maybe you plan on giving away puppies to orphans. That's something worth covering to a local or neighborhood newspaper. Get the word out.

Think Small

Are you Bill Gates? No. Maybe you've developed the antidote for the common cold? No again. Well, the *New York Times* probably isn't knocking on your door quite yet. Go local first. Start a database of newspapers and magazines in your area that might be interested in your content. Try college papers, the neighborhood newspaper, or the free industry digital newsletter you find in your inbox. You'll get the fire started and learn how to deal with reporters in the process.

Make a Reporter Happy

They're a rushed, impatient, always-stressed bunch of over-achievers. Work at their pace and be available whenever they call on you. NEVER blow off an interview, and try to facilitate the contacts they'll need to produce a good story.

Master the Art of the Sound Bite

Tell me why I should write about you in ten seconds or less. If it takes more than ten seconds to pitch your content, a television producer will assume you won't be able to get your point of view across to an impatient audience. And a reporter might try to hustle you off the phone.

Learn to be brief—in both your written and phone pitches. Brevity is cherished in the media. Look at the evolution of the modern sound bite: Some thirty years ago, a presidential nominee was allowed an average sound bite of forty-two seconds. Today, it's somewhere under seven seconds. If the President is only getting a few seconds, how much time do you think you'll get? Think in terms of talking points. Pick the three most interesting points about your story and make them fast, make them colorful, and make them catchy.

Don't Be Annoying

There's a fine line between marketing yourself properly and becoming annoying. If a pitch of mine gets rejected, I'll ask what else it needs to make it publishable. Sometimes it will never be right in the editor's eyes, but other times, you can answer a few more questions or dig deeper and repitch the story. It is okay to be aggressive, but mind the signals, and back off when it's time.

It's All on the Record

Be cautious: What you say can hurt you, and even if you're not quoted or you say something off the record, a reporter will use your words to color the slant of the article. I'm not advocating being tight-lipped. That's what corporate communications directors get paid for, and I don't know anyone in the press who likes them. Just remember: All press is *not* good press, even if they spell your name right.

Trumpet the Message, Not the Messenger

There was a time when I was less aware of the difference between reputation and notoriety. Boy, there is a big difference! Early on in my career, I paid too much attention to getting attention. I was building a brand all right; but as I look back, it just wasn't the brand I wanted for myself. All your efforts at publicity, promotion, and branding need to feed into your mission; if they're only feeding into your ego, you'll find yourself with a reputation you hadn't bargained for that could hold you back for the rest of your life. I was lucky. Looking back, I merely wasted a lot of time.

Treat Journalists as You Would Any Other Member of Your Network or Community of Friends

As in any interview, your primary objective when you meet with a member of the press is to get the person across from you to like you. The reporter is human (at least most are) and your empathy for his or her hard work will go a long way. Even when I feel like a piece did not do me justice, I thank the writer for his hard work. I'll send a short thank-you e-mail no matter the size of the publication. Journalists, by the nature of their profession, are natural networkers. Couple that with a media community that's not all that large, and you'll understand why you want these guys on your side.

Be a Name-Dropper

Connecting your story with a known entity—be it a politician, celebrity, or famous businessperson—acts as a de facto slant. Bottom line: The media wants recognizable faces in their pages. If your story will give them access to someone they otherwise haven't been able to get, they'll make concessions. Or, sometimes, you can link a celebrity to your story without really knowing the person. Leave it to the journalist to track down the star. You've done your job by giving them reason to seek her out.

You've Got to Market the Marketing

Once you've put in all that hard work and landed a nice article, it's no time to be modest. Send the article around. Give it to your alumni magazine. Update your class notes. Use the article to get even more press coverage. I'll attach a recent article about me to an e-mail and in the subject line write, "Here's another one of Ferrazzi's shameless attempts at self-promotion." Most people get a kick out of it and it keeps you on everyone's radar.

There's No Limit to the Ways You Can Go About Enhancing Your Profile

There are literally thousands of different ways to get recognition for your expertise. Try moonlighting. See if you have the time to take on freelance projects that will bring you in touch with a whole new group of people. Or, within your own company, take on an extra project that might showcase your new skills. Teach a class or give a workshop at your own company. Sign up to be on panel discussions at a conference. Most important, remember that your circle of friends, colleagues, clients, and customers is the most powerful vehicle you've got to get the word out about what you do. What they say about you will ultimately determine the value of your brand.

CHAPTER 25

The Write Stuff

This is one of those tricks of the networking trade that may not seem big, but boy, can it come in handy.

If you have any writing skills at all—and yes, the good news is we all have some level of skill—you can get close to almost anyone by doing a piece on them, or with them, even if it's for your local newspaper.

Me, write? I don't have a Shakespearean bone in my body, you say. Well, no one has had that bone for 500 years.

These days, with the Internet and newsstands busting at their seams with publications of every imaginable orientation, everyone can be an author. And writing articles can be a great boost for your career. It provides instant credibility and visibility. It can become a key arrow in your self-marketing quiver, creating relationships with highly respected people and helping you develop a skill that's always in high demand.

First, get over all the romantic pretensions around writing. In business school, when I was dreaming about publishing an article in the *Harvard Business Review,* I had a wonderful encounter with a visiting professor who had written a number of high-profile articles and books. I asked her how I, too, could become a writer.

"Write," she told me.

Brows furrowed, I nodded. When no more advice came from her esteemed mouth, I asked: "Anything else?"

"Write, then write some more. When you're done—and here's the kicker—keep writing.

"Look," she said, "there is no secret. Writing is tough. But people of all talents, at all levels, do it. The only thing necessary to become a writer is a pen, some paper, and the will to express yourself."

Bright woman. Want to write something? Write it. Want to get published? Call an editor and tell him you want to submit an article. Your first time may be a flaming failure. Nothing in life is a sure thing. But that's how people do it.

A lot of business writing is collaborative. While the hunger to be recognized is great, busy people higher up the ladder often don't have the extra time to work alone on something like an article. Instead, they choose to either contribute their expertise or work with others to get it done.

The process I've used to pull these types of things off is simple. First, what's your content? What kind of interesting things are going on in your industry or personal life? Have you learned to do what you do differently or found an easier and more efficient way of doing it?

Once you've got a hook—some subject of interest you'd like to explore that you think others will find interesting—get in touch with the editor of a publication that's likely to publish such material. You don't have to make the op-ed page of the *New York Times*. Community newspapers, professional newsletters, even in-house company publications have white space they need to fill. At this stage, all you're looking for is some tentative buy-in, a small show of interest that you can use to gain access to others in researching the piece. And once you get published, you've got a track record—and samples of your work that you can use to snatch more chances.

What's an editor going to say when you pitch him or her an idea? Probably something like "Sure, sounds great. Very busy. Gotta go. Let me see it when it's done." This is how editors talk and this is what they invariably say.

But now, when you call others to interview them, you're not just Joe Shmo, you're Joe Shmo calling about an article targeted for the *Poughkeepsie Gazette* (or something like that). And these aren't just random people you're calling, either. These are the people you've painstakingly targeted as the top experts and thinkers in the subject you're investigating.

What you've just unknowingly done, by calling these people and setting up an interview, is established a terrific environment for meeting anyone anywhere. The odds will never be stacked so clearly in your favor. The subject of conversation is something you know the other person is fascinated with. And by then, you'll have had the time to become pretty snazzy with the subject yourself. You're offering value through the publicity you'll potentially garner. And the mutual understanding that you're working together toward a common objective will make what would normally be a formal affair into something much closer. It's an opportunity to shine!

Most of the time, I like to share credit and offer a byline to the person who becomes most helpful. Explain that their insights are truly unique and impressive and that you would welcome their coauthorship. You'll do the research and writing and all they have to do is give some time and energy to the project. Then, once you begin to collaborate, ask them (or they more than likely will volunteer) to open their network to you for additional research and interviews. And just like that, you're expanding your network exponentially with contacts that otherwise might have seemed out of reach.

Guess what? By article's end, whether it's been published or not, you've managed to learn a great deal and to meet a group of important people who potentially might be important to your future. And you now have a very good reason to stay in touch with them.

CHAPTER 26

Getting Close to Power

As long as you're going to think anyway, think big.

—Donald Trump

Newt Gingrich, the famous Republican politician and all-about-Washington gadfly, is known to tell a story about a lion and a field mouse. A lion, he says, can use his prodigious hunting skills to capture a field mouse with relative ease anytime he wants, but at the end of the day, no matter how many mice he's ensnared, he'll still be starving.

The moral of the story: Sometimes, despite the risk and work involved, it's worth our time to go for the antelope.

Are you only connecting with field mice? If you are, start turning your attention to reaching out to the sort of important people that can make a difference in your life and the lives of others. The kind of people who can make you, and your network, sparkle.

The conscious pursuit of people with power and celebrity has a bad rap. We're taught to see it as an expression of vanity and superficiality. We regard it as a cheap and easy means of getting ahead. As a result, instead of acting on our impulses, we repress them. We buy celebrity magazines like *People, Us Weekly,* or, in the case of business folks, *Fortune,* to peer safely from a distance into a world we're so obviously hungry to know more about.

I, on the other hand, think there's absolutely nothing wrong with pursuing this world more directly. Seeking the influence of powerful people in our lives is not crass or misguided; it can be enormously helpful. Again, no one does it alone, whatever our goal or mission. We need the help of lots of others.

Why is it that we're so taken with the lives of big achievers? If we measure our accomplishments against the accomplishments of others, it stands to reason that the more accomplished the people we associate with, the greater our aspirations become.

People who fit our conventional notions of fame and celebrity often have qualities or skills that we admire. Many of these people have achieved great things through risk, passion, focus, hard work, and positive attitudes. And so many of them have overcome so much.

Of course, celebrity can mean all sorts of things to all sorts of people. I define celebrity as public recognition by a large share of a certain group. In other words, fame is a matter of context. In college, public recognition is given to tenured professors or well-known deans. In a small midwestern town, the celebrities may be a politician, successful entrepreneur, or outspoken longtime resident. These people have a disproportionate degree of influence over the group they inhabit. That's why it has become popular to use celebrities as spokespersons for major brands. They increase awareness, create positive feelings around a company, and play an important role in convincing consumers of a product's attractiveness. Local mini-celebrities within your own group can do the same for your brand.

That's what social scientists call "power by association": It's the power that arises from being identified with influential people. You can see this phenomenon at work everywhere. Power that arises from internal associations, for example, can include personal assistants and gatekeepers who may not be very high on the ladder in terms of company hierarchy, but who are powerful simply because of their proximity and access to the chief executive officer.

External associations, such as powerful politicians, influential news reporters, mass media personalities, and so on, also help to enhance one's profile inside and outside an organization. That's why a smart start-up company, for example, will seek to populate its board of directors with recognized business personalities who can impart credibility to a new business. Certainly, having the ear of influential celebrities or journalists can mean more favorable coverage of you and your company or an unprecedented amount of coverage for your charity.

Fame breeds fame. The fact is, all my prowess for reaching out to other people would be far less effective if a few of those people in my Rolodex weren't well-known names. The hard truth is that the ones who get ahead are usually those who know how to make highly placed people feel good about having them around. Plus, they add a little magic. Real or imagined, these people have that X factor that can magnify a moment and turn a prosaic dinner party into something magnificent.

Problem is, while we're excited by the idea of meeting "celebrities," they are often not all that anxious to meet us. So how can we get close to them?

There are no easy answers. But if you pursue these people in a sincere manner, with good intentions, you're not being manipulative. And if you are emboldened by a mission and you've put in the time and hard work to establish a web of people that count on you, then the time will come when your growing influence will put you in a place where you'll be face-to-face with someone who can convey a lot of sparkle to your next dinner party. You'll get close to power simply by virtue of reaching out and following the the advice I have offered in this book.

When this does inevitably occur for you, there are a few things to keep in mind that I've learned through the years.

While I'm aware of the impact a recognized persona can have on one's network, and I'm certainly not shy about putting myself in a place where meeting such people can occur, too much fuss and adoration will kill your efforts before they begin. Folks are folks.

This came into play years ago when I was at the *Vanity Fair* party at the old Russian Embassy following the White House Press Corps dinner. When I was standing in line for cocktails, the man beside me seemed awfully familiar. At first, I thought he was a politician. Then I placed his face as someone who was involved in politics, but behind the scenes in some manner, one of the President's key advisors.

I was right—sort of. The man was Richard Schiff, the actor who played the communications advisor to the fictional president played by Martin Sheen in *The West Wing*. Out of context, I'm terrible with recognizing TV stars.

Just as casually as if he were someone I didn't know at all, I introduced myself. He paused slightly, as celebrities are apt to do before engaging with someone they don't know, and politely said hello without introducing himself.

"And you are?" I asked. When he realized I didn't know who he was immediately, he opened up. We ultimately exchanged e-mails and stayed in touch.

I've found that trust is the essential element of mixing with powerful and famous people—trust that you'll be discreet; trust that you have no ulterior motives behind your approach; trust that you'll deal with them as people and not as stars; and basically trust that you feel like a peer who deserves to be engaged as such. The first few moments of an encounter is the litmus test for such a person to size up whether he or she can trust you in these ways or not.

The irony of celebrities is that they often have very fragile egos. In many cases, something in them drove them to want to be famous. Imagine being publicly scrutinized by thousands of people each day! However much the world opens up to celebrities, a part of it also closes. There is a loss of privacy. And because they live in a world of adulation, celebrities struggle every day balancing their private and public personas. They often fret over the fact that their public persona becomes indistinguishable from their private personality. They feel misunderstood and underappreciated for who they really are.

To assure them that you're interested in them for themselves, rather than what the public perceives them to be, stay away from their fame and focus, instead, on their interests. You can certainly let them know that you respect their work, but don't dwell. Take them away from what they are normally barraged with.

Unfortunately, sometimes we make inappropriate exceptions when talking to exceptional people. You simply have to watch and listen with your heart as well as with your eyes. Find out what their passions are.

Not long ago, I saw the then-Governor of Vermont, Howard Dean, give a speech. It was at Renaissance Weekend and people were joking about this unknown governor of this small state and his crazy aspirations to become President. The next time I saw him speak was at a nonprofit event for human rights in D.C. By now, he was indeed running for President, although no one took him seriously.

Intrigued by Dean and his message, I approached one of the people in his campaign staff (which, at the time, was one campaign aide and a state trooper). I told the aide that I was a politically active fellow Yale alum who was interested in meeting the presidential hopeful at some point. The aide and I had a good talk and I did talk briefly with Dean, as did many other folks at the event.

Two weeks later, there Dean was again at the Gill Foundation's annual meeting in California, preparing to deliver the same talk I had heard a couple weeks before. It would be the third time I saw him speak on essentially the same subject, and I had some thoughts on how he might deliver his speech more forcefully. I caught the attention of his aide and asked if I could get a second with the governor. We found him near the podium where he was preparing minutes before he was to go on stage. I told him that I had seen his talk on a number of occasions, I had spoken with his aide, and I had some ideas for how he could deliver his speech with more impact. I suggested that he emphasize a few points here, play down a few points there, and cut down the length. Yes, I was taking some risk, but what did I have to lose? And I was very sincere in my suggestions. I cared about his message on human rights and wanted him to get it across powerfully.

As I sat in the audience, I heard one recommendation after another come to life in his speech. Holy cow! The Governor of Vermont and by now full-fledged presidential candidate (although still a really long shot) was taking my advice. After his talk, I told him how impressive the talk was and that I wanted to devote the rest of the event to introducing him to all the movers and shakers (read: big donors) within the Gill Foundation.

Months later, when I saw the governor again at a fundraising dinner party at the director Rob Reiner's home, he was no longer an obscure candidate but a popular maverick setting the tone for the entire Democratic nomination. Someone introduced the two of us. "Governor, do you know Keith Ferrazzi?" Governor Dean replied, "Of course I know Keith. He's one of the main people responsible for me getting the traction that made such a difference in the early days." And I truly felt at that moment that I had made a difference.

Just remember that famous and powerful people are first and foremost people: They're proud, sad, insecure, hopeful, and if you can help them achieve their goals, in whatever capacity, they will be appreciative. Yes, it helps to be at the right places and invited to the right events. But the fancy weekends and invite-only conferences aren't the only ways to meet important people.

In America, there is an association for everything. If you want to meet the movers and shakers directly, you have to become a joiner. It's amazing how accessible people are when we meet them at events that speak to their interests.

Here are a few more places that I've found particularly rewarding when looking to find people on the rise or who have already risen:

Young Presidents' Organization (YPO)

This organization is for executive managers under the age of forty-four and has regional chapters across the United States. If you're running a business, or want to, there are plenty of entrepreneurial organizations that will put you in front of the corporate chieftains of tomorrow. Similar professional organizations exist for the entire range of vocational pursuits. Graphic artists, lawyers, computer programmers, and garbage collectors—like every other occupation—have a union or group that serves as an advocate for their interests. There is strength in numbers, and when you join such a group, and become a central figure in that group's activities, you'll become someone whom other powerful people will seek to deal with.

Political Fundraisers

Although I once ran for office as a Republican, I no longer openly discuss my political affiliation. Why? First, because I now vote the person and the issues, not the party. Also so I have access to those who are making a difference in both parties. I try and do three to ten fundraisers at my home each year, supporting both regional and national politicians who I believe will make a positive difference from both sides of the aisle. Politics is the nexus of money, passion, and power. In politics, the unknown person you help today is the political heavy that can help you tomorrow. Join a local campaign. Become an outspoken advocate on a particular issue; if it lights your fire, it's sure to light the fire of others: Find them and work together!

Conferences

When you have something unique to say and become a speaker, you momentarily become a celebrity in your own right. Networking is never easier than when people are coming to you. There are thousands of conferences that indulge any number of interests. If you develop a side expertise or passion, as I've suggested earlier, you can find out which well-known people share your interest and attend the conferences that these people will likely attend. Spirituality in leadership and human rights are two passions of mine; I try to participate by being active in several organizations and speaking at several conferences a year. I've met countless prominent people this way.

Nonprofit Boards

Start out by finding four or five issues that are important to you and then support them locally. Successful nonprofits seek out a few famous people to sit on their boards to help them get publicity. Eventually, the goal is to become a board member yourself and sit side by side with these people. But be sure you care and indeed want to help the cause.

Sports (Especially Golf)

Sports and exercise are terrific areas where you can meet new, important people. On the field or court, in the gym or on the track, it's a level playing field. Reputation means little. What does matter is the skill you have and the camaraderie you can create. There's something about athletics that gets people to put down their guard. Maybe competition of this sort taps into our psyche in a certain way that brings us back to a more innocent time when we were kids throwing a ball around on the street. Or maybe it's the venue itself—away from the office, on a squash court or the rolling green hills of a golf course.

Ah, golf. I would be doing you an injustice if I didn't tell you squarely that golf, among all other sports, remains the true hub of America's business elite. I've seen up close and personal how high-profile CEOs and executives lobby desperately—often for years—to be admitted into a private golf club. Why do these men and women of power endure this humiliation to play a round or two? It is, of course, the relationships, the building of friendships, the camaraderie that is created with people who they know could be very important to their company or career.

The rules of conduct are strict. It should never appear to anyone that you are trying to cash in on relationships or your membership in the club. At some clubs, to so much as hint at a future business deal on the course is a breach of etiquette; at others, you can be rather blatant about it. You'll need to feel that out. But most avid golfers will admit that the game has opened up countless opportunities. They do, ultimately, get to do business with one another—even if it's on the nineteenth hole, at the bar, over drinks. Golfers also say that the experience on the course with another person is very telling. It comes down, again, to trust. A CEO can tell if a future business partner is discreet, if he or she plays by the rules, if he or she can handle stress or is a pleasure to be around. It is both a chance to meet new people and see if these new people are up to snuff.

Because the game has proven so useful, there are many ways one can enjoy its extracurricular benefits at any level. Almost all industry associations host regular golf outings and tournaments.

Charities, conferences, and other organizations do the same in hopes of drawing this distinguished group. You can participate in any of these events without being a member.

As for me, despite my years caddying and the fact that I played for my high school team and have won a few tournaments, I don't play golf. It just takes too much time for me. Four-plus hours is just too tough. Now I play only a periodic round with friends at a wedding weekend or at a big event. But for me, it's mostly Barry's Boot Camp for my kind of sports or squash at the Yale Club in New York or a great run in Central Park or around the Hollywood Hills. Whether it's golf, tennis, bowling, or boot camp, the idea is to make it communal—join a league, a club, or an event, and you're bound to meet some new, exciting people.

There's nothing wrong with looking for ways to spend time with people who have accomplished more and have more wisdom than you. Once you put yourself in position to connect with the famous and powerful, the key is not to feel as if you're undeserving or an impostor. You're a star in your own right, with your own accomplishments, and you have a whole lot to give to the world.

CHAPTER 27

Build It and They Will Come

Call it a clan, call it a network, call it a tribe, call it a family:
Whatever you call it, whoever you are, you need one.

—JANE HOWARD

As a young man, I could relate to Groucho Marx. Like the
famous comedian, I, too, had no interest in belonging to any
club that would have me as a member.

It certainly wasn't because of some misplaced belief in self-
sufficiency: I knew then how invaluable and rewarding a gathering of people could be. You wouldn't hear any angry grumblings
out of my mouth about not having enough time. (That excuse
kills me—what could be more important than meeting like-
minded professionals?) And I certainly wasn't shy in large crowds.

It's just that all the clubs that seemed worth attending
had their doors closed to a young, relatively unconnected man
like me.

These clubs and conferences, with their selective memberships
and aura of power, exist for good reason: People are always hungry to congregate with other people with similar interests, to make
a difference in their communities, and to create an environment
that makes it easier to do business. Big company CEOs realize that
to make big things happen—whether it's public policy or a big
deal with a public company—you need others. And the more

connected, powerful, and resourceful these people are, the more you'll accomplish.

That's why the world's premier power and business gatherings, like the World Economic Forum in Davos and Renaissance Weekend, are such tough events to get into. At Renaissance Weekend, we've seen unknown politicians connect with the type of people that would lead them to become nationally known figures. At Davos, we've seen international policies formed and billion-dollar deals hatched over a cup of Swiss coffee. Of course, most of us can't get invited to Davos. But there are always gatherings and clubs to which we are not, at least initially, invited.

So you can't get into the big muckety-muck party tomorrow. Big deal. We all have the entrepreneurial spirit within us—if you can't play on a specific mountain, there's no reason not to build your own.

My friend Richard Wurman, an architect by trade, twenty years ago imagined how a convergence of technology, entertainment, and design was going to shake up the economy. "I was flying a lot, and I found that the only people who were interesting to talk to on airplanes were people in those three businesses," he has said on many an occasion. "And that when they were talking of a project they had passion about, they always included those other two professions." So to bring people in these fields together, he started the TED conference in 1984—with few attendees and his friends as guest speakers.

Opening every year with the same line, "Welcome to the dinner party I always wanted to have but couldn't," TED became the perfect event—a cross between a rollicking party and a mesmerizing graduate seminar. Year after year, more and more people came from all walks of life: scientists, authors, actors, CEOs, professors. At TED, it wouldn't be odd to see musician/producer Quincy Jones having a chat with Newscorp CEO Rupert Murdoch, or movie director Oliver Stone arguing with Oracle's founder and CEO Larry J. Ellison.

From money-losing get-together to exclusive confab, TED eventually took in upward of $3 million a year, almost all profit. Richard paid no speaker fees and organized the event with just a few assistants. He sold TED for $14 million in 2001, and is now busy running a new conference called TEDmed, about the convergence of technology and health, which I highly recommend.

I tried to do something similar when, as a fresh-faced MBA, I moved to Chicago after taking a job with Deloitte. I barely knew anyone in the city. The first thing I did was ask people to introduce me to their friends in Chicago. As I met with the people my friends had suggested, I began to inquire what boards I could join to get more involved in the life of the city. Doing so, I knew, would inevitably lead to increased business for my new company.

I was so young that no one really took me seriously. The traditional options, like the symphony board or country clubs, were not open to me. I had lots of offers to join the junior boards. But they were basically social groups. I wanted to be more of an activist, to make a real difference in the community. I didn't just want to host wine-tastings at a twenty-something dating mixer.

At a time like this, you have to figure out what is your U.S.P.— "unique selling proposition," for all you non-MBA types out there. What secret sauce can you bring to the table? Your proposition can be an expertise, a hobby, or even an interest or passion for a particular cause that will serve as the foundation from which an entire organization or club can be established.

All clubs are based on common interests. Members are united by a similar job, philosophy, hobby, neighborhood, or simply because they are the same race, religion, or generation. They are bound by a common proposition that is unique to them. They have, in other words, a reason to hang out together.

You can take your own distinctive proposition and then take the extra step that most people don't. Start an organization. And invite those you want to meet to join you. Gaining members will be easy. Like most clubs, it starts with your group of friends, who then select their own friends. Over time, those people will bring in even more new and intriguing people.

This is an enormously successful model that even thriving businesses have built upon. Think about the successful Internet sites that pooled people together around a common proposition—like political affiliation, gardening, or even, in the case of iVillage, being a woman—and built profitable enterprises on the feeling of belonging to that community. Think, also, of airline miles or your local grocery store where you get a discount for being a member of a loyalty program. Building a community of like-minded people around a common cause or interest is, and has always been, a very compelling proposition in its own right.

In those days, my proposition came from my personal interest in the popular business concept at the time called Total Quality Management (TQM), which, as I've described, formed the basis of my content that I used to differentiate myself at my first job out of Yale and then during a stint working with one of the professors at business school.

On a national level, the government had established an organization called the Baldrige National Quality Program that rewarded companies who exhibited excellence in TQM. In Illinois, I thought I could create a similar nonprofit organization for local companies. With a federal program already in the works, I figured it would not be too difficult to find others with a similar interest— judges and other members of the national organization who lived in Chicago, consultants, and employees of big corporations whose job it was to deal with TQM.

The first thing I needed to do was enlist the support of an institution or expert in TQM in order to attract other potential members. I asked the head of TQM for First Chicago, Aleta Belletete, to join me as cofounder. She then pulled in her boss and one of the most influential CEOs in Chicago at the time, Dick Thomas, who gave us his blessing and agreed to adopt the initiative as one he personally supported. With Dick's backing, Governor Jim Edgar gladly assigned his Lieutenant Governor to our board. In landing the support of these three people, our start-up organization got a big dose of credibility. Soon a whole host of people was willing to be part of the enterprise, including the leaders of TQM at Amoco and Rush Presbyterian Hospital, who also brought their CEOs on board. The kicker: Because I had started the organization, I was president! Of course, now we had to create, run, and finance this enterprise. But the hard part was now done. We were a credible institution, and from here we all just rolled up our sleeves and got to the nitty-gritty work, which is also critical.

Thus was born The Lincoln Award for Business Excellence (ABE). The organization still exists today as a successful not-for-profit foundation that assists Illinois organizations in building sound businesses. It has hundreds and hundreds of volunteers, a large board, and a full-time staff. Two years after I started it, I knew every major CEO in Chicago on a first-name basis.

The lesson? Even a Harvard MBA or an invitation to Davos is no substitute for personal initiative. If you can't find an outfit to join that allows you to make a difference, then recognize what you do have to offer—your particular expertise, contacts, interests, or experience. Rally people behind them and make your own difference.

The days when clubs were only for wealthy white men to consort with people just like themselves are over. It doesn't matter if it's a group of carpet salespeople meeting weekly to discuss the trials and tribulations of their jobs; a roundtable of female Republicans who are dissatisfied with the stance of the state party; or a group who share a passion for great wines and who come together monthly to do tastings, hear vintners who are traveling through the area, and who plan an annual trip to Napa. Whatever it is and whoever you are don't matter.

As long as it's as an association of people with shared interests meeting in a specified place (even if that place is cyberspace), you'll benefit from belonging to something larger than yourself. You and your fellow members will be strengthened by a collective identity. And whereas with business, where boundaries of most relationships are clearly defined by a specific project or deal and end when that project or deal is done, membership in a club (preferably a club you've started) will lead to friendships that will last for years.

CONNECTORS' HALL OF FAME PROFILE
Benjamin Franklin (1706–1790)
"Can't join a club? Organize your own."

The business term *networking*, as it happens, joined the English language in 1966. But more than two centuries earlier, in Philadelphia, a young Benjamin Franklin used this sweet social science to become one of the most influential men in our as-yet-untitled nation. Before he became a revered patriot, statesman, and inventor, he was one of America's most successful businessmen, rising from indentured servant to printing tycoon.

Flip your calendars, if you will, back to 1723, at which time the seventeen-year-old Franklin was neither wealthy nor accomplished. He was an aspiring entrepreneur—trained in the printing trade by his brother James—and a fresh face in Philadelphia, having moved there after failing to find work in New York. Knowing no one in his new town, but eager to start his own print shop, Franklin began to flex his connecting mojo.

Within seven months, Franklin—who'd landed a job in an established print shop—made the acquaintance of Pennsylvania Governor William Keith. The governor encouraged young Franklin to travel to London to buy whatever equipment he'd need to start his own press. Keith even promised letters of reference and credit, both of which Franklin would need to purchase a printing press and type.

But upon reaching London, Franklin found that Keith had not furnished these letters. Franklin spent the next two years earning enough money to simply sail back to America. On his return voyage, Franklin again displayed his networking virtuosity: His first job, back in Philadelphia, was as a clerk in the store of Thomas Denham, a fellow passenger on his trans-Atlantic voyage.

Before long, Franklin was back in the print trade, employed in the same established print shop as before. In the interest of intellectual stimulation and his own self-advancement, Franklin organized a dozen of his friends into a Friday night social group called the "Junto"—described, as follows, in *The Autobiography*:

> The rules that I drew up required that every member, in his turn, should produce one or more queries on any point of Morals, Politics, or Natural Philosophy [physics], to be discuss'd by the company; and once in three months produce and read an essay of his own writing, on any subject he pleased.

The members of the Junto were young men not yet respectable or established enough to break into the clubs that served Philadelphia's business elite. Like Franklin, they were tradesmen, common people. No doubt about it—the man loved clubs. Indeed, in addition to its lessons of thrift, industry, and prudence, Franklin's autobiography tells us every man should be part of a social group, if not three. He believed that a group of like-minded, achievement-oriented individuals could dramatically leverage each other's success to do things otherwise impossible.

Now flash those calendars forward, if you can, to 1731. Franklin, having earned enough to start his own print shop, invested in a small failing newspaper, the *Pennsylvania Gazette*. Through snappy content and graphics (much of it written or drawn by Franklin himself) and daring distribution, Franklin turned the *Gazette* into a profitable vehicle with the largest circulation in the colonies. The newspaper's prosperity transformed Franklin into an eighteenth-century media magnate. Franklin gained enough renown—and money—to apply himself to public projects, the first

of which was the establishment of the Library Company of Philadelphia, the first circulating library in North America (still in existence).

It was the library campaign—the first of Franklin's several public
projects for Philadelphia—that gave Franklin a deep insight into
one of the crown virtues of networking. The resistance he encoun-
tered, he tells us:

> [M]ade me soon feel the Impropriety of presenting one's self
> as the Proposer of any useful Project that might be suppos'd to
> raise one's Reputation in the smallest degree above that of
> one's Neighbors, when one has need of their Assistance to
> accomplish that Project. I therefore put my self as much as I
> could out of sight, and stated it as a Scheme of a Number of
> Friends, who had requested me to go about and propose it to
> such as they thought Lovers of Reading. In this way my Affair
> went on more smoothly, and I ever after practis'd it on such
> Occasions.

And, oh, would there be "Occasions." Following the library in
1731—for which the Junto helped Franklin find his first fifty sub-
scribers—there came Philadelphia's city watch (1735); its first fire
company (1736); its first college, which would two years later
become the University of Pennsylvania (1749); its first—and also
the colonies' first hospital, through a mixture of public and private
funding (1751); and its first fire insurance company (1751).
Franklin also organized Pennsylvania's first volunteer militia (1747)
and introduced a program of paving, lighting, and cleaning
Philadelphia's streets (1756). Each project depended upon the
assistance of Franklin's network of personal and professional connections, and with each project his network grew, along with his
reputation as a doer of good.

Franklin died in April 1790, about one year into George Washington's first term. More than 20,000 Americans attended his
funeral.

With networking, as in so much else, we follow a trail that
Franklin blazed. From him we also learn the value of modesty and

the power of teamwork—beginning first with a group of young tradesmen that he brought together in his Junto and ending with the powerful men who hammered out the Declaration of Independence and the Constitution of the United States.

CHAPTER 28

Never Give in to Hubris

In my Ph.D. section on connecting, I tried to impart some of the lessons I've learned as someone known as a master at connecting with people. But I'd be remiss if I didn't tell one short, embarrassing story that taught me early on what may be the most important lesson of all.

It is a cautionary tale about what not to do and how not to act.

The pursuit of a powerful network of friends is not in and of itself a bad thing. But the closer you get to powerful people, the more powerful you tend to feel. There is a point where your reaching out to others will pick up momentum; one powerful contact will lead to another and then to the next. It can be a very fun and motivating and important ride.

Don't let a little vanity seep into your actions or excite more expectations or create a deeper sense of entitlement. Don't get your Ph.D. in master connecting, and then, for some reason, forget all the classes and values that were your foundation.

Everyone fails in life. What will you do when the phone calls that were once returned immediately now don't even get a response?

When I ran for City Council of New Haven as a sophomore

against a fellow classmate, the idea of a kid running for local government made a special-interest news item. It wasn't long before a reporter from the *New York Times* showed up to write an article. Little did I know then that that one *Times* article would provide me with one of the more painful and useful lessons of my life. For it would lead to my angering William F. Buckley Jr., the famous Yale alum known for founding the conservative magazine *National Review* and authoring dozens of books.

I ran for office as a Republican. The Republicans needed a candidate, and at Yale, they were the minority as opposed to the many limousine liberals who seemed to a steelworking kid from Pittsburgh insincere and unthinking. Anyway, I was a youngster, and I was still exploring my political sensibilities. I probably also had a certain affinity for the traditionalism of the moderate conservative party on campus called the Tories and a real fondness for their parties and the commitment of their leadership and alumni.

But this story is not about politics. It's about pride and ego.

Back then, I hadn't yet realized that my upbringing could be a well of strength rather than weakness. Insecurity drove me to act in ways I wish I hadn't. My leadership style, for instance, was far from inclusive. While I was racking up accomplishments, my sheer will and ambition alienated a lot of people. I trumpeted my awards and failed to recognize those who had helped make them possible. Too much hubris and not enough humility, as my dad might say, though not in so many words.

I was showing all those kids whom I had caddied for back at the club that I was just as good as they were.

I lost the election, as you know, but the *New York Times* article had been read by quite a number of people, and by a few who thought being a Republican at Yale was a good thing. In my mailbox, weeks after the election, I received a short note.

"So happy to see that there is at least one Republican at Yale. Come see me sometime. WFB."

William F. Buckley Jr. had taken the time to write *me*! I was floored. I became an instant celebrity in our small circle.

Of course, the man had issued an invitation and I, for one, was going to take him up on the offer. I immediately set about contacting Mr. Buckley to set a date for a meeting. He graciously invited me to his home and even suggested I bring a few friends along.

A few months later, with three other classmates in tow, I arrived at a Connecticut train station where we were greeted by none other than Mr. Buckley himself in an old pair of khakis and a wrinkled button-down shirt. He drove us to his home, where we met his wife, who was gardening at the time. It was a glorious day. We shared a few glasses of wine, talked politics, Mr. Buckley played the harpsichord, and then we all sat down for a lengthy lunch. Afterward, we were invited to take a dip in the Buckleys' beautiful pool with tile mosaics reminiscent of a Roman bath.

I couldn't let the opportunity pass. Mr. Buckley wasn't the only Yale alum dissatisfied with the political climate at his alma mater. Other conservative alumni were complaining. Many stopped giving money to Yale outright. I thought I had a solution that would be a real win-win for the campus and for these alums.

What if, I suggested, we create a foundation that allowed disenfranchised conservative alums the ability to give money directly to the undergraduate organizations that represented the traditional values they supported? Yale wins because it would be getting money that it otherwise wouldn't. Conservative alumni win because they could again feel good about their school and their ability to make a contribution. Students win because there would be more organizational diversity and money for campus clubs. What could be better?

Well, I made the pitch and I thought Mr. Buckley embraced the idea. He told me that he had started a foundation to fund a student publication a few years before that had never quite got off the ground. There was, he said, still money in the foundation, and he would be happy to put it toward my idea. That is, at least, what I heard. In my excitement, I left the i's undotted and t's uncrossed for fear of a good thing getting spoiled. "Never sell beyond the close," as they say, and I thought I had the close.

Do *they* ever add that you better be damn sure both parties know what, exactly, is being closed and that both remember thereafter?

When I returned to campus, I didn't conceal my excitement. I made sure everyone knew that I was the new president of a brand-spankin'-new organization. Boy, wasn't I cool? I started searching out other alumni who might be interested in contributing to the cause. I hit the phones, and on weekends, I'd go to New York to pitch other alumni on the new foundation that William F. Buckley and I were starting.

"Bill Buckley put in some money. Would you also like to help out?" I'd ask them. And they did. On each return trip from New York, my head got bigger and bigger as I reveled in the famous and powerful people that were giving me (note the use of "me," not "us") money.

My poor classmates had to suffer my telling stories of my latest escapade to New York. Then, as quickly as it started, my ever-so-brief brush with fame came to a screeching halt.

As luck would have it, Mr. Buckley found himself one day in an elevator with one of the other famous alums who had pledged money. "Bill," this gentleman said, "I matched your contribution to this new foundation at Yale." To which Bill replied, "What foundation?"

It turned out that Mr. Buckley did not recall our conversation. Or maybe he told me one thing and I heard something quite different. Maybe he just thought I wanted to rekindle the magazine. But by then, it was irrelevant. Mr. Buckley could recall only his stalled magazine and a vague reference to restarting it at Yale. He told the other donor he was not the cofounder of a new conservative foundation at Yale, which I'm sure was the way he saw it. At which point, everything unraveled.

The pledges I had received needed to go unrealized, as there was no repository for them any longer. Mr. Buckley didn't return my calls. Most important, and to my shock, my friends who were present and equally excited that day at Mr. Buckley's didn't come to my rescue when I pleaded for them to explain that they had heard exactly what I had heard. My reputation had been tarnished among some important people. I was embarrassed among my friends after I had been gloating. And then to add rock salt to the wound, someone at Yale's college newspaper got wind of all that had happened and created an illustration depicting me as getting wounded by large, famous names being dropped from the sky. Ouch, indeed, and I deserved it.

Looking back now, I'm appreciative of the experience. I learned some valuable lessons. For one, I had to begin the journey to change my leadership style. It wasn't enough to get things done. You had to get things done and make the people around you feel involved, and not just part of the process but part of the leadership. I learned that commitments weren't commitments unless everyone involved knew what was on the table with absolute clarity. I learned how truly small the world is, especially the world of the rich and powerful.

Most important, I learned that arrogance is a disease that can betray you into forgetting your real friends and why they're so important. Even with the best of intentions, too much hubris will stir up other people's ire and their desire to put you in your place. So remember, in your hike up the mountain, be humble. Help others up the mountain along with and before you. Never let the prospect of a more powerful or famous acquaintance make you lose sight of the fact that the most valuable connections you have are those you've already made at all levels. I reach back into my past regularly to touch base with the folks who have meant so much to me since I was a kid. I go out of my way to tell the early mentors what they meant to me and how much they were responsible for my success today.

CHAPTER 29

Find Mentors, Find Mentees, Repeat

To teach is to learn again.

—H. J. BROWN

Great musicians know it. So do professional athletes and world-class public speakers. Successful people in nearly every field know that they can't be their best unless they have a good coach in their corner. And now the business world knows it, too: In a fast-paced, fluid, and dynamic environment, where flattened organizations made up of cross-functional teams must respond rapidly to change, mentoring is one of the most effective strategies to get the best out of each and every individual.

Many companies have developed formal mentoring programs with the idea that sharing what you know and learning what others have to teach is just smart management. At FerrazziGreenlight, we have worked with many companies to create such formal programs with the idea that helping employees build relationships for career success reduces turnover and ultimately leads to stronger external relationships for revenue growth as well. One of the more historically successful programs was established in 1997 at one of Intel's largest chip-making facilities in New Mexico.

The people responsible for developing that program wanted to go beyond the traditional notion of mentoring as a one-way process that teamed seasoned executives with ambitious up-and-comers. To the people at Intel, organization-wide mentoring meant creating an inclusive learning network matching people not by job title or by seniority but by specific skills that are in demand. The company uses an intranet site and e-mail to break down departmental barriers and create partnerships between two people who can teach each other different valuable skills that they need to be better employees. The system enables Intel to spread best practices quickly throughout the global organization and develop the best and brightest employees in the industry.

While it's wonderful the business world is finally catching on, mentoring—a lifelong process of giving and receiving in a never-ending role as both master and apprentice—has always been the Holy Grail for those who love to connect people with people.

No process in history has done more to facilitate the exchange of information, skills, wisdom, and contacts than mentoring. Young men and women learned their trade by studying as apprentices under their respective craftsmen. Young artists developed their individual style only after years working under elder masters. New priests apprenticed for a decade or more with older priests to become wise religious men themselves. When finally these men and women embarked on their own, they had the knowledge and the connections to succeed in their chosen field.

By studying the lives of those who know more than we do, we expand our horizons. As a child, I realized that many of the opportunities other kids had that would expose them to new things and new people, like summer camp or extra tutoring, were unavailable to me. I quickly learned that success in my life would require determination, exploration, self-reliance, and a strong will. I also learned to rely on other people who *were* available: my father and some of the more professional people he knew in our neighborhood.

My mom and dad instructed me to observe how the most successful people we knew worked and talked and lived. My parents told me I could learn how to live my life by watching others live their lives. My dad, of course, did all he could to nurture and teach me what he knew. But he wanted me to know more than that; like most fathers, he wanted me to be more than he was. He gave me the confidence I needed to go out, without pride or insecurity, and develop relationships with the men and women he knew whom he respected.

Perhaps the value he placed on mentors came from Damon Runyon, one of my father's favorite authors. A tough guy who dropped out of school by the sixth grade and bootstrapped his way to success, Runyon's tough-luck stories about equally tough characters had a lot of emotional resonance for my dad. His favorite quote of Runyon's was "Always try to rub up against money, for if you rub up against money long enough, some of it may rub off on you." No surprise, then, that my dad wanted me rubbing up against people with more money, more knowledge, and more skills than he had.

Before I was even ten years old, I remember him encouraging me to bike down our dusty driveway to hang out with our neighbors. By the time I was in grade school, I had reached out to George Love, the father of one of my friends and a local attorney. Dad would take me to see Walt Saling, a stockbroker, every so often just to visit. I'd sit close by and pepper Walt with questions about his job and the people he worked with. When I came home from prep school, Dad and I would go on our "rounds." We'd go visit those people Dad thought I'd learn something from: Toad and Julie Repasky, who owned the local cement plant and whom Dad used to work for, or the Fontanella sisters, who used to tutor me in Latin and math when I was growing up. These men and women of our town were the celebrities for our working-class family. They were professionals with a good education, and that meant they had something to teach.

The fact is, from my father's perspective, everyone had something to offer. When he'd go out for his weekly sit-down at a local diner with his friends, he took me along. He wanted me to be comfortable with older, more experienced people and to never fear seeking their help or asking them questions. When my dad would show up with me in tow on a Friday night, his buddies would say, "Here's Pete [my father's name] and Re-Pete [my nickname to his buddies]."

I look back on those times with so much gratitude and emotion. At every turn, and to this very day, I still try to connect with trailblazers, head honchos, and people who have experienced a different life than I've had.

My father and Runyon were onto something in a way, perhaps, that was even more profound than they imagined. Research now backs up their belief that whom you associate with is crucial to who you become. Dr. David McClelland of Harvard University researched the qualities and characteristics of high achievers in our society. What he found was that your choice of a "reference group," the people you hang out with, was an important factor in determining your future success or failure. In other words, if you hang with connected people, you're connected. If you hang with successful people, you're more likely to become successful yourself.

Let me explain how important mentoring became for me through an experience I had early on in my career. It was toward the end of the summer before my second year at business school. Deloitte and Touche, the accounting and consulting firm I had been interning with during that summer, was having its annual end-of-the-summer cocktail party for its interns from all around the country.

Off to the corner, amid all the clink of drinks and polite chatter, I saw a bunch of the partners and senior staff hanging around this big, gruff, white-haired guy who was holding court. Other interns stayed in their comfortable cliques, keeping their distance from their bosses, but I headed straight for the poobahs. It was, really, no different from riding my bike down the road to see the neighbors.

I went straight up to the man in the center of all this action, introduced myself, and asked him point blank, "Who are you?"

"I'm the CEO of this firm," he said with an abruptness that signaled I should have known that, while the partners around him smiled and chuckled mischievously.

He was about six-foot-three, barrel-chested, and very, very direct. He's the kind of guy who just fills the room with his presence.

"Well, I guess I should have known that," I responded.

"Yeah, I guess you should have," he said. He was joking, and as is often the case with people in positions of power, he liked my candor and chutzpah. He introduced himself as Pat Loconto.

"Loconto," I said. "That's a good Jewish name, isn't it?"

He laughed, and I talked with him in the little Italian that he and I knew. In short order, we were fully engaged, talking about our families and our similar upbringing. His dad was also a first-generation Italian-American who instilled in him many of the same values my father had taught me. I did, in fact, know Pat, but only by reputation. I had heard about his no-nonsense style—tough and tireless but warmhearted, too. I decided then and there that getting to know him better might not be a bad idea.

That I approached him at the cocktail party and discovered we were cut from similar cloth deepened my respect for the man and his respect for me. I found out later that quickly after that exchange, he followed up and found out everything about me and my summer with the firm. That night I hung out with Pat and the senior partners into the wee hours of the morning. I didn't try to be anyone I wasn't. I didn't overstretch and pretend to know more than I did. Many people believe that's what it takes when reaching out to those above you, but in truth that often results in making a jerk out of yourself.

I remembered that my father and mother had told me to speak less in such situations; the less you say, the more you'll likely hear. They were warning me, given my predisposition for dominating a conversation from an early age. That's the way you learn from others, Dad said, and glean the small nuances that will help you engender a deeper relationship later on. There's also no better way to signal your interest in becoming a mentee. People tacitly notice your respect and are flattered by the attention. That said, quiet for me isn't exactly quiet. I asked tons of questions, suggested things that I saw from the summer, and conspired with these leaders of the firm on what was important to them—making the firm a success.

Mentoring is a very deliberate activity that requires people to check their ego at the door, hold back from resenting other people's success, and consciously strive to build beneficial relationships whenever the opportunity arises. Other interns at that party looked at Pat and the other senior partners with intimidation and boredom (What do I have in common with them?) and therefore kept their distance. They looked at their job titles versus the bigwigs' and felt excluded, and because of it, they were.

When I finally graduated from school, in typical MBA fashion, I interviewed with several companies. My choice was coming down to Deloitte Consulting and one of their competitors, McKinsey. McKinsey was then considered the gold standard of consulting companies. For most of my peers, the choice would have been obvious.

Then, one afternoon, I got a call the day before my final McKinsey interview. When I picked up the phone, I was met with a familiar gruff voice. "Accept our offer now and you can come down to New York for dinner this evening with me and some of my partners." Before I had a chance to respond, he said, "It's Pat Loconto. I want to know if you're coming to Deloitte or not?"

I told Pat, uncomfortably, that I hadn't decided on where I'd end up. But I had an idea that might help me through the process. "Listen, I'm still up in the air," I told him. "But it would help if I had dinner with you and a few partners to get a better feel for what I'd be doing and where the organization is headed."

"I'll have dinner with you only if you accept my offer," he said. Pat was joking again, and I liked him even more for his unorthodox recruiting practices. Then he let me off the hook with, "OK, get your butt down to New York, and don't worry, we'll get you out to Chicago in the morning for your interview." Now, how did he know about my interview?

So I found myself with Pat and a few partners around a table at Grifone, their favorite Italian restaurant in Manhattan. The banter was hard and heavy, as was the drinking. We had gone through bottles and bottles of great wine and a few cognacs on top of that. Near the end of dinner, Pat threw out his pitch and actually launched into a fairly shocking tirade.

"Who the hell do you think you are? You think McKinsey gives a damn about Keith Ferrazzi?" Before I could answer, he continued. "You think the CEO of McKinsey knows who you are? You think any of the senior partners would take a Sunday night to have dinner with you? You'll be just another number-crunching MBA grad lost in the shuffle. We care about you. We want you to be successful here. More importantly, we think you can make a difference in our firm."

Was I in? Pat demanded to know.

Wow, his pitch was compelling, and right then my instinct told me he was right. I knew he was right. But I wasn't about to leave that dinner without making a small pitch of my own.

"Look, I'll make you a deal," I said. "If I accept your offer, all I ask is that you give me three dinners a year at this very restaurant for as long as I'm at Deloitte. I'm in if you're in."

He looked me in the eyes and then with the biggest smile said, "Great. Welcome to Deloitte."

By the way, I then asked him for more money. He just shook his head and laughed. Well, it never hurts to ask; the worst he could have said was no. So, after three hours in a restaurant, this man convinced me to make a life-changing career decision without one word about title, salary, or even one detail of how he expected I might make a difference.

Honestly, I still had my doubts at the beginning that I had made the right move. In consulting, Deloitte's was smaller potatoes those days; its prestige didn't compare with McKinsey's.

But what a right move I had made—in fact, it was the best of my life. First, because I went to Deloitte Consulting, I was given more responsibilities and I learned more about consulting in the eight years that followed than most people learn in twenty. Second, I found I could make a difference given my access to the senior partners. Third, and most important, I realized that finding a talented, experienced mentor who is willing to invest the time and effort to develop you as a person and a professional is far more important than making career decisions based purely on salary or prestige.

Besides, back then the money wasn't important. You learn in your twenties, as the saying goes, and earn in your thirties. And boy, did I ever learn. Each year, Pat and I had at least three dinners at Grifone, that same Italian restaurant. For my entire tenure at Deloitte, I had the ear of the CEO, and he kept asking about me among his partners. He was looking out for me the entire time.

Ultimately, of course, I got to work closely with Pat and other amazing men and women at Deloitte, and it taught me the importance of attaching yourself to great people, great teachers. Not that working with Pat and his right-hand man Bob Kirk was easy. They taught me some hard lessons about staying focused; that bold ideas weren't enough if they couldn't be executed; that the details are as significant as the theories; that you had to put people first, *all* people, not just those above you. Pat probably should have fired me a few times. Instead, he invested time and energy into making me the kind of executive—and more important, the kind of leader—he wanted me to be for the sake of the firm and for the sake of his role as mentor.

There were two crucial components that made my mentorship with Pat—and makes any mentorship, for that matter—successful. He offered his guidance because, for one, I promised something in return. I worked nonstop in an effort to use the knowledge he was imparting to make him, and his firm, more successful. And two, we created a situation that went beyond utility. Pat liked me and became emotionally invested in my advancement. He cared about me. That's the key to a successful mentorship. A successful mentoring relationship needs equal parts utility and emotion. You can't simply ask somebody to be personally invested in you. There has to be some reciprocity involved—whether it's hard work or loyalty that you give in return—that gets someone to invest in you in the first place. Then, when the process kicks in, you have to mold your mentor into a coach; someone for whom your success is in some small or big way his success. I owe so much to Pat. If it were not for him, I would not be the man I am today. And that goes for so many others, starting with my Mom and Dad and Jack Pidgeon from the Kiski School, and my "Uncle" Bob Wilson, to so so so many others I've mentioned in this book, as well as those left unmentioned but to whom I feel so close.

The best way to approach utility is to give help first, and not ask for it. If there is someone whose knowledge you need, find a way to be of use to that person. Consider their needs and how you can assist them. If you can't help them specifically, perhaps you can contribute to their charity, company, or community. You have to be prepared to give back to your mentors and have them know that from the outset. Before Pat would consider having dinner with me three times a year, he had to know that I would be committed to his firm. That's how I found myself so early on in a trusted position that later turned into a friendship.

If, however, there are no immediate opportunities to help, you must be prudent and conscious of the imposition you're placing on that person. Almost every day, some ambitious young man or woman sends me an e-mail that states all too directly, "I want a job." Or, "I think you can help me. Take me on as your mentee." I shudder at how deeply these young folks misunderstand the process. If they're going to get my help, and they haven't even offered their help in return, then at minimum they should attempt to endear themselves to me. Tell me why you're special. Tell me what we have in common. Express gratitude, excitement, and passion.

The problem is often that these people have never had mentors before and they have a limited view of how it works. Some people think there is just one special person out there waiting to be all things at all times to them. But as my father taught me, mentors are all around you. It's not necessarily your boss or even someone in your business. Mentoring is a nonhierarchical activity that transcends careers and can cross all organizational levels.

A CEO can learn from a manager, and vice versa. Some smart companies, recognizing this fact, actually have programs in place that view new hires as mentors to the company. After a month on the job, they'll ask these new employees to jot down all their impressions with the idea that a pair of fresh eyes can see old problems and make innovative suggestions that others can't.

In fact, the people I've learned so much from are my own young mentees, who help me periodically to update my skills and view the world anew.

As much as you stretch yourself by reaching up, be sure you are stretching just as far to reach back and help others. I've always taken the time to give young people a helping hand. Most of them actually end up working for me at some point, either as interns or employees. People like Paul Lussow, Chad Hodge, Hani Abisaid, Andy Bohn, Brinda Chugani, Anna Mongayt, John Lux, Jason Annis. The list goes on and on.

There are those who don't get it at first. They sheepishly ask, "How can I ever repay you for all that you are doing?" I tell them they're repaying me now. All I really expect is sincere gratitude, and to see them apply all that they are learning.

To see Brinda moving up at Deloitte, Hani becoming a partner in one of my businesses and "graduating" into a new company I had a hand in forming, Chad becoming one of Hollywood's most successful young writers, Andy becoming a player in Hollywood himself, or Paul attending Wharton is a total thrill. It's even more so when they get to a point in their careers when they start becoming mentors themselves.

I can't stress enough how powerful the process is and how important it is that you give your respect and time to it. In return, you'll be more than compensated with spirit, enthusiasm, trust, and empathy—all things that will ultimately far exceed the value of any advice you gave.

If you take mentoring seriously, and give it the time and energy it deserves, you'll soon find yourself involved in a learning network not unlike the one Intel uses. You'll be the recipient of more information and more goodwill than you ever imagined, as you play the role of both master and apprentice in a powerful constellation of people all simultaneously teaching and being taught.

CONNECTORS' HALL OF FAME PROFILE
Eleanor Roosevelt (1884–1962)

"Connecting should advance, rather than compromise, your principles."

If connecting can be described, loosely, as the commingling of friendship and mission, then First Lady Eleanor Roosevelt was one of the twentieth century's premier practitioners. In her autobiography, she wrote: being "drawn together through the work . . . is . . . one of the most satisfying ways of making and keeping friends." Through groups such as the International Congress of Working Women and the Women's International League of Peace and Freedom (WILPF), Roosevelt befriended a wide circle of friends—and a few foes—in advancing some of the great social causes of our time.

The First Lady was not timid about using her personal network to tackle testy social issues. For example, she fought for women's rights in the workplace—their inclusion in labor unions and their right to a living wage. Today, those seem like uncontroversial issues, but during the late 1920s and early 1930s, many Americans *blamed* working women for displacing male "breadwinners" in the midst of the Great Depression.

Roosevelt believed the beauty and obligation of living in a democracy was to make a stand for what you believe in; and she proved you could do so while gaining the trust and admiration of your peers. She also proved that sometimes it was *your peers* whom you need to stand up *against*.

In 1936, thanks largely to the First Lady, an opera singer named Marian Anderson became the first black person to perform at the White House. But Anderson's acceptance at 1600 Pennsylvania Avenue was unusual. Though Anderson was the country's third-highest concert box-office draw, her success did not exempt her from the racial biases that pervaded her era. When traveling, she was restricted to "colored" waiting rooms, hotels, and train cars. In the South, newspapers rarely called her "Miss Anderson," opting for "Artist Anderson" and "Singer Anderson" instead.

In 1939, Anderson's manager and Howard University tried to arrange a performance at Constitution Hall in Washington, D.C. The Daughters of the American Revolution (D.A.R.), the organization that owned the Hall, refused them. Roosevelt, herself a member of the D.A.R., promptly—and publicly—resigned her membership to protest. In a letter to the D.A.R., she wrote: *"I am in complete disagreement with the attitude taken in refusing Constitution Hall to a great artist . . . You had an opportunity to lead in an enlightened way and it seems to me that your organization has failed."*

Mrs. Roosevelt arranged for Anderson to perform on the steps of the Lincoln Memorial. The show, on April 9 (Easter Sunday), 1939, was seen by a crowd of 75,000.

Yes, loyalty matters. But not when it means sacrificing your principles.

Though Eleanor Roosevelt's positions on civil rights hardly seem radical today, they were far in advance of her time: All of this was *decades* before the Supreme Court, in its 1954 *Brown v. Board of Education* case, rejected the "separate but equal" doctrine.

Every time the First Lady advocated for a social cause, preached tolerance in a black church or Jewish temple, or even when, acting as a delegate to the newly formed United Nations, which passed the controversial Universal Declaration of Human Rights, she lost friends and received vicious criticism for going against the tide.

Still, this amazing woman persisted in successfully building influence for a progressive agenda. She left a legacy to which we are all indebted. What can we learn from Eleanor Roosevelt? It's not enough simply to reach out to others; instead, we all must be vigilant that our efforts to bring people together are in line with our efforts to, in part, make the world a better place.

Of course, when you're driven by principles, there are always sacrifices involved. But your determination to connect with others should never come at the expense of your values. In fact, your network of colleagues and friends, if chosen wisely, can help you fight for causes you believe in.

CHAPTER 30

Balance Is B.S.

Balance is a myth.

You can't call my schedule "balanced" by conventional standards. Let's take a look at a typical day. Monday: I was up at 4 A.M. in Los Angeles to make calls to my team in New York. Then I worked the phone for a few more hours, trying to organize a fundraiser for a candidate friend of mine. By 7 A.M., I was at the airport for a flight to Portland, Oregon, to meet a new customer (with two cell phones buzzing, fidgeting with my BlackBerry, sending short e-mails, and my laptop never far away with spreadsheet access). After the meeting, I'm back in the car on my way to Seattle and back on the phone, setting up meetings for tonight, tomorrow, and a week from now. I'm in constant contact with my assistant, trying to get invitations out for a big dinner party I'm throwing in a month. In Seattle, I have a scheduled dinner with the folks organizing Bill Gates's CEO conference this year, after which I'll have drinks with some close friends. And tomorrow, there will be another 4 A.M. wake-up call to do it all again.

Welcome to what my friends jokingly refer to as "Ferrazzi

Time," a zone of operations in which the switchboards are always open and the rush of humanity is ongoing.

Witnessing such a schedule begs a number of very important questions: Is this a life? Operating in such a way, can one have balance between work and having a life? And do you—God forbid— have to operate in Ferrazzi Time to be successful?

The answers are: Yes, it is a life, albeit my own; yes, you can find balance, albeit your own; and no, thank heavens, you don't have to do it my way.

For me, the best thing about a relationship-driven career is that it isn't a career at all. It's a way of living. Several years ago, I started to realize that connecting was actually a way of seeing the world. When I thought and behaved in that way, dividing my life between professional and personal spheres no longer made sense. I realized that what made you successful in both worlds were other people and the way you related to them. Whether those people were family people, work people, or friend people, real connecting insists that you bring the same values to every relationship. As a result, I no longer needed to make a distinction between my career happiness and my life happiness—they were both pieces of me. My life.

When it became clear to me that the key to my life was the relationships in it, I found there was no longer a need to compartmentalize work from, say, family or friends. I could spend my birthday at a business conference and be surrounded with warm and wonderful friends, as I recently did, or I could be at home in Los Angeles or New York with equally close friends to celebrate.

The kind of false idea of balance as some sort of an equation, that you could take this many hours from one side of your life and give it to this other side, flew out the window. And with it went all the stress of trying to achieve that perfect state of equilibrium we read and hear so much about.

Balance can't be bought or sold. It doesn't need to be "implemented." Balance is a mind-set, as individual and unique as our genetic code. Where you find joy, you find balance. My wacky schedule works for me and perhaps only for me. The blurring of professional and personal lives isn't for everyone. The important thing is to see connecting with others not just as another manipulative tool used toward achieving a goal but rather as a way of life. When you're out of balance, you'll know because you'll be rushed, angry, and unfulfilled. When you're balanced, you'll be joyful, enthusiastic, and full of gratitude.

Don't worry about trying to develop your own version of Ferrazzi Time. The way you reach out to others is the way you eat an 800-pound gorilla: one small bite at a time.

In the end, we all live one life. And that life is all about the people we live it with.

More People, More Balance

If you buy into the myth of balance (the one that sees life as an equation), as I once did, the answers to such questions as "If I'm so 'accomplished,' why aren't I having more fun?" or "If I'm so 'organized,' why do I feel so out of control?" is to "simplify," "compartmentalize," or "reduce" your life into its most essential components.

So we try to save time by eating our lunches at our desk. We have less serendipitous conversations with colleagues, strangers, and other "nonessentials" at the water cooler. We consolidate our schedules to include only the most important actions.

People tell us, "If you just get more organized, if you strike a balance between work and home, and limit yourself to the *important* people in your life, you'll feel better." That's just totally misguided. What they should be saying is "I gotta get a life filled with people I love." The problem, as I see it, isn't what you're working on, it's whom you're working with.

You can't feel in love with your life if you hate your work; and, more times than not, people don't love their work because they work with people they don't like. Connecting with others doubles and triples your opportunities to meet with people that can lead to a new and exciting job.

I think the problem in today's world isn't that we have too many people in our lives, it's that we don't have enough. Dr. Will Miller and Glenn Sparks, in their book *Refrigerator Rights: Creating Connections and Restoring Relationships*, argue that with our increased mobility, American emphasis on individualism, and the overwhelming media distractions available to us, we lead lives of relative isolation.

How many people can walk into our homes and just open up the fridge and help themselves? Not many. People need "refrigerator rights relationships," the kind that are comfortable, informal, and intimate enough to let us walk into one another's kitchens and rummage through the refrigerator without asking. It is close relationships like these that keep us well-adjusted, happy, and successful.

America's focus on individualism works against reaching out to others. Comparative studies on levels of job stress and worker dissatisfaction show that people of individualistic cultures typically report much higher stress levels than do the people who work in more community-oriented cultures. In spite of our high standard of living, wealth and privilege haven't produced emotional well-being. Instead, as these studies show, it's a sense of belonging that brings us happiness.

When our lonely lives catch up with us, we turn to self-help literature for answers, but it isn't SELF-help we need, I'd argue, it's help from others. If you buy this, and I hope that you do, then what I teach in this book is the perfect antidote to all this talk of imbalance. Connecting is that rare thing that lets us have our cake and eat it, too. We end up serving the interests of both our work and our life, ourselves and others.

Oscar Wilde once suggested that if a person did what he or she loved, it would feel as if they never worked a day in their life. If your life is filled with people you care about and who care for you, why concern yourself with "balancing" anything at all?

CHAPTER 31

Welcome to the Connected Age

> We human beings are social beings. We come into the world as
> the result of others' actions. We survive here in dependence on
> others. Whether we like it or not, there is hardly a moment of our
> lives when we do not benefit from others' activities. For this rea-
> son, it is hardly surprising that most of our happiness arises in
> the context of our relationships with others.
>
> —Dalai Lama

There has never been a better time to reach out and connect
than right now. The dynamic of our society, and particularly
our economy, will increasingly be defined by interdependence and
interconnectivity. In other words, the more everything becomes
connected to everything and everyone else, the more we begin to
depend on whom and what we're connected with.

Rugged individualism may have ruled for much of the nineteenth and twentieth century. But community and alliances will
rule in the twenty-first century. In the digital era, when the Internet has broken down geographic boundaries and connected hundreds of millions of people and computers around the world,
there's no reason to live and work in isolation. We've come to realize, again, that success is not contingent on cool technology or
venture capital; it's dependent on whom you know and how you
work with them. We've rediscovered that the real key to profit is
working well with other people.

We've taken some lumps getting back to this fundamental
truth. All the changes, all the fads, all the technologies of the last
decade too often foundered on the human factor, leading the busi-

ness world to treat people less as human beings than as just so many bits and bytes. We placed our faith in gadgets, processes, new organizational structures, stock market prices. When these things didn't deliver on their promise, we returned to us, you, and me.

Life is about work, work is about life, and both are about people. "The most exciting breakthrough of the twenty-first century will occur not because of technology, but because of an expanding concept of what it means to be human," said the futurist John Naisbitt. Technology has proved no substitute for personal relationships. To the contrary, it seems to be enhancing them. Look around you and you'll see this expanded view of what it means to be human, and how we interact with one another, in action. Here's just a small sampling:

- The hottest trend these days is found in social-networking software tools, and services like Spoke Software, Plaxo, Ryze, and LinkedIn. People are now finding new ways to use technology to connect people with bonds of trust and friendship. Some are calling it a social revolution.

- Blogs, part of the same phenomenon, are allowing passionate individuals with good content to reach literally millions of other people. These self-sustaining communities are flourishing. In the future, as personal branding continues to solidify itself as a mainstay in the economy, blogs will become as ubiquitous as résumés.

- Social scientists are making remarkable discoveries about the power of social networks. Recent research findings are proving that people who are more connected with other people live longer and are healthier. In communities where people are connected, the schools work better, the crime rate is lower, the economic growth rate is higher. Bringing people together by building personal relationships is becoming far more than a career strategy; it's increasingly regarded as one of the most effective ways to enhance America's civic and social health.

- Old-style labor unions and guilds are showing signs of revitalization. As the outsourcing of jobs outside the United States continues, and more and more of us become free agents, Americans are finding strength in membership to something larger than themselves. We're giving our loyalty and our trust not to companies but to our peers.

That's just a small taste of what's to come. We are in the formative stages of a new era of connectivity and community. You now have the skills and knowledge to thrive in this environment. But to what end? *How* will you thrive? What does it mean to live a truly connected life?

Certainly, some of us will tally success in terms of income and promotions. Others will cite their newfound celebrity or the exciting expertise that they've amassed. For others still, it will be the fabulous dinner parties they throw or the aspirational contacts they've befriended.

But will such success feel empty? Instead of being surrounded by a loving family and a trusted circle of friends, will you only have colleagues and clients?

Sooner or later, in one way or another, we all will ask ourselves these questions. Moreover, we'll look back on our life and wonder, What is my legacy? What have I done that is meaningful?

How many of you can recall the names of the last three CEOs of General Motors, IBM, or Wal-Mart? Are you struggling to come up with names? Now try and recall three important figures in the Civil Rights Movement. Ah, here people usually can name six or more.

Ultimately, making your mark as a connector means making a contribution—to your friends and family, to your company, to your community, and most important, to the world—by making the best use of your contacts and talents.

It's funny what events in life will make you question where you're headed and what you value most. I remember as a young man, for instance, dreaming of owning my own Brooks Brothers button-down shirt. All throughout my years growing up, I wore hand-me-downs from my mom's cleaning customers' kids or I'd find my clothes in secondhand thrift shops. I thought that when the day came that I could walk into a shop like Brooks Brothers and buy my own *firsthand* shirt (for retail!), well, that would be the day I arrived.

That day came. I was in my mid-twenties and I proudly bought the finest, most expensive button-down shirt Brooks Brothers sold. The next day I wore that shirt into work as if it were a rare, emerald-studded gown from the Victorian era. Then I washed it. I remember pulling my shirt from the washer and—gasp!—two buttons had fallen off. I kid you not. This, I asked myself, is what I've been waiting for all my life?

As noted author and speaker Rabbi Harold Kushner once wisely wrote, "Our souls are not hungry for fame, comfort, wealth, or power. Those rewards create almost as many problems as they solve. Our souls are hungry for meaning, for the sense that we have figured out how to live so that our lives matter so the world will at least be a little bit different for our having passed through it."

But it would take many more missing buttons before I truly started to ask myself what meaning, exactly, my soul was hungry for.

That time finally came with what I call my own personal mini-revolution. Revolutions sometimes begin in the least likely of places with the least likely of heroes. Who could imagine that a small Indian man with a very strong accent could challenge what I wanted out of life and how I was going to attain it? Or that doing nothing and remaining silent for ten days, rather than trying to do everything all at once, could change the course of my life?

The first shot in my revolution happened, in all places, while I was in Switzerland for The World Economic Forum, attending an oversubscribed talk entitled, simply, "Happiness." The room was jam-packed with the world's rich and powerful—a clear indication that there were others in my midst who had experienced a few missing buttons of their own.

We were gathered together to hear a short, stout, and thoroughly happy-looking man named S. N. Goenka deliver a speech on how he, as a businessman-turned-guru, found health and happiness through an ancient tradition of meditation known as Vipassana.

Goenka slowly shuffled to the podium and launched into a talk that enraptured the entire audience for the next hour. With his words, we were all transported into our own heads, forced to confront the feelings of inadequacy, stress, and imbalance that still accompanied our seemingly successful lives.

Not a word was spoken about business, per se. There was no talk of balance sheets or influential contacts. Happiness, he told us, had nothing to do with how much money we made or how we made it.

There is only one place to find real peace, real harmony. That place is within, Goenka told us. And while we may be masters of business, it was clear that we were not masters of our own minds and souls.

There was a way, he said, to ask the right questions and become masters of our mind. Vipassana, we were told, is an insight meditation technique that means "to see things as they really are." It was a technology for inner peace that could drive fear from the heart and help us have the courage to be who we really are. Goenka described a grueling ten-day course, during which practitioners sit for hours-long stretches in absolute silence, without eye contact, writing, or communication of any kind except with teachers at the end of each day.

It was up to us. No, it was within us to live a happy and meaningful life. We just had to ask the right questions and spend the time looking and listening.

While I'm not sure how many of my fellow executives were intent on learning Vipassana, it was clear that Goenka had touched us . . . deeply. He made us feel, at least for that moment, that we had the power to make our work and lives mean something, that it could be important, that it could make a difference, and that we could learn to be happy if only we took the time to listen to what our souls were telling us.

I left refreshed and inspired, but I was sure that I would never learn Vipassana. Ten days with no conference calls, no power lunches, no talking . . . ten DAYS! Impossible. I could never find the time.

Then, suddenly, I had all the time in the world. After my departure from Starwood, one too many buttons had gone missing and I was in need of clarity—and happiness.

Until that moment, I thought I didn't have enough time, or courage, for ten days of introspection. But eventually I took the Vipassana course and learned, for what seemed the first time in my life, to slow down and truly listen. In the process I shed many—though not all—of the thoughts of what I "should" and "ought" to be doing.

If you commit yourself to finding your passion, that blue flame, it's interesting how that commitment is rewarded with answers. The answers that came to me after all that meditation helped me to reevaluate my pursuit of prestige and money and refocus on what I've always known matters most: relationships.

Vipassana certainly isn't the only way to get clarity, but so few of us give ourselves the time and space we need to come to a better understanding of who we are and what we really want. How had I—along with so many other perfectly capable and intelligent people I knew—allowed my life to get so far out of whack? By failing to ask ourselves the kinds of questions that are the most important: What is your passion? What truly gives you pleasure? How can you make a difference?

When I left the meditation course and got back to the routine of my life, I was like a kid in a candy store. There were so many people I wanted to meet! So many people I wanted to help! The pursuit of achievement could be, I realized, so much fun and so inspiring when you knew what was worthy of achieving.

We've been taught to see life as a quest, a journey that ends with, hopefully, meaning, love, and an IRA that will keep our golden years golden. There is, however, no end, no final arrival; the quest never quite ends. There is no one job title or one Brooks Brothers shirt or one dollar amount that can ever act as the ultimate finishing line. Which is why the achievement of some goals can feel as disappointing as failure.

Living a connected life leads one to take a different view. Life is less a quest than a quilt. We find meaning, love, and prosperity through the process of stitching together our bold attempts to help others find their own way in their lives. The relationships we weave become an exquisite and endless pattern.

There is a line in a lovely movie called *How to Make an American Quilt* that sums up this philosophy nicely: "Young lovers seek perfection. Old lovers sew shreds together and see beauty in the multiplicity of patches."

What will be the legacy of your own quilt? How will you be remembered? These questions are potent measuring sticks for anyone who cares about making a difference, not just making a living. There's nothing wrong with wanting to be the best in the world, as long as you remember that doing so also means wanting to be the best *for* the world.

Remember that love, reciprocity, and knowledge are not like

bank accounts that grow smaller as you use them. Creativity begets more creativity, money begets more money, knowledge begets more knowledge, more friends beget more friends, success begets even more success. Most important, giving begets giving. At no time in history has this law of abundance been more apparent than in this connected age where the world increasingly functions in accord with networking principles.

Wherever you are in life right now, and whatever you know, is a result of the ideas, experiences, and people you have interacted with in your life, whether in person, through books and music, e-mail, or culture. There is no score to keep when abundance leads to even more abundance. So make a decision that from this day forward you will start making the contacts and accumulating the knowledge, experiences, and people to help you achieve your goals.

But first be honest with yourself. How much time are you ready to spend on reaching out and giving before you get? How many mentors do you have? How many people have you mentored? What do you love to do? How do you want to live? Whom do you want to be part of your quilt?

From my own experience, I can tell you the answers will come as a surprise. What's important probably won't come down to a job, a company, or a cool new piece of technology. It will come down to people. It's up to each of us, working together with people we love, to make the world a world we want to live in. As the anthropologist Margaret Mead once said, "Never doubt that a small group of thoughtful, committed citizens can change the world. Indeed, it is the only thing that ever has." It is my hope that you have the tools to make that a reality. But you can't do it alone. We are all in this together. Make your quilt count.

Index

ferrazzigreenlight

BUSINESS IS HUMAN

Ferrazzi Greenlight is a strategic consulting and professional development firm specializing in transformations through improved relationships with customers, partners, and employees.

Our clients share our passion to develop the relationships that drive their business success and include many of the most innovative and respected companies in the world.

SERVICES

Developing Strategy

Designs product and marketing solutions which fulfill the most important needs of our clients' key stakeholders.

Driving Sales

Enables business leaders and sales forces to develop, nurture, and expand relationships at every stage of the sales pipeline.

Instilling Culture

Strengthens and aligns the relationships between individuals within organizations to achieve collective success.

Enhancing Skills

Focuses on developing behaviors needed to grow business, lead effectively, and accelerate careers.